LIFE'S PURPOSE

"WRITE IT. I WILL GUIDE YOU!"

ALFONSO JOSEPH CAPITO

LIFE'S PURPOSE
"WRITE IT. I WILL GUIDE YOU!"

First published in Australia by Alfonso Joseph Capito 2018

A catalogue record for this book is available from the National Library of Australia

ISBN: 978-0-6484645-0-1(pbk)

Typesetting and design by Publicious Book Publishing
Published in collaboration with Publicious Book Publishing
www.publicious.com.au

Front cover photo is a close up of the image of the Cross described in the author's Preface and resembles the view seen by the author at the time. It is the spire on the Convent of San Lucchese, Poggibonsi, Italy.

Back cover is the actual photo taken of the Cross by the author some moments after driving by it from a passing bus on the trip described in the author's Preface; and is the Lighted Cross on the spire of the Convent of San Lucchese, Poggibonsi, Italy.

Contents

Preface and Thanks

"Write it. I will guide you!"

Whilst I was the only person to write this book there was a certain "energy" in me guiding me all the way through.

I don't fully know what this energy was but I have a clear idea of when it both entered and exited my psyche. This energy not only compelled me to write, it also kept me totally passionate about what I was writing, as well as led me to much of the content and insights that are expressed in the book.

It exited my psyche exactly at the point when a final draft of the book was handed by me to my partner Giselle in early 2017. At that point it was as if a load of bricks was removed from my shoulders and I could at last live, breathe and sleep without being obsessed with the book.

What is it that I could, as an accountant and at best a tax lawyer, offer towards writing a book on metaphysics, religion and philosophy? What could someone like me, being uneducated in the ways of such disciplines, offer towards an in-depth discussion of such paramount topics?

At most only two things – a logical mind (now

THAT I could claim to have from my many years of education and practice in accounting, economics and law) and most importantly, a passion for the search for meaning. The latter as a consequence of a personal black patch I went through in my life wherein I then searched passionately for a meaning to life. In the course of writing the book, I subsequently came to learn, through several Sacred Scriptures of varying religions, that those who search for meaning will be assisted to find it.

If you want to find meaning in life, then the most important thing you can do, indeed must do, is to search for it passionately. Don't wait for a life crisis situation to throw you into despair in order to start your search.

Perhaps the more interesting point to mention here is how I first acquired this so called "energy" that propelled me to write such a book. Especially when you consider that I have never written a book before (or felt in any way inclined to do so since, now nearly two years after having completed the final draft I mentioned earlier). Moreover, i was certainly not motivated to seek financial reward from having written such a book. My only drive was to write it for myself as a result of being prompted to do so; and once completed, I merely wanted to ensure that the book was widely available for anyone who might be guided to it.

My personal black patch occurred in late 2012 and by early 2013 I was well and truly looking for the meaning of life. I started to read many sources and consulted a number of people on it. By mid to late

2015 I had a rough idea of what I thought life was really about. So much so that I would make notes of thoughts that I had on the subject and started to think about whether I should write an essay incorporating such notes.

The trigger point that led to my decision to write such a book occurred whilst I was on a trip to Florence, Italy with my daughter Vanessa in late December/early January 2015/16. I vividly recall being on a bus tour of the Florentine country side just as dusk was setting in. I was sitting on the bus next to my daughter and I was somewhat tired of the day's proceedings and half asleep, eyes closed and thinking about whether I should or should not write such a book.

I recall saying to myself that it would be totally preposterous of me with no philosophic or religious training to attempt to write an essay on the subject. I then made a very clear decision NOT to write anything. Just at that very point it was as if someone slapped me across the back of the head, and I heard in a very clear voice in my head, in a way that i had never heard before or since, the words "Write it. I will guide you!"

At that point the impact on me was so great that i leapt forward in my bus seat, opened wide my eyes and looked out the window as if whoever whacked me across the back of the head had done so from outside rather than from behind me. When I looked out the window I knew then that I had been called to write this book from a high, if not the highest, authority possible. For when I looked out the widow I saw we were driving past a monastery that was perched high upon a hill, and on top of this monastery was a large cross lighted up in white lights burning brightly against the darkening sky. I scrambled and took an iPhone picture of this as best I could as I knew this was a special sign of sorts.

There was no doubt whatsoever that, having just decided NOT to write anything, I had been told by no other than possibly Christ himself, to get on with it and that I didn't need to be a scholar to write this because he would guide me. So naturally from that day onwards I started to piece the book together.

As I did I found that whenever I had a difficult question, the answer would come. Either overnight in some new early morning thought, or during the day someone would say something, or I'd see something in the media, or by some other mode of delivery, the jigsaw pieces would gradually all be given to me in such a way that the whole story came together in a coherent way.

In this regard I'd like to pay special respects and thanks to my amazing partner Giselle who, apart from being incredibly supportive and helpful, also introduced me to regular Sydney Baha'i Temple visits. And the resultant weekly exposure I therefore received to readings of many non-Christian Sacred Scriptures helped filled my mind with possibilities and wisdom well beyond my capabilities.

Of course thanks also goes to my spiritual guide whoever that may be, if not perhaps various guides, who assisted me as I put words to pages, for the benefit of myself as well as perhaps others, to gain insight and understanding.

Dearest Love and Thanks also to my children, family and close friends.

Finally, I should say that there is an age old tussle between Reason, Revelation and Personal Experience that has defined metaphysical conflicts for centuries. Do I believe only what I can reason out for myself? ; Or should I also believe what we are told in Sacred Scriptures? Or perhaps I should only believe in whatever aspects of spirituality that I have personally experienced for myself?

The process of writing this book leads me to believe that the most unshakable belief system is that based on believing those aspects of spirituality that intersect all three of these circles of purported truth. If you believe in something that makes logical sense to you AND resonates with a personal experience you have had or seen firsthand AND is supported by Sacred Scripture, then and only then, are you likely to be on unshakable ground worthy of defending with all your heart, mind and strength.

In this sense, Revelation is important because it can provide the context without which Reason or Personal Experience alone will be unhelpful, if not misleading. Imagine for a moment walking into a movie half way through. You could be the smartest guy in the world and try and make sense of what was happening using reason and your own experiences- but without someone next to you whispering in your ear and giving you some context, you may never really know what's going on.

Revelation is that whisper in your ear that is there to help you put the pieces together. Does it mean you should believe it blindly if it does not make sense? No. But equally don't easily dismiss it since you haven't yet seen the end of the movie. And perhaps in your own lifetime, you will never get to see it all.

All you can do, and these are worthy attributes, is to keep an Open Mind and to keep Searching for the Truth; Never Surrender.

(Preface and Thanks included in November 2018)

Chapter One

The Problem of Evil and Suffering in the World

Let's start with what many people struggle with; the age old problem of evil and suffering in the world.

Recently, I saw a TV documentary wherein five people who all had a terminal illness were asked whether they believed in God. All of them said "No". One in particular, who was 21 years old and had contracted cancer 5 years earlier and sadly had died before the program aired on TV, said that if indeed there was a God, why would he allow a sixteen year old to contract cancer?

It reminded me of a comment made by a well-respected Jewish author who, referring to the Holocaust, said something along the lines of,

"How could there be an all loving, all knowing and all powerful God and yet this same God would allow such a protracted, vial and systematic murder of innocents?"

Indeed, this is the conundrum that many non-believers, and believers also, face; namely, the so called Problem of Evil (or constant Suffering) in the world; especially when focussed on pain suffered by innocents. It is what dissuades many from a belief in an all loving God.

There are other issues that equally dissuade people from a belief in God. For example, if God existed why wouldn't he (or she - please read these terms interchangeably) clearly and obviously reveal himself?

Why create all this uncertainty about his existence and have people rely on a so-called doctrine of Faith, when he could simply "out" himself publicly and obviously, and thereby do away with all non-believers?

Why has he created, or allowed to endure, so many contrasting religions which often are the cause of bitter rivalry, discrimination and hatred in the world?

Why hasn't he made clear to all the masses what purpose there is in life?

Why do good things seem to happen to seemingly bad people, and bad things happen to seemingly good people (whether innocents or not)?

No wonder people struggle with a belief in matters spiritual, let alone an all loving, all knowing, all powerful God.

What if?

Now what if I said to you that there is indeed a theory or master plan, you could even call it a simple storyline, that could explain the meaning of life with God as the central player? And that it could answer rationally and sensibly all these questions; and that none of it relies per se on revelation or a leap of faith, but relies solely on basic logic and reasoning?

Yes it's true that the story would likely be

supported by sacred scripture, as it would have to be if it were true, but it would not be dependent on it.

If such a story existed, would this be a worthwhile story to share with you and others?

Moreover, what if this story brought together the key fundamental beliefs of the main religions of the world so that no one religion was right and the others wrong?

Furthermore, what if this theory was immersed in, and indeed depended on, the basic fundamental scientific principles of Evolution, as well as natural and economic notions of the primacy of Freedom and Competition?

Finally, what if this story was not only logically sound, but also to some extent shown to be capable of verification by looking at some obvious and logical facts, especially given developments in scientific research?

If all these "What Ifs" came to pass, would you think this story was worth sharing?

I came to the conclusion that not only is it worthwhile sharing but anyone who had such a theory was duty bound to share it.

So here are my thoughts:

Let us first develop a reasoned hypothesis and then test it against both facts and reason; and finally, let us see if it is consistent with holy scriptural writings.

This hypothesis can be one of various hypothesises one could propose, but it has to be a reasonable possibility, as well as one capable of being rationally justified by what I later cover as corroborative evidence.

Therefore, I am not asking you to agree with me that this hypothesis is the only possibility. But I am asking you to accept that it is a reasonably plausible one; even if it's not the one that you yourself would choose to put forward as your preferred starting one.

Now having said it must be a reasonable hypothesis, I know I am about to ask you to make a big assumption to start with; and an assumption that you might consider unreasonable. However, I assure you that I will revisit this assumption later and demonstrate, by reason alone, why it is a perfectly reasonable assumption with which to start our hypothesis.

The assumption is this. Assume there is an all loving, all knowing, all powerful God.

Now given that assumption, I'd like to lead you through logically how I got to my hypothesis. But so as not to leave you in doubt until then, let me state upfront what my hypothesis is.

My Hypothesis as to Life's Purpose

I believe that the purpose of Life is to give us one long schooling experience to develop and perfect ourselves. To evolve and perfect, into our soul DNA or soul memory, a natural immunity from worldly desires, fears and anger; and to re-enliven our innate love of both, the supreme cosmic consciousness (which I call God), as well as a love for mankind in general.

That we are born to learn, and be tested on, certain lessons involving both joy and suffering and that

over time, indeed a very long time as I shall explain later, we "purify" ourselves of worldly attachments and become immune to their allures as well as the anger such attachments breed; and we develop a virtuous and loving character and thereby evolve into perfect souls.

The real "we" are our spiritual selves (or soul essences), which are immortal (or perhaps quasi immortal as I shall also explain later); and our bodies and the material world are illusory (i.e. they are not true reality).

The purpose of this illusory world is to test and subject our souls (the real "us") to multiple character building experiences over many lifetimes; and all through a process of reincarnation and transmigration of soul essences.

And that there is a higher organising consciousness (or God, in my terminology) which, through various means, including the provision of teachers and guides, oversees our long schooling and training program.

Moreover, that we can at any time connect with this overarching consciousness by "awakening and turning towards it"; and if we do, our material existence is more meaningful and much more rewarding, and our awareness of both self and the real world is heightened.

That the purpose of giving us multiple character building experiences over many lifetimes, is to develop our innate "freedom fighter" trait. This trait has been given to us so that once we have evolved and perfected it, it will insulate and keep us free of worldly restraints such as fears, desires, temptations and anger, which all distract us and make us forgetful of our end life purpose objectives; namely, to learn to love intensely and unconditionally (to the point of loving worship, as opposed to slavish worship) this higher organizing consciousness (or God in my terminology), and to learn to love our fellow souls.

Finally, the schooling process will at some stage come to an end. And those that have purified and detached themselves, and connected with this higher consciousness and achieved the love of God and mankind generally, will "graduate"; and thereby exit the reincarnation cycle and become eternally "blissful" to the point of acquiring a divine nature.

***This is life's ultimate long term purpose.* Those that do not graduate will likely cease to exist as soul identities.**

The Logic to the Hypothesis

I will, through the course of this work, logically explain all aspects of this hypothesis.

For now though, let me continue leading you through some of my logic as to how I arrived at the hypothesis, which we then review and test throughout the course of this work.

As noted earlier, let's temporarily assume there is an all loving, all knowing and all powerful God (which assumption I will review in depth later).

Assume that he (again please feel free to use she or it, interchangeably here) is alone, in the sense that no one or thing is like him and so has, by definition, no comparable or competitive counterpart.

If you were a "one off" being and were all loving and all powerful, what might you do? You could of course choose to do nothing, but that would seem to be a great waste of your powerful talents. You could also choose to do many things but nonetheless love no one, or alternatively, to love things that were second in nature to yourself.

If it were me, I'd like to have someone that I could both love, and be loved by in return. In other words, there would be little point in being an "all loving being", if you could neither love anyone, nor be loved in return. But if you wanted to love someone and be loved in return, what or who would that be?

Clearly, if you were all powerful you could simply create a being or beings, and create them in a way to ensure they loved you and you them. However, is this the highest form of love? You would think rationally that such an all knowing, all powerful loving God would want to experience the highest form of love.

Surely, the highest form of love is to be loved by someone who has a choice, or the freewill, to love you or not. Anything short of that involves a creation with a "robotic love" trait. Having that creation's love is hardly satisfying for you, since no matter how poor a lover you were, their love of you was always guaranteed.

In addition, not only would I want to be loved by someone who had freewill to love me in return, but that person would ideally be someone like me or my kind. It's true that in my lifetime, I have enjoyed very much being loved by pets from time to time, but I'd much rather be loved by a human if it were possible.

But how could God choose to be loved by someone "like him" when there is no one like him? The closest being he could therefore be loved by that was like him would naturally be something, or somethings, that emanated from him; i.e. his, for want of a better word, children; and children that would be made in his image; that is, really like him, even if not perfectly identical to him.

So returning to our hypothesis, let's assume there is an all loving, all knowing, all powerful God that has created or emanated beings that are in his image (i.e. they are like him in the sense that they have a divine nature) but they are not gods in their own right and they have freewill.

Moreover, that God loves them dearly and they reside in God's kingdom in a state of great happiness. However, true to their freewill character to love or not love, they can at any time succumb to temptations and turn away from God's preferred path for them. That is, they are completely free to choose not to love God and to instead focus their love and attention on other things; including, a desire to be more like God than they currently are. In other words, despite their state of great happiness and benefaction, they may well be tempted to become more knowledgeable and powerful than their present state.

Assuming these creatures are exposed to such temptations over time, what do you think would logically flow from this?

Chances are some, or all of the so-called, children are going to exercise their freewill and explore other paths involving temptations that lead them away from total commitment to God's love.

God, being all knowing, would of course have known this from the start. Indeed, if he wanted them to truly love him in the highest sense, he may prefer to see their love tested by such temptations. Clearly, a lover who has been tempted to move away but resists this and stays true to ones love, is all the more worthy of God's love in return.

Imagine a pet dog that is being enticed away from your home by a passer-by's wayward gifts but resists this and stays true to you. Knowing this, would you not feel more in love with such a being in recognition of its loyalty towards you, despite the best efforts of a sinister passer-by to lure it away?

So continuing the story, let us therefore assume that some children were successfully tempted away from God's love and went over to, for want of a better term, the "Dark Side", and some stayed in God's realm. What to do about those who were tempted and had "fallen" away?

Clearly, an all loving God would be merciful and afford them an opportunity to return to the fold, rather than banish them for eternity. In other words, an all loving God would likely be a forgiving God, especially in circumstances where his creations were made by him intentionally with the freewill to choose temptations ahead of his love and care.

As you might have gathered by now, I am asking you to temporarily imagine that WE are his children and are made in his image. If we are really made in his image, then how might we have approached the problem of the "fallen ones"? Logically, this may indicate how God might have approached it.

Ideally, just as we would treat our own children who have made an error of judgment, we would wish to somehow support and educate the wayward ones and show them the error of their choice.

Ok, so then how best to educate fallen ones who have chosen the temptations of bad vices over God's virtuous kingdom? Logically, the answer is to show them that bad vices don't provide them with long lasting and meaningful satisfaction - i.e. ultimate happiness.

This, by necessity, has to be through a meaningful course of education. Otherwise, a quick return to "paradise" will be of little value if the lesson is not well learnt in a sustainable way, since they will likely again be tempted away over time.

The fallen ones need to be able to both ENJOY (i.e. experience good) and ENDURE (i.e. suffer) a diverse variety of experiences, in order to realize that what God wanted for them in terms of perfect love (i.e. for them to love him and each other and be loved in return), comprises complete utopian happiness. And that anything they have chosen, or could choose, in place of that will be inferior.

If utopian happiness as described above, is what God would have considered as perfect love, he would have likely embedded the desire for it in their hearts; despite giving them freewill to reject it in substitution for inferior temptations. Those hearts, made in likeness to his own, therefore crave only this highest form of utopian happiness.

And so each child may need to experience a multitude of pains, joys, sorrows and challenges before coming to a slow realization that returning to God's realm is the highest form of happiness; and that desiring more than what God has endowed on them is a futile exercise. That is, they need to taste both the good and the bad (i.e. Good and Evil) that comes from being away from God's love, to realize that "the grass is not greener" outside of God's realm.

Moreover, God being all knowing, all powerful and all loving, would provide his children guidance and teachings along the way, rather than simply abandon them to the ravages of an unsaintly and unruly world; just as we would guide and mentor someone we took under our wing in order to develop them. In other words, God would provide them with a guided Schooling and training program to educate them back into the fold.

So the above is the theory, or so called, hypothesis.

Now let's see if the objective facts verify such a hypothesis. But we need to revisit one thing first.

Chapter Two

Does God exist?

We need to revisit one aspect of our hypothesis that is critically important.

I started off our hypothesis by asking you to assume that there is a God. I want to first test this before moving forward using purely reason rather than Faith, and ignoring for the time being the ultimate findings of our main inquiry into whether or not the objective facts support our hypothesis, (which on its own would suggest proof for the existence of a God in any event).

There is in my view an easier way to prove God's existence, although this on its own, will not prove the key thesis of our hypothesis; namely, that Life is one big illusory school; nor will it prove that God is all loving, or that he wishes us to return ultimately back into his fold.

A god can only exist either because one existed from the beginning of time (or if one was created, its creator must have also been a god who existed from the start), or if one did not exist from inception, then one must have evolved over time without being itself created by a god.

There is not much research or reading that I could find about a god evolving over time, but I think it is a subject worthy of serious consideration.

Let's say for an instance that the atheists are right when they say God did not create the universe (or many universes as the new science of quantum physics might suggest). Let's also say therefore that physical matter existed from the outset and that life developed on its own without the aid of anyone external. All incredibly big assumptions I know, but let's assume these atheistic tenets to be true for the sake of the argument.

In essence, atheists say that we and life in general "evolved" to the point we are now. Of course, one could not credibly dispute Darwin's theory of Evolution. And so the atheists response to the religiously motivated age old saying, that "the world is so complex as to resemble a Swiss watch masterpiece found on the side of a beach and therefore only a crafty super intelligent Watchmaker like God could have made it", is to say, "No, you don't need a watchmaker because combining evolutionary forces and eons of time, the watch evolved on its own."

In essence, they would say that we became an intelligent race in an amazingly unique and precarious environment by a combination of chance, evolutionary forces and extraordinary lengths of time throughout which chance and evolution danced together to form both us, and our world.

Ok, let's say for the sake of the argument that this is correct. What is its logical extended conclusion? If indeed chance and evolution and eons of time can dance together to evolve a Swiss watch masterpiece, then why could they not, indeed how could they not, evolve also to create the Masterly Swiss Watchmaker?

I recently watched a Neil Tyson documentary (Cosmos) that plotted out the time spanning the original birth of our universe from the so called "Big Bang" to now, over a hypothetical 12 month period. A 15 billion or so time span divided into 12 months. As you can image, the human race only came into the picture during the last hour on December 31st. All that has ever been written about Kings, battles and human civilization spanned only the last 14 seconds before midnight. Moses roughly appeared with six seconds to go, Jesus with four seconds to go and Mohammad with three.

Indeed, this is exactly the point made by our atheist brothers and sisters. Time is so immense to the point of incredulity and, given that much time, it's not surprising that life and mankind can readily evolve without the help of a god.

Ok I can understand this argument, although I struggle with the age old question of who created (and how) the original matter from which matter and therefore life started. But that aside for now, unquestionably immense eons of time coupled with pre-existing matter can lead to life through evolutionary processes.

Look how far we have come in just 14 seconds of our universe's life - from primitive civilizations to landing men on the moon. Well then imagine where we will be in 14 seconds from now?

We already understand DNA and can grow body parts and are well advanced in artificial intelligence. So just imagine the advancement in the next 14 seconds of time. Indeed, what will civilization look like after a full 60 secs from now? Or five minutes from now; or even a full hour from now?

When you couple eons of time bordering on infinity with an immense spacious universe, let alone other possible universes, how could the forces of evolution *not* give rise to a civilization, or individuals, of unimaginable intelligence and power?; assuming of course, you had something to start with in the first place.

Why would it be beyond credulity to think that an all loving all knowing all powerful being could not have evolved? Indeed, if you look at how far mankind has come in 14 secs, would not a quasi-infinite time span lead to infinite possibilities of creations, including a god like creation? It is indeed the obvious logical conclusion of what the scientific atheist world is telling us.

Again I say, if time and evolution together are so powerful on their own to be capable of producing a Swiss Watch Masterpiece, they are just as potent enough to produce someone who is capable of making it.

The final point I would make is another statistic that was raised in the same documentary I referred to above (the Cosmos series by Neil Tyson). That is, that science, despite all its advancements, acknowledges that it only really understands 4 % of the known universe (noting that this "known universe" could, of course, be even bigger than we think; potentially much bigger) with the rest comprising "dark matter" or "dark energy" (being terms scientists tend to use to describe something they typically know little or nothing about). Therefore, we need to take with a grain of salt what science tells us as being possible, or more importantly, impossible.

Add to this the fact that scientific advancements in history proceed in phases, with each phase showing that what was thought as scientifically true in an earlier phase, was not quite the whole truth and was therefore incorrect or needed modifying.

The point I've tried to make here is that even if you accept the scientific based atheist view that God did not create the Universe, the same forces they say created life and human kind, by logical extension, can reasonably, if not obviously, be shown to have eventually created an all knowing and powerful force that we might call God.

In fact, the reasoning I have employed to reach this conclusion is less of a leap of faith than the scientific atheists would have us make in believing that matter could come from nothing; or alternatively, and just as much a chasmic jump, that matter was in existence from inception without ever needing a cause.

For this reason alone, of course there is a God, whether you believe that one always existed or, alternatively, that one evolved.

Moreover, and separate to this proof, if the tenants to my Hypothesis can be shown to be sound, as I endeavour to do so in this work, then this will not only be a further reasonable basis of proof for the existence of God, but more importantly, of a God that is an all Loving and all Merciful God.

Chapter Three

Tenets of the Hypothesis that can be tested

Reverting back to our hypothesis, what are its tenets?

Having built a hypothesis that says that there is an all loving all knowing all powerful God that is desirous to educate his children and reunite them to his realm, what are the tenets of this hypothesis that could be tested against objective facts?

In other words, what would you expect to find in such a scenario and do the facts support those expectations?

As a starting point, you would expect to see progress over time and that such a process was resulting in some success in the progress of either certain individuals, or groups of individuals, and mankind in general. **Progress**.

From an all loving, and therefore supposedly just God, you would also expect the system to be universal and open to all his children, not just those "chosen" or predestined to succeed.

In other words, freewill is just as much relevant here in the decision to succeed as it was in the decision to fall in the first place. It doesn't mean that one can necessarily succeed without God's intervention, benevolence or grace. But it does mean that each individual soul must be universally capable of succeeding or failing, albeit over the relatively long period of time during which it would take to learn all the lessons required for it, to both desire and be ready, to reconnect with God.

It also doesn't mean that everyone will be saved in the end but only that everyone has the opportunity of being saved. **Universality**.

You would expect to find an intense world class education process in place, including guidance and teaching. **Best in class education system**.

You would also expect, from an all loving God, to see love, mercy and compassion embedded into the system of education and it not be a process based on ruthless discipline, mere chance or one lacking empathy. **Love, mercy, compassion**.

The first two tenets of **Progressivism and Universality** go hand in hand. The progress to be observed you would expect would be visible across all of humanity although it may, by definition, progress along a time frame and geographical reach that is phased in both respects. However, evidence should exist of its gradual extension and reach across all boundaries and throughout time to a great, and increasingly greater, number of souls.

The final two tenets of **Best in Class Educational System tempered with Love Mercy and Compassion** also go hand in hand; Love, Mercy and Compassion need to be necessary traits of the Educational System itself and so, evincing a World's Best Educational System based on love, mercy and compassion.

Let's look at both these tenets commencing with the later first; namely, World's Best Educational System based on love, mercy and compassion.

However, before you can determine whether and to what extent there exists a world class education system, you first need to determine WHO the students are.

In this hypothesis the students are obviously us, God's supposed children. However, importantly we are represented not by our bodies here but by our souls or spiritual selves. (I will use reference to our spirit selves and to our souls interchangeably even though we could, if we chose to, distinguish the two in certain respects).

This is a critical point. We are not mere physical bodies but rather bodies that have, coexisting within us, souls. Indeed, you could more correctly say, that we are souls that have bodies. These souls survive the body once it dies and then exist separately in either spirit form, or are reincarnated back into a bodily form in another life reborn again. (I will provide evidence for the existence of souls later in this work).So, yes, before we can sensibly understand WHO is the student, we have to rationally explore the notion of reincarnation, and either accept or reject its existence. If we reject its existence, then there is no basis to my hypothesis. It cannot be rationally supported.

If we accept it, then we are left with an inescapable conclusion that the student must be our spiritual selves not our bodily selves. Although I should say that i also believe that our spiritual selves, through the transmigration of our souls, retains elements or trace memories of our bodily ailments and traits in general. And therefore one could say that to the extent that our souls carryover bodily traits, then there are bodily aspects of us that also survive death, and when combined with our souls, comprise the entire "student" spiritual self. More on this later.

Chapter Four

Does Reincarnation exist and why is it relevant to our education?

So what do we know about reincarnation and can we rationally accept its existence?; acknowledging of course, as if it were merely a minor matter, that an acceptance of reincarnation by definition requires acceptance of the notion of a soul and spiritual essence that survives the body upon death.

For myself, I can say without equivocation, yes, I can rationally accept the existence of reincarnation.

I say this not just because a large part of the world's population (in excess of a billion people and circa 25% of the population of the USA) currently accept it. For instance, eastern religious groups such as the Hindus, Taoists and Buddhists, as well as Jewish Kabbalist's and not to forget the great civilisation of the ancient Egyptians.

Nor do I say it just because of the many learned and well respected identities that have openly supported it over the centuries i.e. Plato, Pythagoras, Socrates, Voltaire, Hume, Goethe, Schopenhauer, Kant, Nietzsche, Shakespeare, Thoreau, Mark Twain, Edgar Allen Poe, Charles Dickens, Oliver Wendell

Holmes, Thomas Edison, Benjamin Franklin, Origen of Alexandria etc.

For instance, here are some eye-opening thoughts on reincarnation from various renowned personalities. (I should note that I do not intuitively agree with all the comments made).

Socrates

"I am confident that there truly is such a thing as living again, that the living spring from the dead, and that the souls of the dead are in existence."

Ralph Waldo Emerson

"The soul comes from without into the human body, as into a temporary abode, and it goes out of it anew… it passes into other habitations, for the soul is immortal."

William Jones

"I am no Hindu, but I hold the doctrine of the Hindus concerning a future state (rebirth) to be incomparably more rational, more pious, and more likely to deter men from vice than the horrid opinions inculcated by Christians on punishments without end."

Henry David Thoreau

"As far back as I can remember I have unconsciously referred to the experiences of a previous state of existence."

Walt Whitman

"I know I am deathless...We have thus far exhausted trillions of winters and summers, / There are trillions ahead, and trillions ahead of them."

Voltaire

Doctrine of reincarnation is neither absurd nor useless. "It is not more surprising to be born twice than once."

Goethe

"I am certain that I have been here as I am now a thousand times before, and I hope to return a thousand times."

Jack London

"I did not begin when I was born, nor when I was conceived. I have been growing, developing, through incalculable myriads of millenniums... All my previous selves have their voices, echoes, promptings in me... Oh, incalculable times again shall I be born."

Isaac Bashevis Singer

"There is no death. How can there be death if everything is part of the Godhead? The soul never dies and the body is never really alive."

Herman Hesse, Nobel Laureate

"He saw all these forms and faces in a thousand relationships... become newly born. Each one was mortal, a passionate, painful example of all that is transitory.

Yet none of them died, they only changed, were always reborn, continually had a new face: only time stood between one face and another."

Count Leo Tolstoy

"As we live through thousands of dreams in out present life, so is our present life only one of many thousands of such lives which we enter from the other more real life... and then return after death. Our life is but one of the dreams of that more real life, and so it is endlessly, until the very last one, the very real life of God."

Richard Bach

"Do you have any idea how many lives we must have gone through before we even got the first idea that there is more to life than eating, or fighting, or power in the Flock? A thousand lives, Jon, ten thousand!... We choose our next world though what we learn in this one... But you, Jon, learned so much at one time that you didn't have to go through a thousand lives to reach this one."

Benjamin Franklin

"Finding myself to exist in the world, I believe I shall,

in some shape or other, always exist."

Arthur Schopenhauer, 19th century German philosopher

"Were an Asiatic to ask me for a definition of Europe, I should be forced to answer him: It is that part of the world which is haunted by the incredible delusion that man was created out of nothing, and that his present birth is his first entrance into life."

Zohar, one of the principal Cabalistic texts

"The souls must reenter the absolute substance whence they have emerged. But to accomplish this, they must develop all the perfections, the germ of which is planted in them; and if they have not fulfilled this condition during one life, they must commence another, a third, and so forth, until they have acquired the condition which fits them for reunion with God."

Jalalu 'D-Din Rumi, Sufi poet

"I died as a mineral and became a plant, I died as a plant and rose to animal, I died as animal and I was man. Why should I fear? When was I less by dying?"

Giordano Bruno

"The soul is not the body and it may be in one body or in another, and pass from body to body."

Emerson

"It is a secret of the world that all things subsist and so not die, but only retire a little from sight and afterwards return again... Nothing is dead; men feign themselves dead, and endure mock funerals and mournful obituaries, and there they stand looking out of the window, sound and well, in some new and strange disguise."

"The soul is not born; it does not die; it was not produced from anyone... Unborn, eternal, it is not slain, though the body is slain." (quoting *Katha Upanisad).*

Honore Balzac

"All human beings go through a previous life... Who knows how many fleshly forms the heir of heaven occupies before he can be brought to understand the value of that silence and solitude whose starry plains are but the vestibule of spiritual worlds?"

Charles Dickens

"We all have some experience of a feeling, that comes over us occasionally, of what we are saying and doing having been said and done before, in a remote time - of our having been surrounded, dim ages ago, by the same faces, objects, and circumstances."

Henry Ford

"Genius is experience. Some seem to think that it is a

gift or talent, but it is the fruit of long experience in many lives."

Carl Jung

"I could well imagine that I might have lived in former centuries and there encountered questions in was not yet able to answer; that I had to be born again because I had not fulfilled the task that was given to me."

Thomas Huxley

"The doctrine of transmigration... was a means of constructing a plausible vindication of the ways of the cosmos to man; ... none but very hasty thinkers will reject it on the grounds of inherent absurdity."

Erik Erikson

"Let us face it: 'deep down' nobody in his right mind can visualize his own existence without assuming that he has always lived and will live hereafter."

J D Salinger

"It's so silly. All you do is get the heck out of your body when you die. My gosh, everybody's done it thousands of times. Just because they don't remember, it doesn't mean they haven't done it."

John Masefield

"I hold that when a person dies / His soul returns again to earth; / Arrayed in some new flesh disguise / Another mother gives him birth / With sturdier limbs and brighter brain."

W Somerset Maugham

"Has it occurred to you that transmigration is at once an explanation and a justification of the evil of the world? If the evils we suffer are the result of sins committed in our past lives, we can bear them with resignation and hope that if in this one we strive toward virtue out future lives will be less afflicted."

[End of Quotes]

The notion of reincarnation also helps explain child prodigies like Mozart and many other individuals who seem to have unexplainably acquired natural talents at an incredibly early age.

All the above reasons are themselves quite powerful and not to be skimmed over in a dismissive manner. For example, the Dalai Lama, who I and countless others respect, is probably reincarnation's most public proponent.

There is also the existence of affirmative biblical quotes from none other than Jesus himself (which we examine later). These are all matters that cannot be easily bypassed.

Nonetheless, despite all this I would not be an unequivocal believer in reincarnation if it were not for two sources of evidence that I believe, for me at least, places the matter beyond doubt.

The first of these is the pioneering work of Dr Ian Stevenson and the ongoing work of Dr Jim Tucker after Stevenson's death, both from the University of Virginia. This is not mystical storytelling. It is hard core modern medical research from people of unassailable integrity and qualification.

The second reason is my own personal experience with the notion of reincarnation as it applies to my private life experiences. This is not something I can ask any reader to understand, much less accept. Whilst I cannot ask any one reading this to believe in reincarnation simply because I do, I can ask you to look at the work of doctors Stevenson and Tucker, and do your own research on the subject and come to your own conclusion on the matter. There's much to be read on the subject that is accessible via the internet. I would also pay particular attention to the well documented cases of the reincarnation story of Anne Frank (already famous WW2 heroine). As well as the case of a small American boy documented in the book "Soul Survivor" and related YouTube stories.

I cannot here try to convince you of the existence of reincarnation. That would require a much more devoted effort than I can offer. However, if I can ask you to keep an open mind to its existence then we can better examine the tenants of the original hypothesis.

It's worth remembering when you read up on reincarnation evidence, that if only one case of reincarnation were ever conclusively confirmed, then that is enough to prove not only that souls exist, but also that they Pre exist and enter bodies at some stage of pregnancy, and that they transmigrated from body to body after death.

Refer below to a knowledgeable online article on the subject which also references the work of Doctor Ian Stevenson from the University of Virginia.

"Reincarnation: Best Evidence" by Stephen Wagner (updated January 16, 2017).

In this article, Wagner analyses the question of "Have we lived before?" And under five headings as follows, he presents some of the best known evidence, gathered by researchers to date on the subject.

This article, and the cases and references it refers you, to are definitely well worth examination and research.

"PAST LIFE REGRESSION HYPNOSIS

The most famous case of past life regression through hypnosis is that of <u>Ruth Simmons</u>. In 1952, her therapist, Morey Bernstein, took her back past the point of her birth. Suddenly, Ruth began to speak with an Irish accent and claimed that her name was Bridey Murphy, who lived in 19th century Belfast, Ireland.

Her story was told both in a book by Bernstein and in a 1956 movie, *The Search for Bridey Murphy.*

ILLNESSES AND PHYSICAL AILMENTS POINTING TO REINCARNATION

In "Have We Really Lived Before?", Michael C. Pollack, Ph.D., CCHT describes his lower back pain, which grew steadily worse over the years and limited his activities. He believes he found out a possible reason during a series of past life therapy sessions: "I discovered that I had lived at least three prior lifetimes in which I had been killed by being knifed or speared in the low back. After processing and healing the past life experiences, my back began to heal."

Nicola Dexter, a past life therapist, has also discovered correlations between illnesses and past lives in some of her patients.

PHOBIAS AND NIGHTMARES

In "Healing Past Lives through Dreams," author J.D. tells of his claustrophobia and a tendency to panic when his arms and legs were confined or restricted in any way. He believes that a dream of a past life uncovered a trauma from a past life that explained this fear.

PHYSICAL APPEARANCE AND REINCARNATION

In his book *Someone Else's Yesterday*, Jeffrey J. Keene theorizes that a person in this life can strongly resemble the person he or she was in a previous life. Keene, an Assistant Fire Chief who lives in Westport,

Connecticut, believes he is the reincarnation of John B. Gordon, a Confederate General of the Army of Northern Virginia, who died on January 9, 1904.

Another case is that of artist Peter Teekamp, who believes he could be the reincarnation of artist Paul Gauguin.

CHILDREN'S SPONTANEOUS RECALL AND SPECIAL KNOWLEDGE

Many small children who claim to recall past lives express thoughts, describe specific actions and environments, and even know foreign languages they could only know or have learned from their present experiences. Many cases like this are documented in Carol Bowman's *Children's Past Lives*:

HANDWRITING

Can past lives be proved by comparing the handwriting of a living person and the deceased person he or she claims to have been? Indian researcher Vikram Raj Singh Chauhan believes so. Chauhan has undertaken a study of this possibility, and his findings have been received favourably at the National Conference of Forensic Scientists at Bundelkhand University, Jhansi.

BIRTHMARKS AND BIRTH DEFECTS

Dr. Ian Stevenson, head of the Department of Psychiatric Medicine at the University of Virginia

School of Medicine, Charlottesville, Virginia, is one of the foremost researchers and authors on the subject of reincarnation and past lives. In 1993, he wrote a paper entitled "Birthmarks and Birth Defects Corresponding to Wounds on Deceased Persons" as possible physical evidence for past lives."

Assuming that Reincarnation is a real phenomenon, why is this relevant to the tenant of a world class education system?

Consistent with the Darwinian notion of evolution, if souls exist and can transmigrate then why can they also not evolve? If a soul can survive and have many life experiences over eons of time, why would it not evolve by learning from each life experience and become a more experienced, and by definition, a more learned entity. Is this not what human, animal and plant DNA does as it evolves over eons of time, to adapt life to ever changing conditions in its quest for improvement of the species?

A soul's progress through many lifetimes would be the equivalent of a student progressing though a school curriculum, or someone spending their lives in undertaking a multitude of educational courses.

The soul might not remember the individual bodily characters it assumed over time (and with few exceptions they don't), but it recalls the many lessons learnt through lifetime experiences. These lesson memories (as opposed to factual lives memories) then shape the nature and progress of the spiritual development that the soul undertakes.

We all know instinctively that the best way to learn something is to experience it. You can explain to a child, or even an adult for that matter, that if you were to touch a flame that it would cause pain. However, we know that the best way to learn that lesson is to be burnt at least once. Similarly people tend to drive a little more carefully after they have had their first car accident.

If a teacher wanted us to learn what it is like to be a tyrant or hedonist, the best way would be to make us either live the life of such, or equally to live the life of someone who bore the painful brunt of tyrannical or hedonistic behaviour.

If a teacher wanted us to learn what it is like to be a loving and selfless individual, the best way would be to make us either live the life of such, or equally live the life of someone who was blessed to be in the company of such a loving individual; or indeed live both lives on one, or perhaps even more than one, occasion.

If the concept of Love was an important facet of an all loving God, then is it surprising that the lives of people are constantly preoccupied with dealing with loved ones; new lovers; ex-lovers; tolerating existing lovers, etc.? Moreover, this seems to be reflected in our artistic works, especially music. As a famous song writer once put it, "people say the world is full of silly love songs". As a result, constant reincarnations into earthly life should give us an education in the meaning of Love Par Excellence!

Can there be any real doubt that such a system of learning by real life experiences would be world class and unparalleled?

But why would it be attendant with love, mercy and compassion, as the tenent suggests? We all know that some schooling systems can be brutal and uncompromising.

If a soul is made to endure a life of constant physical or mental abuse, or is plagued for life from an early age with a debilitating illness, then is this not a brutal learning system that lacks mercy and compassion?

Certainly yes, if the soul was to endure this permanently over its entire soul life existence, with no prospect of improvement. However, the mere fact that it may endure pain and suffering in one of its worldly life experiences, or many in fact, does not lead to a conclusion that the system lacks compassion.

We all have had experiences in life where things have been tough. Indeed, it is often said that much good comes from being put through challenging times ("No pain No Gain" or "It's only outside your comfort zone that great things are achieved"). So enduring painful experiences for part of one's earthly life, or for even a large part of it, may in fact lead to great advancements. I don't believe it is coincidental that many great writers, poets and artists generally seem to have undergone difficult life experiences.

The fact is that if the student is really the soul (i.e. the spiritual self), then enduring painful life time existences in bodily form for one or more lives is not unmerciful or uncompassionate. It's what's needed to bring that spiritual being to a learned state of advancement.

Do we not see this in Darwin's evolutionary theory on the advancement of the species, based on struggles that nature provides at almost every turn?

You could say that for a soul to have had a tough and seemingly uncompassionate life is akin to having had a tough year at school. Provided the whole schooling curriculum is not infested with pain and uncompromising brutality, then some hard lessons in pain and even brutality along the way are not only instructive, but necessary for evolutionary advancement.

If someone needs to appreciate how bad and evil it is to be a child abuser, then living a life as a victim of child abuse is an intensive learning experience.

The mercy and compassion that is inherent in the system comes from the fact that God has endowed us with souls that are capable of learning right from wrong and retaining this, as well as from giving us many lifetimes which to learn our lessons.

It's true that on its own, having countless lives without the ability to learn and retain the learnings of each lesson and to therefore advance our spiritual selves, would not be a feature of a world class education system. Indeed, it would be akin to an indefinite spiritual lifetime of constant pain and struggles for no ultimate reward. This would be my definition of eternal hell.

Why do I say we (i.e. our souls) can retain our

learning? I think it's evident in people's character from an extremely early age that they are born with certain personalities, traits and even obvious gifts of talent that could only have come from experiences had before birth.

How else could you explain a young child with a gift for music or mathematics or literature or even meditation? It's clear to me that we retain things from earlier experiences or past lives and carry them over into the next world. I also know this from personal experience but I'm not asking you to believe me on this.

The work of Doctors Stevenson and Tucker independently and objectively also suggests we carry over certain physical traits, such as birth marks, where some trauma has occurred in a past life. Moreover, mental ailments such as phobias may also be carried over e.g. someone burnt to death in a fire in a past life may have an acute aversion to fire in this life. This, to me at least, shows we learn from prior life experiences.

It's this ability to retain and learn lessons endowed upon us and inherent in our soul capacity that, in part at least, provides the mercy and compassion to compliment the school of hard knocks that painful lives reflect.

It's also important to note that we ALL go through this whether we believe in a God or not. We are all learning. We are all at school. We are all in one big illusory world universe. It's just that some of us may understand and appreciate the world class education system we are in better than others. For this reason, many non-believers are still therefore advancing and therefore incredibly moral and upstanding individuals. Equally many believers who may not be as advanced, or who although incredibly advanced, may be in a tough year of schooling, can be incredibly immoral in nature.

This can explain the apparent contradiction as to why apparent so-called "spiritual believers" can often seem immoral when compared to non-believers. Belief in God or religion does not of itself mean that you are morally virtuous.

However, belief in both God and the hypothesis I am putting forward, does mean that you can better understand what life is about; and how to better reconcile the many apparent injustices we see that militate against the existence of a spiritual meaning to life.

True belief in God (or a higher consciousness) and an awareness of the illusory world we are in, also means we have become truly aware; truly conscious. We have discovered our real selves and put ourselves in a position whereby we can manifest around us the lives we wish to lead.

Finally, on the illusion point, the world is better starting to understand this phenomenon. I recall a very striking comment made by Deepak Chopra in a recent lecture I heard him give, together with Eckhart Tolle, entitled "Awakening to your higher Consciousness", wherein he said,

"If you can see it, touch it, smell it, measure it, then it's not real ".

The world we think we live in is clearly illusory; but it's there for a reason; namely, to develop our real innermost selves, our spirit essences.

Chapter Five

Some Basics: Teachers, Teachings, Faith and the notion of Resurrection

Ok so now let's ask some obvious questions. For example, if life is meant to be one long schooling experience, who are our teachers and what exactly are we supposed to learn or achieve?

Where does the age old notion of Faith come into this? If you are expected to have Faith in God or a religious set of values, how does that advance your learning process and does this hypothesis still require a leap of faith, rather than reliance on reason to justify itself, contrary to what I suggested at the outset?

Moreover, if God is the same God as that of the Bible and other religious faiths, where is the evidence in all these faiths and their attendant scriptures that life is a lifelong schooling process based on recurring reincarnations of the soul?

Furthermore, and related to this reincarnation point, given that many religions (Christians, Muslims and some Jews) talk about an eventual "resurrection", how can this be if our bodies are but dispensable cloaks for our soul? How can the body be resurrected if the real person is the soul and the soul has had many bodies over many lives? Which body is resurrected come Judgement Day?

All great questions and probably part of the reason why this hypothesis I've put forward has not had much of an uptake throughout history. I believe I can answer these questions in a way that is not only entirely consistent with the hypothesis, but in fact, the answers will actually help corroborate the hypothesis.

Who are our Teachers?

This is an easy one. Let me name just some of the best and not in chronological order.

Moses (Judaism), Jesus (Christianity), Mohammad (Islam), Zoroaster (Zoroastrian), Krishna (Hinduism), The Buddha (Buddhism) and more recently Bahaullah of the Baha'i Faith. Confucius (Confucianism) and Mahavira (Jainism) may be others in this category.

Undoubtedly, there are others that we either don't have a record of, or who have been divinely inspired but are not regarded as religious teachers as such.

In my view, this category encompasses great scholars and personalities such as Pythagoras, Socrates, Plato as well as Aristotle. Although these are not regarded as spiritual leaders, all of them believed in a spiritual existence, recognized the illusory nature of our world and, as we will touch on later, provided the philosophic foundation for later generations of both Gnostics and Orthodox Christians.

In today's world, although the jury is still out on this, their disciples may be people like Eckhart Tolle, Deepak Chopra and Joe Dispenza.

The Teachings: What exactly are we supposed to learn or achieve? - The "Turn" to God.

Again, a relatively simple question.

Consistent with my earlier comments on the reason for The Fall, we are supposed to learn how to resist all the temptations that are around us and that distract us from being devoted solely to the love of God and our fellow souls. In other words, to develop an eternal discipline that enables us to detach ourselves from all worldly illusory desires and related fears and anger, and to "turn" fully towards, and therefore live 100% by reference to, or belief in, God; i.e. loving Him unconditionally to the point of worship, and also loving (but not worshipping, which is reserved only for God) our fellow souls in the form of the men and women we know, as well as mankind in general.

We are to learn this by tasting both good and evil. In other words, to experience life away from God and thereby learn that life, in the Darkness away from the Light, is an unpleasant and unsatisfying existence; involving periods of pain and suffering, and never feeling that one has truly lived a purposeful or fulfilling life.

Life is therefore meant to be hard and to teach us that we can never be truly happy until we turn away from a godless world, recognise and repent our failures and seek to connect with God. And then become devoted to what he would like from us; namely, to recognize him, love him, be loved by him and to love the other souls he has created for both our benefit and his.

In Life, there are of course, instances of joy. These are typically either, joy arising from worldly pleasures, including satisfying material desires and addictions; all of which joy is temporary and meaningfully unsatisfying.

There is also the joy coming from tasting some of God's heavenly virtues; for example, the love of one's family, or the broader community, or even one's pet, or animals and plants generally. That is, joy coming from what God would like us to be; namely a loving, caring, compassionate and just soul (i.e. The Good). This form of joy is given to us in this world so we can taste, and get a sense of, the ultimate joy that comes from being connected with the ultimate cosmic creator consciousness (God).

This type of joy is a taste of the Good that goes with the Bad, so that we can learn to tell the difference. There would be little point in having a schooling system encouraging us to be better souls, if we didn't have a sense of what being better souls felt like; we need to experience some of the heavenly Good in order to appreciate it, want more of it.

This is reminiscent of the Buddhist fable of the Burning House, where the Buddha (playing the role of a father) reveals some modest rewards to occupants of a house (the father's children) which is on fire, in order to encourage them to leave it. But once they leave it and join him, he then gives them rewards which are much greater than those initially revealed. They needed a taste for the Good to free and extract themselves from their environment of crisis and poverty and in turn seek to follow their father.

Here are some other examples from various Faiths which demonstrate these common themes, involving detachment from worldly desires, fears and resulting anger; a realisation of what is real versus temporary or illusory; good actions towards others (i.e. akin to the Platonic notion of Eudaimonia); and an unconditional focus on either God or some form of cosmic consciousness or deity.

In Hinduism :

Hindus believe that there is one true god, the supreme spirit, called Brahman. Brahman has many forms, pervades the whole universe, and is symbolised by the sacred syllable Om (or Aum). Most Hindus believe that Brahman is present in every person as the eternal spirit or soul, called the *atman.*

Shree Krishna says :

"O Arjuna! The scorcher of your foes (passions) it is by single-minded devotion alone that I can be known, seen in Reality and also entered into (as rivers enter the oceans). O Son of Pandu! He/she who performs actions for Me who considers Me as the Supreme Goal, who is My devotee and is devoid of attachments; who is without animosity towards all living beings, he or she alone attains Me (Self,

Realization)." – Bhagavad Gita 11:54, 55

Bhagavad Gita 2.61 – (Explained by Paramhansa Yogananda as remembered by his disciple, Swami Kriyananda)

"There are two requirements for attainment of wisdom.

First, withdraw the mind not only from sense objects but from the senses themselves.

Second, to remain merged in the consciousness of God as the most desirable of all goals.

Yogis who seek only to control their bodies and physical senses and those also who seek only the abstraction of divine union without proper physical and mental discipline, can never achieve true fixity of purpose. Uprooting the weeds of ego gratification on the one hand to their last tendril, and on the other becoming lovingly absorbed in the infinite, both of these are essential.

Many yogis seeks ego gratification not only through sensory pleasures but in the development of spiritual powers, many others again, seek the ego gratifying abstraction of intellectual wisdom. The true yogi seeks only to unite his soul with God."

B Gita 2.62 and 2.63 as explained by Yogananda

"Dwelling mentally on sense objects breeds attachment to them. From attachment arises craving. From craving, when frustrated, springs anger. Anger produces delusion. Delusion causes forgetfulness of the self. Loss of memory as to what one is in truth, causes decay of the power of

discrimination. From loss of discrimination ensues the annihilation of all right understanding."**["my emphasis"]**

Every step in this descent has a single lynchpin, the ego. To rise again towards wisdom the deluded ego must reach the point where it realises that what it has understood of life so far has bought it nothing but pain. Its first question must therefore be – Do I like suffering? No obviously. Next it should ask, What increases suffering and what lessens it? The answer is that suffering diminishes when there is a decrease of self-interest. The discernment of this truth leads to the first faint stirrings of recollection that a reality exists that is more than ego and the body. The fog of delusion begins to lift from the mind and one no longer strikes out at the world for not giving him what he wants. From acceptance of what is, comes a gradual decrease of worldly attachment. From lessening attachment comes lessening interest in objects of the senses and an increase of longing for true wisdom; a longing which awakens devotion in the heart, a love of truth and intense aspiration to know true and lasting bliss."

B Gita 2.64 as explained by Yogananda

"The man of perfect self-control is able to act in this world unaffected by it. Inwardly free from attraction and repulsion, he has attained unshakable inner calmness. That state, as we have seen from what Yoganada has said above, comes only when one's consciousness … has become so established with oneness with God, that there is no possibility of a return to outward-ness and the limitations of the ego."

Hinduism

Mahabharata 3.181.11-20

"Formerly Prajapati brought forth pure creatures, who were truthful and virtuous. These creatures joined the gods in the sky whenever they wished, and they lived and died by their own wish. In another time, those who dwelt on earth were overcome by desire and anger, and they were abandoned by the gods. Then by their foul deeds these evil ones were trapped in the chain of rebirth, and they became atheists."

In Judaism :

Deuteronomy 10:12-22

12 And now, O Israel, what does the LORD your God ask of you but to fear the LORD your God, to walk in all his ways, to love him, to serve the LORD your God with all your heart and with all your soul, 13 and to observe the LORD's commands and decrees that I am giving you today for your own good? 14 To the LORD your God belong the heavens, even the highest heavens, the earth and everything in it. 15 Yet the LORD set his affection on your forefathers and loved them, and he chose you, their descendants, above all the nations, as it is today. 16 **["My emphasis"] "Circumcise your hearts, therefore, and do not be stiff- necked any longer". (Note, first the notion of "circumcising your hearts" means detach**

yourself from other passions or desires; second, the notion of not being "stiff-necked" means be prepared to "Turn to God", which we shall look at later in some depth). 17 For the LORD your God is God of gods and Lord of lords, the great God, mighty and awesome, who shows no partiality and accepts no bribes. 18 He defends the cause of the fatherless and the widow, and loves the alien, giving him food and clothing. 19 And you are to love those who are aliens, for you yourselves were aliens in Egypt. 20 Fear the LORD your God and serve him.

In Islam :

For Muslims life is a period of testing and temptations. People have to find their own solutions to these problems but Allah will provide them guidance:

"If, as is sure, there comes to you guidance from Me, whosoever follows My guidance, on them shall be no fear, nor shall they grieve."

Surah 2:38

Muslim Theology teaches that after Adam's banishment out of paradise, man is still able to live righteously, if he resists the whispering of Satan. And that Temptation approaches from the outside to him, not from his inner heart. Sin is not rebellion against God, but only "transgression" or a "trespass" (2,36).

With this view, life on earth is like a time of probation and test which Allah poses upon man.

Refraining from worldly pleasures is exemplified in Islam by the observance of Ramadan. During the month of Ramadan observant Muslims do not eat or drink during daylight hours. This is because Fasting is one of the Five Pillars of Islam. The other acts of worship are the shahadah, which is the declaration of faith (i.e. There is only One God and Mohammed is his Prophet); salat, the five daily prayers; zakat, or almsgiving; and the hajj, the pilgrimage to Mecca.

Fasting in Ramadan is obligatory for Muslims, and in the Qur'an it states:

O you who believe! Fasting is prescribed for you as it was prescribed for those before you, that you may attain Taqwa [God-consciousness]. – The Qur'an, Al-Baqarah:183

Fasting, or sawm in Arabic, literally means "to refrain" – and not only is it abstaining from food, drink and sex, but also actions such as smoking cigarettes, talking about others behind their backs, or using foul language.

"How can the heart be illumined while the forms of creatures are reflected in its mirror?

Or how can it journey to God while shackled by its passions?

Or how can it desire to enter the Presence of God while it has not yet purified itself of the stain of forgetfulness?

Or how can it understand the subtle points of mysteries while it has not yet repented of its offences?"

(Aphorism 13 from The Book of Wisdom, by Sufi Saint Ahmed Ibn Ata Allah Al-Iskandari d1309, third master of the tariqa Shadhiliyya).

For Buddhists :

Buddhism is very much focused on the elimination of suffering and Buddhists believe in the 'Four Noble Truths'—1) to live is to suffer (Dukha), 2) suffering is caused by desire (Tanha, or "attachment"), 3) one can eliminate suffering by eliminating all attachments, and 4) this is achieved by following the noble eightfold path. The "eightfold path" consists of having a right 1) view, 2) intention, 3) speech, 4) action, 5) livelihood (being a monk), 6) effort (properly direct energies), 7) mindfulness (meditation), and 8) concentration (focus).

Behind these distinguishing Buddhist teachings are teachings common to Hinduism, namely reincarnation, karma, Maya (i.e. the world is illusory), and a tendency to understand reality as being pantheistic in its orientation. Buddhism also offers an elaborate theology of deities and exalted beings. However, like Hinduism, Buddhism can be hard to pin down as to its view of God. Some streams of Buddhism could legitimately be called atheistic, while others could be called pantheistic, and still others theistic, such as Pure Land Buddhism. Classical Buddhism, however, tends to be silent on the reality of an ultimate being and is therefore considered by some as atheistic.

For Christians :

From the Gospel of Thomas:

"Logion 27. If you do not fast from the world, you will not find the (Father's) kingdom."

Mark 10:17-27 New American Standard Bible (NASB)

"The Rich Young Ruler

17 As He was setting out on a journey, a man ran up to Him and knelt before Him, and asked Him, "Good Teacher, what shall I do to inherit eternal life?"
18 And Jesus said to him, "Why do you call Me good?
No one is good except God alone. 19 You know the
commandments, 'Do not murder, Do not commit adultery, Do not steal, Do not bear false witness, Do not defraud, Honor your father and mother.'" 20 And
he said to Him, "Teacher, I have kept all these things
from my youth up."21 Looking at him, Jesus felt a love for him and said to him, "One thing you lack: go and sell all you possess and give to the poor, and you will have treasure in heaven; and come, follow Me."
22 But at these words [a]he was saddened, and he went away grieving, for he was one who owned much property.

23 And Jesus, looking around, *said to His disciples, "How hard it will be for those who are wealthy to enter the kingdom of God!" 24 The
disciples were amazed at His words. But Jesus *answered again and *said to them, "Children, how hard it is to enter the kingdom of God! 25 It is easier
for a camel to go through the eye of a needle than for a rich man to enter the kingdom of God." 26 They
were even more astonished and said to Him, "[b] Then who can be saved?" 27 Looking at them, Jesus
*said, "With people it [it, here meaning, a camel passing through the eye of a needle] is impossible, but not with God; for all things are possible with God."

For the Brahma Kamari's :

Dadi Janki Of the Brahma Kamari's, from her book called "Inside out" 2007 says,

"The essence of spiritual knowledge is very simple. It is to know who we really are, as souls; that our original home, the ground of our being (as opposed to our doing), is non-material; and that this home is also where we connect with the Supreme Soul.

But without inner purity, the connection is weak and therefore power does not accumulate. So, it is essential to give ourselves time to really understand what purity is.

...

Knowledge in the spiritual context means to know the truth about the soul. The impurities that used to cover that truth made me ignorant about the self and others. The sun of knowledge burns away those impurities and reveals the truth to me. It shows the harm I did to myself in allowing my consciousness to be trapped by the material world, and the joy and power I receive when I learn to connect again to God."

Teachings continued: Plato and The Platonic Notion of Worldly Illusion.

I believe that the Platonic notion of worldly illusion is integral to the teachings of all the key Faiths mentioned herein.

And so moving away from religious beliefs, for philosophers and logicians, we must examine :

Plato's Allegory of the Cave

I earlier noted in this chapter, and in my starting hypothesis, what is the life purpose objective which forms the key plank of my hypothesis; namely, that we are here to learn the art of :

"Detaching ourselves from all worldly illusory fears and desires and learning how to "turn" fully towards, and therefore living 100% by reference to or belief in, God; i.e. loving Him unconditionally to the point of worship, and equally learning how to love (but not worship, which is reserved only for God) our fellow souls in the form of the men and women we know, as well as mankind in general."

This ideal, at least in part, as it applies to the notion of detachment from fears and desires, as well as the "turn to" God, should resonate to those who are familiar with the Platonic notion of the "Form of the Good" and Plato's Allegory of the Cave.

An anonymous writer online has aptly, in my view, summarized the Allegory of the Cave broadly as follows:

"In the Allegory of the Cave, Plato has given a description of people living in an illusory cave world. The cave is very dark due to there being little light inside it and people can hardly see things. There are some people, sitting against one wall facing another wall, who are chained to chairs by chains on their necks as well as feet. Onto the wall they are facing, shadows are projected via a fire burning high up behind the wall against which the chained people are sitting. These people because of their chains cannot move easily and cannot therefore see

anything but the wall in front of them.

Similarly, there is also another world of light outside of the cave world, which is the true world. There is a steep ascent out of the cave that leads to this outer world. On the high raised wall above where the people are chained, and in front of the burning fire, cave dwellers of sorts move along this wall holding different forms or objects in their hands, and parading them in front of the burning fire so as to project the shadows of those things onto the wall which the chained people are facing. The chained people inside the cave cannot raise their heads due to the chains so they only see the shadow like illusions, which they fully believe to be real but, of course, what they are viewing is one big illusory fabrication.

In the outer world, there is light and everything is clearly visible. If one of the chained people is released from the cave world, and if he is taken to the outside world, he cannot see anything at first because his eyes dazzle in the light. But if he stays in the outer world, slowly and gradually he begins to identify everything and he comes to realize that the outer world is the real world and the cave world is the unreal world.

He becomes gratified with himself and remembers the other people in the cave. He has pity and sympathy over the cave people who are trapped and lost in darkness. He thinks that it is better to be a slave in the outer world rather than being the king inside the cave.

Even though he does not want to go back to the cave world, he does so to tell the others about the true world outside. But his eyes dazzle even more if he is taken back to the cave world as now, having seen the light, he struggles to see or relate to anything inside the darkness, and therefore acts very oddly, in the eyes of the chained people, to the person he was before. If he attempts to persuade the people inside the cave, by saying that the outer world is the real world and the cave world is unreal, his ignorant friends will dislike the change he is advocating for them and will kill him.

The allegory of the cave has clear allegorical meaning because so many symbolic suggestions are used in this writing. The dark cave symbolically suggests the contemporary world of ignorance and the chained people symbolize ignorant people in this ignorant world. The high raised wall over which the chained people cannot see symbolizes the limitation of our thinking by reason, and the shadows symbolically suggest the world of sensory perception which Plato considers an illusion. In his opinion, the appearance is false and reality is somewhere else, which we cannot see.

Plato, as an ideal philosopher, says that the appearing projected world is just an imitation of the real world. The shadows represent thus illusions and reality is possible to know only through spiritual knowledge. The chains symbolize our limitation in this material world so that we cannot know the true reality; we have to break the material world.

The outer world of the light symbolically suggests the world of spiritual reality, which we arrive at only by breaking the chains that are used to tie us.

The dazzling of our eyes for the first time when we exit the cave symbolizes our difficulty in denying the material world. The second time dazzling of the eyes, when we to return to the cave, symbolizes our difficulty to accept ignorance after knowing the reality.

Hence, in the allegory of the cave, Plato has given a criticism over our limited existence in the material world. Plato also says that there are two types of perception: sensory perception and spiritual perception. Sensory perception is the world of appearance, which we perceive, with the help of our sensory organs. For this world is the world of illusion. It is the world of shadows. So in Plato's view it is the world of falsehood. The reality or truth is impossible to perceive with our senses. It is only possible through spiritual perception, which is divine enlightenment. Spiritual perception is only possible once we reject the world of sensory perception. So until, and unless, we break the material chains, we do not get spiritual perception".

Some commentators focus on the non-spiritual aspects of the Allegory. But as you will see from Plato's own words below, there can be no doubt that he intended a spiritual meaning.

Plato mentions, in a dialogue with his friend Glaucon, the following (and note the reference to the "journey upwards" as being the ascent from the cave to the outside world; and the reference to the outside sun as being the "idea of the good" meaning, as we shall see later in this work, is a reference by him to The Good or God):

"This entire allegory", I said, "you may now append, dear Glaucon, to the previous argument; the prison-house is the world of sight, the light of the fire is the sun, and you will not misapprehend me if you interpret the journey upwards to be the ascent of the soul into the intellectual world according to my poor belief, which, at your desire, I have expressed -- whether rightly or wrongly God knows. But, whether true or false, my opinion is that in the world of knowledge the idea of good appears last of all, and is seen only with an effort; and, when seen, is also inferred to be the universal author of all things beautiful and right, parent of light and of the lord of light in this visible world, and the immediate source of reason and truth in the intellectual; and that this is the power upon which he who would act rationally, either in public or private life must have his eye fixed".

"I agree", he said, "as far as I am able to understand you".

"Moreover", I said, "you must not wonder that those who attain to this beatific vision are unwilling to descend to human affairs; for their souls are ever hastening into the upper world where they desire to dwell; which desire of theirs is very natural, if our allegory may be trusted".

To me the Allegory of the Cave is a quintessential summation of both the WAY life works, as well as what our PURPOSE in life is.

The Allegory is often limited to explaining the Platonic

Idea of Forms. But of course, the Allegory is much more meaningful than this. There's no doubt that for Plato the idea of "Contemplation of the Divine" was an important part of his philosophy. As was also the case for Aristotle as we shall touch on later. Plato thought that through contemplation, the soul may ascend to knowledge of the Form of the Good or other divine Forms.

In my view, the Allegory of the Cave summarises much of the work in this essay and does so as follows. What I outline below builds on Plato's Allegory.

- In the spirit world before birth we, as souls, exercise our freewill by choosing who we will be in human form once we are born.

- We effectively choose the seats we will sit in inside Plato's prison theatre. From those seats, we will visualise the illusory material world and take on an Avatar that plays out our existence in this illusory realm. We typically agree to do this in conjunction with a small group of other souls (soul mates perhaps) who tend to play Life theatrical roles together.

- In the spirit world before birth, we also agree the experiences that our Avatar will experience in the illusory material theatrical world. For example, will they have caring or uncaring parents, loving or spiteful siblings, personal tragedies involving ourselves or close family or friends, loving or onerous relationships, number and nature of offspring, success or failure in business or wealth, personal health problems, addictions or inhibitions etc.

- As we sit through this illusory life drama, we are chained to our seats by desires and fears which are inherent in us from birth, or which we develop throughout our earthly lifetimes. These chains are a product of our bodily senses, and are intended to prevent us from escaping the illusory theatre and venturing outside the cave to discover Truth, Tranquillity and Freedom from worldly attachments. The chains can be so strong that we may never escape them before physical death in our material world, and so never realise that we live entirely in an illusory world governed by our physical senses and their attachment to earthly pleasures, fears and addictions.

- However, at times the painful experiences in our life, which we may have predestined for ourselves pre-birth, may shake us so strongly so that we want to change our lives; so that we start to search for what life is really about, or for meaningful change. We start to fight our way out of our entanglements by choosing to jettison our desires and fears. We may then begin to realise that there is more to life than simply satisfies the bodily senses, and we start to seek a way out of our self-imprisonment. We begin to detach ourselves from desires and try to jettison our fears, and thereby start to place our faith in a higher consciousness. We then start to connect with this higher consciousness, which i call God.

- There are dark forces in the Cave that will seek to prevent us from liberating ourselves from such a prison existence. Whether you call these forces demons, jinn or something less dramatic, these forces exist to test us and to intentionally dissuade us from becoming free. They will sometimes tell us that there's nothing wrong with wanting what we desire, or that our fears are justified, all in an attempt to distract us from walking the Path or Way out of the cave to the Light (i.e. the Path of the Righteousness).

- Those successful at freeing themselves and walking that Path, are truly "righteous warriors or freedom fighters". They have overcome temptations and negative forces and connected with God by placing their fate in his hands.

- In so doing, they have demonstrated to themselves (as soul and spirit beings) that they have the righteous qualities that can overcome temptations, fears and desires. They have had sufficient faith in their belief that the world they live in is devoid of true and worthy purpose, and that another world exists which, as Plato says, reveals a much stronger power that must be aimed for and upon which our eyes must be fixed. And that Faith in this has carried them through all that the Dark forces of Desire can throw at them.

- God, through the Holy Spirit and his guides and messengers, helps and encourages them to break free and exit the Prison Cave. But the climb out must be of their own volition and effort. Only in this way can their souls mutate sufficiently (in a Darwinian evolutionary sense), so that they become gradually and permanently immune from Temptation and Transgression of the kind that led to their demise in the first place; and they do so out of their own freewill.

- In this regard, God wants us to develop this immunity naturally, and through a long course of evolutionary phases so that it is something we can say we have earned ourselves, and therefore earned the right to his eternal love and beneficence if we manage to exit the Prison Cave and permanently connect with him. He could, of course, inoculate us and carry us out of the cave into the Light himself, but as will be covered later in this work, this would be pointless as we would not have developed our innate resistance to Evil of our own accord.

Again, to demonstrate how interrelated the key belief systems are that we have been looking at here, below is an extract from the Bhagavad Gita of the Hindu faith, which echoes a number of the points I've made above in respect of Plato's Allegory and, in particular, makes the point that, the Will governed sets the Soul at peace (i.e. free).

"KRISHNA:

When one, O Prithâ's Son!—
Abandoning desires which shake the mind—
Finds in his soul full comfort for his soul,
He hath attained the Yôg—that man is such!
In sorrows not rejected, and in joys
Not overjoyed; dwelling outside the stress
Of passion, fear, and anger; fixed in calms
Of lofty contemplation;—such an one
Is Muni, is the Sage, the true Recluse!

He, who to none and nowhere overbound
By ties of flesh, takes evil things and good
Neither desponding nor exulting, such
Bears wisdom's plainest mark! He who shall draw,
As the wise tortoise draws its four feet safe
Under its shield, his five frail senses back
Under the spirit's buckler from the world
Which else assails them, such a one, my Prince!
Hath wisdom's mark! Things that solicit sense
Hold off from the self-governed; nay, it comes,
The appetites of him who lives beyond
Depart,—aroused no more. Yet may it chance
O Son of Kunti! that a governed mind
Shall some time feel the sense-storms sweep,
and wrest
Strong self-control by the roots. Let him regain
His kingdom! let him conquer this, and sit
On Me intent. That man alone is wise
Who keeps the mastery of himself! If one
Ponders on objects of the sense, there springs
Attraction; from attraction grows desire,
Desire flames to fierce passion, passion breeds
Recklessness; then the memory—all betrayed—
Lets noble purpose go, and saps the mind,
Till purpose, mind, and man are all undone.
But, if one deals with objects of the sense
Not loving and not hating, making them
Serve his free soul, which rests serenely lord,
Lo, such a man comes to tranquillity;
And out of that tranquillity shall rise
The end and healing of his earthly pains,
Since the will governed sets the soul at peace.

The soul of the ungoverned is not his,
Nor hath he knowledge of himself; which lacked,
How grows serenity? and, wanting that,
Whence shall he hope for happiness?
The mind
That gives itself to follow shows of sense
Seeth its helm of wisdom rent away,
And, like a ship in waves of whirlwind, drives
To wreck and death. Only with him, great Prince!
Whose sense are not swayed by things of
sense—
Only with him who holds his mastery,
Shows wisdom perfect. What is midnight-gloom
To unenlightened souls shines wakeful day
Is known for night, thick night of ignorance,
To his true-seeing eyes. Such is the Saint!

And like the ocean, day by day receiving
Floods from all lands, which never overflows;
Its boundary-line not leaping, and not leaving,
Fed by the rivers, but unswelled by those;—

So is the perfect one! to his soul's ocean
The world of sense pours streams of witchery;
They leave him as they find, without commotion,
Taking their tribute, but remaining sea.

Yea! whoso, shaking off the yoke of flesh,
Lives lord, not servant, of his lusts; set free
From pride, from passion, from the sin of "Self,"
Toucheth tranquillity! O Prithâ's son!
That is the state of Brahm! There rests no dread

> When that last step is reached! Live where he will,
> Die when he may, such passeth from all 'plaining,
> To blest Nirvâna, with the Gods, attaining.
>
> Here endeth Chapter II. of the Bhagavad-Gîtâ, entitled "Sânkhya-Yôg," or "The Book of Doctrines."

I should mention here again, that Plato says that those who have exited the cave and seen the Light (in his words, who have had a "beatific vision"), and who have then sought to convince others of their enlightened views, such will be vilified or worse persecuted. Evidence of this, of course, lies in the history of all religious martyrs, of which there are innumerable instances.

Teachings continued: Aristotle on God and Divine Contemplation

Before moving onto the question of Faith and its relevance, we should also consider the thoughts of the other giant philosopher and logician of Plato's and Socrates' time, and that is of course, Aristotle. It's particularly important to look at Plato's view and contrast it to Aristotle's view, since whilst they may have disagreed on the notion of Divine Platonic Forms, they both certainly agreed on the existence of a monotheistic Creator God who overshadowed Greek and Pagan versions of lower gods.

Moreover, both approached the subject of the existence and importance of the Divine from a pure logical and philosophical standpoint, without any reliance on Revelation or reference to holy scriptures.

Like Plato, Aristotle clearly and for purely logical reasons believed in a supreme divine power referred to from time to time as "The One" or "The Unmoved Mover". But unlike Plato, Aristotle believed God played no role in day to day affairs but that he simply created the material world and then spent his time contemplating matters divine, including supreme virtues.

Most importantly, Aristotle believed that apart from man seeking to lead a morally virtuous life (which he said was the second highest purpose a man may strive for), the highest purpose in man's life is the contemplation of the Divine.

As one anonymous writer on the subject put it:

"Aristotle believes that "contemplation is the highest form of moral activity because it is continuous, pleasant, self-sufficient, and complete" (Nichomachean Ethics X 8).

"Aristotle believes that God ...is the only entity that can transcend past itself while still being of itself. He is eternal, unchanging, and therefore does the best thing. God believes that contemplating is the best of things. He believes that the best things are those that are good and simple in nature. Because of his own contemplation of his thought, Aristotle believes in God's existence. One of human nature can reach fulfilment and enlightenment through contemplating God's existence.

The following premises state:

(Premise 1) If Happiness is a virtuous activity, then

it will be in accord with the most supreme virtue.

(Premise 2) The most supreme virtue is theoretical study and contemplation.

(Premise 3) The most supreme object of contemplation is the divine.

(Conclusion) It follows that happiness consists in the activity of contemplation of the divine.

This conclusion emphasizes why God exists, and it is a fair assumption to believe that God is needed for the fulfilling life. Aristotle's main philosophy is all about how we as humans can have a fulfilling life. He lays out some of the most prominent doctrines concerning human ethics that we still use and discuss today. His definition of Happiness has been used to shape much of our thinking in the western world. For one to be happy, they must simply be a virtuous person.

*Where does God fit into Aristotle's plan though? For Aristotle, happiness is something that we can work towards. We achieve it through our life style. So in that sense, we do not need God to be happy. We can be happy all on our own. "**However, human fulfilment is an entirely different thing" ["My emphasis"].***

The God of Aristotle is described as the first mover. He is the One who started the universe in motion. But that's where He left it for Aristotle. God is far too busy contemplating the things that He has created and span the vast universe to care too much about the few humans that live on earth. But the best that we can do is to try and focus on the divine intellect of God. "The intellect is the highest thing in us, and the objects it apprehends are the highest things that can be known." This means that the greatest Good that we can do for ourselves in this lifetime is to think about the highest things, or the things that God would think about.

"It is in that sense that we need God for the complete fulfilment of our lives" ["My emphasis"]"

As Aristotle himself says:

"Happiness is a bringing of the soul to the act according to the habit of the best and most perfect virtue, that is, the virtue of the speculative intellect, borne out by easy surroundings and enduring to the length of days."

(Aristotle, Â Nicomachean Ethics (trans. Joseph Rickaby, S. J.), Book 1, Sec 7, 15, 16)

The more one engages in contemplation, the more complete one's happiness will be and so the more one will be closer to the divine.

One of the problems pointed out by those who oppose Aristotle's view, was that this kind of life is very difficult to lead in a world plagued with so much trouble and suffering. Understanding this problem, Aristotle concedes,

"But such a life would be too high for man; for it is not in so far as he is man that he will live so, but in so far as something divine is present in him."

(Aristotle, Â Nicomachean Ethics (trans. William David Ross), Book 10, Sec 7).

Thus, in situations where it is not possible to exercise contemplation, man can forego this for a secondary (and less divine) form of moral values. In effect, Aristotle says that because it is likely to be too hard for man to constantly contemplate God, the second best existence one can lead is a virtuous life based on moral values.

And so both Plato and Aristotle believed that to achieve human fulfilment, man's eye should be fixated on the Divine, albeit both differed slightly in why and how this should be done.

Faith: What's the relevance of Faith in all this?

By reference to the Christian world, the notion of Faith can best be evidenced and summarised by Christ's words in John's Gospel:

John 11:25 to 26 ▸

New International Version

Jesus said to her [Martha], "I am the resurrection and the life. The one who believes in me will live, even though they die; and whoever lives by believing in me will never die."

New Living Translation

Jesus told her [Martha], "I am the resurrection and the life. Anyone who believes in me will live, even after dying; and everyone who lives in me and believes in me will never ever die.

This passage also raises the question of what is meant by "living" and "dying"; as well as the notion of immortality of the soul. But more on that later.

For now, let's simply ask: What's the relevance of Faith in all this?

This is a harder question than the earlier ones,

but an excellent one.

Why does all this learning and devotion require faith in a God? Why can't God just come out and demonstrate to all of us that he actually exits and spare us all the effort of guessing, along with this ridiculous need for faith? Then we would all be believers and surely the world would be a better place?

Here is the answer; and it's a really important point - ***Having Faith is part of the test.***

In other words, part of our school assessment requires you to believe in something that is not obvious or scientifically provable. But why?

This is my belief to the key to understanding the relevance of Faith. God does not want people to follow or believe in him simply because he can make himself obviously factual and can then be shown on a YouTube video or be the subject of scientific testing.

Moreover, if he was to show himself, people would be so overawed with him and all the amazing benefits of connecting with him that they would, of course, drop all interest in worldly fancies and wish to be with him. The problem is that they would all want to be with him for the wrong reasons. Namely, to satisfy their wants for association with power, for greed and a lust for self-gratification.

It would be like an incredibly beautiful woman who is rich and learned and wants to find a man to love her and be her partner. If she was to reveal to her suitors how beautiful and wealthy she was, all would be desirous of her. But of course she is after the suitor who loves her deeply, not for what she owns, nor her beautiful looks, but for what is in her heart and mind. She is also after someone who thinks like her, is incredibly generous, caring of others and the world at large, can resist the most tempting of temptations; i.e. generally, someone who has her innate virtuous qualities.

And so in her pursuit of a suitor, she cloaks her herself as a poor and unattractive woman so as to find a truly worthy and meaningful lover.

Perhaps even a more apt analogy would be that of a lonely king, who lives in a distant and inconspicuous castle full of riches compared to the poverty, pain and anguish that exist in the lands nearby where the rest of the people live. He wants to help all of his subjects, but more importantly he wants to love each of them and for them to love him; but to love him not for all the wealth and benevolence he can bestow on them, but rather to love him because of his personal characteristics; his warmness of heart, his compassion, his lack of desire for vain and temporary riches, his fortitude and courage in the face of evil and temptation, his fairness and justice etc. He wants them to be his subjects, but to first become like him, so that eventually he can bring them into his castle realm knowing that they think and act like him and have the same values he has.

Unfortunately, he knows that currently very few of them have his values, and this would continue to be the case even if he were to reveal himself and his riches; knowing full well that people unworthy of his love would want to then flock to him. Instead, he believes that by him reaching out to them he can find those few who do love him for what he is, rather than his riches. Moreover, by engaging with all his subjects he can educate many of them to eventually become of similar purity and virtuosity.

To enable this to happen, he sends out his closest emissaries to spread the word of how mankind will need lift itself in order to be able to be worthy enough to enter his realm. He may even undertake such a mission himself. But whether he does it personally, or by sending emissaries, or even by recruiting some of his subjects to the cause, he will never seek to recruit followers by simply revealing the extent of his power and riches.

His castle, his benevolence and the majesty of himself will remain hidden from his subjects, so that those that turn to love him do so for the right reasons, rather than the wrong ones.

Accordingly, whilst he spreads his word to his subjects that his kingdom exists and is open to them if they adopt his values, they must take his word for it and trust him on this. They must have Faith. Even a minute revelation of the magnificence of himself and his kingdom would make it impossible, whilst recruiting, to distinguish those followers who had become genuine to his cause, versus those who simply were overawed by the riches of his kingdom.

This is why Faith is important. To believe in and love someone whose magnificence is virtually hidden from you, and often in circumstances where this love can be the subject of worldly oppression, derision

and persecution, is indeed a true test, if not the truest test, of genuine love and commitment.

Perhaps this is best described by a Baha'i scriptural passage from Bahaullah as follows,

"He Who is the Day Spring of Truth is, no doubt, fully capable of rescuing from such remoteness wayward souls and of causing them to draw nigh unto His court and attain His Presence. "If God had pleased He had surely made all men one people." "**His purpose, however, is to enable the pure in spirit and the detached in heart to ascend, by virtue of their own innate powers, unto the shores of the Most Great Ocean, that thereby they who seek the Beauty of the All-Glorious may be distinguished and separated from the wayward and perverse" ["my emphasis"]**. Thus hath it been ordained by the all-glorious and resplendent Pen...."

"That the Manifestations of Divine justice, the Day Springs of heavenly grace, [read God's emissaries] have when they appeared amongst men always been destitute of all earthly dominion and shorn of the means of worldly ascendancy, should be attributed to this same principle of separation and distinction which animateth the Divine Purpose **["my emphasis"]. "Were the Eternal Essence to manifest all that is latent within Him, were He to shine in the plentitude of His glory, none would be found to question His power or repudiate His truth. Nay, all created things would be so dazzled and thunderstruck by the evidences of His light as to be reduced to utter nothingness. How, then, can the**

godly be differentiated under such circumstances from the froward" [Note 'froward' here, meaning subjects unfit to enter his kingdom. Also note the reference here to dazzling light, is similar to the comment in Plato's Allegory of the Cave, that outside the Cave walls, the Light would bedazzle anyone who had lived their life within the Cave]?"

Bahá'u'lláh - Gleanings from the writings of Bahá'u'lláh (p.72)

The Buddhist story of the Burning House is also an example of how God encourages us to leave behind (i.e. detach from), a painful corrupted world (the burning house), by Him showing us some modest benefits (i.e. not all the riches of his kingdom) of following him out of the burning house, only to ultimately reward those that leave the house (i.e. those who had Faith in him even though they were only shown some modest benefits when compared to all the allures and temptations of worldly desires), with rewards many times in excess of such benefits.

If we consider for a moment the relevance of what we have said here about Faith and how it references back to Plato's Allegory of the cave, some useful observations can I think be made.

In the Cave Allegory God, represented by the Sun in the outside world, could readily manifest itself in the Cave and show all the chained prisoners its splendour and dazzling beauty. However, if this happened all prisoners would be awestruck initially and then once it became obvious that the outside world was the real world, they would readily, albeit begrudgingly perhaps, leave the cave and wonder outside.

The problems with this scenario are, first, that their hearts are still no different than when they were in the cave. That is, they have not gradually evolved from ignorant, self-centred beings into self-less and enlightened faithful followers of God. The transition is too great to have been of long lasting value and their true character has not changed.

Moreover, because they did not endure the battle of fighting off desire, fear, anger and temptation in order to exit the cave with effort, they have not developed their "righteous warrior" or "freedom fighter" skills. As a result, if they were to be tempted again by Desire or Transgression, they would no doubt easily succumb and again be easily lead astray from God.

For this reason, the Prison Cave is needed by God to train our souls in the "righteous warrior" skills, i.e. with prayer, meditation, patience, courtesy, kindness of heart, love, faith, immense courage, self-discipline and willpower, to defeat the negative influences of desire, fear, envy, anger and temptation. And to have these fighting qualities gradually, but permanently, embedded in our soul DNA (i.e. soul memory). And we need to do all this of our own volition; it must be of our own freewill, using our own inner strength, albeit with God's graceful help once we have made the decision to "turn to Him".

As Bahaullah says earlier, "His [God's] purpose, however, is to enable the pure in spirit and the detached in heart to ascend, **"by virtue of their own**

innate powers", ["my emphasis"] ... "

It is the equivalent of a training camp for "freedom fighters". Once these qualities are embedded in our souls, we retain them when we ultimately retreat to the spirit world upon our physical death from this material world. We then use those qualities in the spirit world to similarly avoid being forgetful of (forgetfulness being a great Islamic sin), or tempted away from, God.

Furthermore, inherent in what I've said is the Mankind has built into it from interception, a desire to be free. The yearn for FREEDOM is already part of our soul DNA.

Also inherent is the obvious notion that we have true freewill to decide whether to remain prisoners in the cave to seek to fight our way out. We shall touch on this in later chapters.

I should add that even though our hypothesis suggests that God waits until mankind is sufficiently worthy before embarking on a full reunion with him, (i.e. the coming of God's kingdom on earth, as it were), it is of course possible, and indeed part of the Schema, for worthy individuals, to connect with God in the interim in the present world. More on this also later.

Resurrection - and its apparent conflict with Reincarnation

Ok, so let's go back to the other two questions we posed earlier, which are interrelated; namely, if God is the same God as that of the Bible and other religious faiths, then where is the evidence in all these faiths and their attendant scriptures that life is a lifelong schooling process based on recurring reincarnations of the soul?

Furthermore, how can the concept of "reincarnation" be consistent with the notion of "bodily resurrection"? In other words, since many religions (Christians, Muslims and some Jews) believe in an eventual "resurrection of the body", how can this be the case if our bodies are but dispensable cloaks for our soul? How can the body be resurrected if the real person is the soul which has had many bodies over many lives? Which body is resurrected come Judgement Day?

Let's start with the last question first. This is such an important question since it's a principal reason why such religions, and speaking from my own Christian upbringing, the Christian religion in particular, has refused to accept the notion of reincarnation.

On the face of it, reincarnation is completely at odds with the very clear Biblical notion of the coming resurrection of the dead on Judgement Day; and specifically of the resurrection of the body which forms part of the Catholic Nicaean creed; but let's examine this carefully.

First of all, it goes against all reason to think that if the notion of bodily resurrection exists (and I believe that it does in a particular context), that it could possibly refer to our flesh and blood human bodies as we know them today. No eternal world, where things are meant to be everlasting and free of pain and suffering could possibly involve us having the bodies we have now. Our bodies do not last forever; are in need of sustenance and environmental patterns that could hardly exist in an eternal world, and are prone to pain and ailments; let alone of course those poor individuals who may have been born at the outset, with ill or defective bodies.

Saint Paul himself recognised this where at 1st Corinthians Chapter 15 (NIV), he notes the body to be raised will be a spiritual body.

"The body that is sown is perishable, it is raised imperishable; it is sown in dishonor, it is raised in glory; it is sown in weakness, it is raised in power; it is sown a natural body, it is raised a spiritual body."

So first point is, if we are to have resurrected "bodies" they cannot be of a type or substance as we currently see and know them.

Second, you might recall from our earlier discussion that the soul has some form of "memory" that retains not only the lifetime lessons learnt along the way of reincarnated history, but also some of the bodily human traits we have had in the past. I mentioned for example the retention of birth marks in the work done by Drs Stevenson and Tucker; which marks indicate bodily traumas in prior lives. Just as importantly there appears to be visual similarities in the facial features of reincarnated persons. I know this for a fact from my own experience but again I'm not asking you to take my word for it. You only need to research for yourself the many writings that exist on reincarnation to see the similarities in the often made photo comparisons between people who have been apparently reincarnated.

As a result, I think it's clear that transmigrating souls carry over bodily features from one life to the next. These features must, by definition, withstand the transition from one life into the next and do so in a spiritual form. It follows that in some form of spiritual context, the bodily features that we have when we are in flesh and blood can carry over to the spirit world. It is this form of the "body" that will be subject to being resurrected at a future point.

In this way, each so-called individual soul could have a "Name" (as sometimes mentioned in sacred scripture) which would reflect the amalgamation of that soul's spiritual and bodily forms of existence over eons of time.

The notion of reincarnation and the immovable Christian principal of the resurrection are not therefore incompatible; indeed, you could say that when viewed in this context, they are fully compatible and actually give powerful support to the notion of a bodily resurrection which, without the possibility of spiritual memory, is impossible to fathom in a fleshy existence for the reasons mentioned earlier.

This compatibility between reincarnation and resurrection was clearly understood and accepted by certain early Church Christian theologians; indeed, arguably by some of the best Christian theologians ever known, namely the Alexandrian Church Fathers in Origen and Clement of Alexandria.

Chapter Six

Does Holy Scripture support the Hypothesis?

So now returning to the first question, where is the evidence in the teachings and scriptural writings of the key religious faiths, that life is a lifelong schooling process based on recurring reincarnations of the soul?

The Search for Reincarnation in holy scriptures.

Of course, we already know that the concept of reincarnation is widely evidenced in holy scriptures belonging to the Hindu and Buddhist faiths. However, it has only made rare appearances in the "Religions of the Book" (Judaism, Christianity and Islam), except for Jewish Kabbalist thinking where reincarnation is critically important to its tenants.

There are some obvious reasons for the absence of reincarnation concepts, at least in the context of Christianity.

First, as we have already touched on, reincarnation was perceived as being in direct contrast to the notion of bodily resurrection.

Second, it was apparently contradictory to the

notion that Christ came to earth and died for us to atone for our sins. The notion of reincarnation did not, at least for some Christian theologians, apparently sit well with the importance of the Atonement theory of the resurrection. Nonetheless, we already noted that probably the greatest Christian theologian of all time Origen, along with certain of the other the Alexandrian Church Fathers, had no problem in incorporating reincarnation into the Christian theological milieu.

Finally, it was in my view, contrary to what was in the best interests of keeping the Church and its clergy in a position of power. The Church wielded great power from telling the masses that, "You only have one life and you'd better do what we say and give to the church what it asks of you, otherwise you will end up in eternal hell".

If the masses came to know that they had many lives to become perfect enough to enter the kingdom of God; and so if they did not get it right this lifetime, they could always try better next time, the Church's power would naturally be diminished.

Of course, the Church did not have the means or clout to suppress all free thinking intellectual clergy and theologians until it became the official Roman religion in 313 AD. Up until then, various incredibly well respected Church fathers, such as the Alexandrian fathers in Origen and Clement, were able to write freely about the incorporation of reincarnation concepts wholly compatibly with Christian tenants and scripture.

After 313 AD, and as early as the Council of

Nicaea in 325AD, the Church started to impose a regimented and censorship style regime towards free thinking Christian writers aimed at repressing all thinking inconsistent with the line of orthodoxy agreed at Nicaea.

The Holy Roman Emperor Justinian was also convinced by his advisers to do so, and so in the Council of Constantinople called by Justinian around 543 AD, Origen and his notion of the transmigration of souls were anathematised, despite the early resistance of the then Pope Vigilus, who ultimately succumbed to agreeing with the anathema under threat of physical arrest and imprisonment by Justinian.

The period after the Council of Nicaea (and certainly by the time of Council of Constantinople) was one of the most critical and tragic turning points not only in the Christian Church, but for western philosophy and civilisation in general. Since from that point on, no western theologian (who tended to be church men in any event in medieval times), including the great scholarly theologians of Saint Augustine and Saint Thomas Aquinas, contemplated reincarnation in their thinking, since it carried the risk of heresy charges and inquisitorial investigation. Neither did western philosophers of any note thereafter. The concept became foreign to western thinking and relegated to Eastern mythology.

However, the point remains that before the advent of Christianity's rise to official Roman religious status, the great scholarly Alexandrian fathers wrote openly about it and took authority for it from biblical sources. In the case of the New Testament this authority came from none other than Jesus himself and his Apostles.

There are various Bible verses which are suggestive of reincarnation. One episode in particular from the healing miracles of Christ seems to clearly point to reincarnation:

"And as he was passing by, he saw a man blind from birth. And his disciples asked him, 'Rabbi, who has sinned, this man or his parents, that he should be born blind?" Jesus answered, 'Neither has this man sinned, nor his parents, but the works of God were to be made manifest in him.'" (John 9:1)

The disciples ask the Lord if the man himself could have committed the sin that led to his blindness. Given the fact that the man had been blind from birth, we are confronted with a provocative question. When could "he" have made such transgressions as to make him blind at birth? The only conceivable answer is in some prenatal state. The question, as posed by the disciples, explicitly presupposes prenatal existence. It will also be noted that Christ says nothing to dispel or correct the presupposition.

Also very suggestive of reincarnation is the episode where Jesus identifies John the Baptist as the return of the Prophet Elijah. Elijah, under Old Testament prophecies, was predicted to return before the coming of the Messiah.

"For all the prophets and the law have prophesied until John. And if you are willing to receive it, he is Elijah who was to come." (Matthew 11:13-14)

"And the disciples asked him, saying, 'Why then do the scribes say that Elijah must come first?' But he answered them and said, 'Elijah indeed is to come and will restore all things. But I say to you that Elijah has come already, and they did not know him, but did to him whatever they wished. So also shall the Son of Man suffer at their hand?' Then the disciples understood that he had spoken of John the Baptist." (Matthew 17:10-13)

By identifying the Baptist as Elijah, Jesus is also identifying himself as the Messiah. Throughout the gospel narrative there are explicit references to the signs that will precede the Messiah. "Behold I will send you Elijah the prophet, before the coming of the great and dreadful day of the Lord." (Malachi 4:5)

Although Christendom has sought to refute these passages as having other meanings, they are obvious references to the ability of souls and spirit essences to pass from one person into another. The fact that John the Baptist himself, in Gospel narrative, denied that he was Elijah is not surprising since, by design, we are not intended to remember who we once were.

The Old Testament also has references to reincarnation notions (see below). The Jewish Kabbalists, of course, fully believe in it.

"Jeremiah 1:4

Then the word of the LORD came unto me, saying, 5 Before I formed thee in the belly I knew thee; and before thou camest forth out of the womb I sanctified thee, and I ordained thee a prophet unto the nations."

Indeed, the reincarnationist can even find scriptural support for personal disincarnate pre-existence. The following Bible verse alludes to proof of pre-existence:

"He chose us in him before the foundation of the world, that we should be holy and without blemish in his sight and love." (Ephesians 1:4)

Malachi 1:2-3 and Romans 9:11-13 both state that God loved Jacob, but hated Esau even before they were born. These verses are highly suggestive of the soul's pre-existence, at least of Esau's, who God apparently hated pre-birth; a necessary tenet associated with reincarnation.

Unfortunately, this verse has been used by advocates of Predestination to argue that it is scriptural evidence for the fact that God chooses who he will favour even before they are born. This not only does injustice to the real meaning of the verse, but uses the verse to propose a predestination notion which no God having compassion and true love for all souls could possibly espouse.

Ok, so having dealt with the scriptural reincarnation question, where is the reference in scripture to life being a lifelong learning process?

The Search for Life's Purpose of Schooling in Holy Scriptures

First, it's evident throughout the Bible, the Quran, and Kabbalist Jewish scripture and of course, Hindu and Buddhist religious writings, that souls and spirit essences exist separate from bodies. If reincarnation exists, and souls can retain the lessons learnt in life from one incarnation or transmigration to another, both of which I have argued for rationally above, then Darwin's theory of evolution alone would make clear that life must be a lifelong evolutionary, improvement, learning process.

In other words, a soul, being itself something that exists, albeit spiritually, should just as equally be subject to Darwin's laws of Evolutionary nature as all other things are. That is, if every animate thing we know is constantly subject to change and evolutionary forces, then why wouldn't souls (i.e. "animae" in Latin, from where the very word "animate" derives from) be subject to the same laws of animal nature? Certainly, the reincarnation Faiths I mentioned earlier such as Buddhism and Hinduism, believe that souls "learn" lessons from reincarnation experiences.

In this context, any animate thing or being that exists, can innately retain the lessons of experience in its constituent makeup, (i.e. Memory during our lives and, upon replication, DNA for us and animals; and "soul memory" for souls). And must, by nature's own evolutionary laws, be capable of learning and developing and modifying its nature to meet the changing circumstances and experiences it undergoes.

Second, both in the Bible as well as in non-conical writings, there is evidence that our lives are to be used to learn about ourselves and improve and perfect ourselves. I set out some examples below.

But we need to appreciate one significant point

here which naturally militates against there being clear and conclusive recognition in holy scriptures that life is immortal at the soul level; and that we (in bodily form) are but avatars of our true selves living in an illusory world. At that is this. ***If God wants us to learn hard lessons by experiencing many lives on earth, or in other worlds or other dimensions, then people need to "think" (which they do instinctively anyway) that the life they are living is REAL, and not just a big illusion created for them as a learning experience***.

For this reason, we cannot expect to find absolute clarity in holy scripture that life is just a schooling process, and the world we think we live in is purely illusory. It would be somewhat self-defeating if you knew you were being taught a lesson simply by enacting a role play of an event, as opposed to living out the real thing. But nonetheless, lessons learnt through role plays can still be good learning experiences; indeed, just as lessons learnt through hearing a parable can be a great learning experience, even though we realize that it does not depict a real life event.

If it were obvious to all and sundry that life was lived by us all in some avatar format, I certainly would not need to be making this point here. It would already be part of our western philosophical and theological learning.

There is often reference to secret teachings of Christ (and other holy teachers) and I suspect, but can't prove, that such secret teachings cover this notion.

For example in Mark:10-12 (NIV) it is noted as follows

"When he was alone, the Twelve and the others around him asked him about the parables. He told them, "The secret of the Kingdom of God has been given to you. But to those on the outside everything is said in parables so that, they may be ever seeing but never perceiving, and ever hearing but never understanding; otherwise they might turn and be forgiven!"

To me this is evidence that God's schema is for us to be under an illusion that the physical world we live in is real, and for us to experience its ups and downs in order for our souls to gradually elevate themselves to perfection so that we might be of a calibre to then truly unite with God and see him "face to face".

Importantly, Faith in God is a key aspect of this ascension to "enlightenment" and as a result we cannot be given total proof of his manner of training us nor even of his existence. Otherwise, even without having undergone the soul mutation required to bring us to becoming a selfless, loving and compassionate pure spirit worthy of God's ultimate reward, it would become obvious to us that God does actually exist and the training game would be given away, so much so that we would simply repent and, in his mercy, God would forgive us.

BUT we would never have "toiled" on our own account to have effected a permanent mutation to our "Soul DNA" in order to become like him (i.e. Godly in nature). We effectively would have "turned" (i.e. converted to believers) not from toil, sacrifice and self-learning (albeit this may still require God's assisting grace), but from the obvious "outing" of God's plan and himself. Nonetheless God, being All Merciful, would forgive us. However we would never have reached the elevated status that God's ultimate plan has in store for us; and as a result would not be eligible to receive our maximum potential reward of unification with him. More on this notion later.

Both in the Bible as well as in non-conical writings, there is evidence that our lives are meant to be challenging and to be used to learn the truth about ourselves; and to encourage us to detach ourselves from idle worldly vanities and improve and perfect ourselves to the point worthy to ultimately be reunited with God.

For example in the Gospel of Thomas, Jesus says,

"2. Jesus said, "Those who seek should not stop seeking until they find. When they find, they will be disturbed. When they are disturbed, they will marvel, and will reign over all. [And after they have reigned they will rest.]"

3. Jesus said, "If your leaders say to you, 'Look, the (Father's) kingdom is in the sky,' then the birds of the sky will precede you. If they say to you, 'It is in the sea,' then the fish will precede you. Rather, the (Father's) kingdom is within you and it is outside you.

When you know yourselves, then you will be known, and you will understand that you are children of the living Father. But if you do not know yourselves, then you live in poverty, and you are the poverty."

27. "If you do not fast from the world, you will not

find the (Father's) kingdom."

88. Jesus says:

(1) "The messengers and the prophets are coming to you, and they will give you what belongs to you.

(2) And you, in turn, give to them what you have in your hands (and) say to yourselves: 'When will they come (and) take what belongs to them?'"

"98. Jesus said, "The Father's kingdom is like a person who wanted to kill someone powerful. While still at home he drew his sword and thrust it into the wall to find out whether his hand would go in. Then he killed the powerful one."

I examine these sayings later in Chapter 10.

In Matthew 5:48

"48 Be perfect, therefore, as your Heavenly Father is perfect".

This training and learning process will come from subjecting men and women to pain, suffering and challenges.

We already know from evolutionary science and daily life experiences, that human and specie advancement comes from trials, challenging situations and often outright crises. It is this sense of crisis that serves well the purpose of educating people to change their ways and reform.

For example, in the Gospel of Thomas

"10. Jesus said, "I have cast fire upon the world, and look, I'm guarding it until it blazes."

"16. Jesus said, "Perhaps people think that I have come to cast peace upon the world. They do not know that I have come to cast conflicts upon the earth: fire, sword, war.

For there will be five in a house: there'll be three against two and two against three, father against son and son against father, and they will stand alone."

And in Matthew 10:34

"The Sword of the Gospel

33 But whoever denies Me before men, I will also deny him before My Father in heaven. 34 Do not assume that I have come to bring peace to the earth; I have not come to bring peace, but a sword. 35 For I have come to turn 'A man against his father, a daughter against her mother, and a daughter-in-law against her mother-in-law..."

An Old Testament quote also alludes to this as follows.

"The Law was given to be a tutor to lead people to the understanding that they were sinners in need of God's grace"

(Galatians 3:24).

From the Quran we also see clearly the notion that our lives are given to us as a test, refer the following Quranic quotes:

"Have the people thought that they would be left to say "We Believe" without them being tested? 29:2

[29:3] We have tested those before them, for God must distinguish those who are truthful, and He must expose the liars.

also:

[2:155] We will surely test you through some fear, hunger, and loss of money, lives, and crops. Give good news to the steadfast."

God tests all people, even God's chosen messengers

and prophets were put to the test. In 38:34 we read that God tested Solomon, Moses in 20:40, David in 38:24 and the severe test which the prophet Job had to endure is also told in the Quran.

From 29:2, we know that God tests all people. Further to this truth, we also read that God tests people through adversity as well as prosperity:

"Every person will taste death. We put you to the test through <u>adversity and prosperity</u> then to Us you shall be returned." 21:35

"You should know that <u>your money and your children are but a test</u> and that a great reward lies with God." 8:28

On the surface it may seem that the one tested in prosperity has been given a much more lenient test than one who is in poverty, but for the Quranic answer to this we need to look at the following quote.

"God does not demand from any soul <u>more than He has given it</u>." 65:7

This confirms that what is expected from every person is <u>directly related to what he/she has been given</u>, no more and no less.

"[14:34] If you count God's blessings, you can never encompass them. Indeed, the human being is transgressing, unappreciative.

[41:51] <u>When we bless the human being, he turns away</u>, and drifts farther and farther away, and <u>when he suffers any affliction, he implores loudly</u>."

Adversity and hardship is also a very effective reminder for those who are too much absorbed in the worldly life, and thus they may not be as devoted to God as they should be. Due to their being too preoccupied with this worldly life they do not seek God nor call on God as they should:

"[10:22] He is the One who moves you across the land and sea. You get onto the ships, and they sail smoothly in a nice breeze. Then, while rejoicing therein, violent wind blows, and the waves surround them from every side. This is when they implore God, sincerely devoting their prayers to Him alone: "If You only save us this time, we will be eternally appreciative."

"[10:23] But as soon as He saves them, they transgress on earth, and oppose the truth. O people, your transgression is only to the detriment of your own souls. <u>You remain preoccupied with this worldly life</u>, then to us is your ultimate return, then we inform you of everything you had done."

This last quote suggests not only that life is clearly a training ground, but that upon our death in this life, there will be an accounting to God of what we have done. A "Reckoning Day" as the Quran calls it, or a "final result" I would say, of our schooling days (i.e. Judgement Day in Biblical terms):

"And you (O Muhammad) will see the criminals (disbelievers, polytheists] that Day bound together in fetters. Their garments will be of liquid pitch, and fire will cover their faces. That Allah may requite each person according to what he has earned. Truly, Allah is Swift at reckoning. [Quran 14: 49-51]"

Another example:

"And the earth will shine with the light of its Lord and the record [of deeds] will be placed, and the

Prophets and the witnesses will be brought, and it will be judged between them in truth, and they will not be wronged. [Quran 39: 69]"

Baha'i writings evidencing Life as an illusory training ground

Evidence of the world having been created as a training ground for us can also be found in the Baha'i writings, for example

"O SON OF BOUNTY!

Out of the wastes of nothingness, with the clay of My command I made thee to appear, **"and have ordained for thy training every atom in existence and the essence of all created things" ["my emphasis"]**. Thus, ere thou didst issue from thy mother's womb, I destined for thee two founts of gleaming milk, eyes to watch over thee, and hearts to love thee. Out of My loving-kindness, 'neath the shade of My mercy I nurtured thee, and guarded thee by the essence of My grace and favor. And My purpose in all this was that "thou mightest attain My everlasting dominion and become worthy of My invisible bestowals" ["my emphasis"]. And yet heedless thou didst remain, and when fully grown, thou didst neglect all My bounties and occupied thyself with thine idle imaginings, in such wise that thou didst become wholly forgetful, and, turning away from the portals of the Friend didst abide within the courts of My enemy."

Baha'u'llah

The Hidden Words - Persian (p.29)

The above passage also mentions part of the learning and loving infrastructure God set in place for us when he talks of "eyes to watch over thee and hearts to love thee."

"XXXIV. All praise and glory be to God Who, through the power of His might, hath delivered His creation from the nakedness of non-existence, and clothed it with the mantle of life. From among all created things He hath singled out for His special favor the pure, the gem-like reality of man, and invested it with a unique capacity of knowing Him and of reflecting the greatness of His glory.

This twofold distinction conferred upon him hath cleansed away from his heart the rust of every vain desire, and made him worthy of the vesture with which his Creator hath deigned to clothe him. It hath served to rescue his soul from the wretchedness of ignorance.

This robe with which the body and soul of man hath been adorned is the very foundation of his well-being and development. **"Oh, how blessed the day when, aided by the grace and might of the one true God, man will have freed himself from the bondage and corruption of the world and all that is therein, and will have attained unto true and abiding rest beneath the shadow of the Tree of Knowledge!" ["My emphasis"]."**

Baha'u'llah

Gleanings from the writings of Baha'u'llah (p.78)

In the quote below Bahaullah clearly contemplates a time when God created us "rich" and "noble" and we subsequently reduced ourselves down to "poverty" and abasement. To me it's clear he is talking about the Adam and Eve story and the Fall, rather than having created us rich and noble at a prenatal time whilst in our mother's womb.

Man, having suffered the Fall from God's realm, now needs to "turn" towards God by examining himself, purifying himself from worldly detachment and finding God within himself.

"O SON OF SPIRIT!

I created thee rich, why dost thou bring thyself down to poverty? Noble I made thee, wherewith dost thou abase thyself? Out of the essence of knowledge I gave thee being, why seekest thou enlightenment from anyone beside Me? Out of the clay of love I molded thee, how dost thou busy thyself with another? Turn thy sight unto thyself, that thou mayest find Me standing within thee, mighty, powerful and self-subsisting."

Baha'u'llah

The Hidden Words - Arabic (p.13)

In the quote below Bahaullah notes God's urge to us to "rise" above our abasement (indeed, a reference to the Christian notion of Resurrection, but Resurrection not after bodily death but whilst we are alive) and become purified and worthy of reconnecting with God.

"O SON OF SPIRIT!

Noble have I created thee, yet thou hast abased thyself. Rise then unto that for which thou wast created."

Baha'u'llah

The Hidden Words - Arabic (p.22)

This "rising" and "turning" towards oneself can only be accomplished in our present state by worldly detachment and purification. But how can anyone achieve this in just one lifetime. Maybe some exceptional souls can but most of us require many lifetimes.

It's worth noting that although the Baha'i Faith does not specifically mention the notion of reincarnation, there is on death, a clear passing of the soul from one world to another, and it is not clear to me at least whether this is a permanent heaven / hell notion, as opposed to a journey involving many potential worlds.

It's also worth noting that the Baha'i Faith, having been born in the repressive environment of the Islamic Ottoman Empire, had to be circumspect about its teachings and so the notion of reincarnation, being an anathema to the Muslim environment surrounding the faith, may have been downplayed. But I should quickly add that this is conjecture on my part. The reality is that the faith talks about a passing from this world to another world and there is uncertainty, at least for me, about what this really means.

Finally, Baha'i reference to multiple lives can be seen in the quote below. The quote also brings out the notion that true lasting happiness can only be achieved by reconnection with God.

"O SON OF JUSTICE!

Whither can a lover go but to the land of his beloved? And what seeker findeth rest away from his heart's desire? To the true lover reunion is life, and separation is death. His breast is void of patience and his heart hath no peace. **"A myriad lives he would forsake" ["my emphasis"]** to hasten to the abode of his beloved."

Baha'u'llah
The Hidden Words - Persian (p.4)

Biblical stage plays and the Tree of Knowledge of Good and Evil

A further point I would like to make in this Chapter that also affirms the role of worldly illusion as a teacher of mankind, is as follows.

There are a few examples I would like to give that connect to both the Old and New Testament that make this point. In my view, all these demonstrate how biblical history (and indeed, perhaps all history) is but a stage upon which God, potentially through Jesus The Logos, plays out a story aimed to teach us lessons and in which the actors often have little say; that is, our life phases (as opposed to God's love and grace) are Predestined; and which therefore demonstrate powerfully the role of Destiny. (Note this does not mean that *how we perceive* such life phases, or *how we react* to them, is always predestined. There's naturally room for Freewill in our thoughts and actions, otherwise the notion of karma or, in the Abrahamic religions, the notion of being ultimately "judged" for our moral choices would have little or no relevance).

Exodus

The first is in the Old Testament in the story of the Exodus wherein God "hardened the heart "of Pharaoh so that he would not easily agree to let the enslaved Jews leave Egypt. Otherwise, there would be little need for a series of plagues and unnatural events to be levied on the Egyptians.

◀ Exodus 9:12 ▶

New International Version

"But the LORD hardened Pharaoh's heart and he would not listen to Moses and Aaron, just as the LORD had said to Moses."

Clearly, he did so to enable the Exodus story to be a dramatic and memorable record, depicted with plagues and unnatural phenomena, of God's power and might to all; both at the time, and also for posterity by having such recorded in the Old Testament and Jewish Torah. Like any good book or movie, without a great and dramatic story, it is hard to get across a profound and lasting teaching message.

Curing the man born blind

Another example is one we have touched on earlier from the New Testament; namely, the story of the blind man who was blind from birth. As we noted, Jesus's own words, when asked by his apostles why this man was born blind, clearly indicate that it was so he could be present in time during Christ's earthly reign; and so that Christ could heal him and so demonstrate to all, both at the time, and by recording the story in The Gospels for posterity, the great power Jesus had to heal the sick and be shown therefore as a great messenger from God and a Light for the world.

Gospel of John, 9:1-12.[1]

According to the Gospel, Jesus saw a man who had been blind since birth. His disciples asked him, "Rabbi, who sinned, this man or his parents, that he was born blind?"

Jesus replied:

"Neither this man nor his parents sinned," said Jesus, "but this happened so that the works of God might be displayed in him. As long as it is day, we must do the works of him who sent me. Night is coming, when no one can work. While I am in the world, I am the light of the world."

Raising Lazarus

Another example is the background to the well-known miracle involving the raising of Lazarus. Here Jesus, having received word of Lazarus's illness, waited for two more days before heading to Judea where Lazarus was, ensuring Lazarus would be dead by the time he arrived. He explained to his Apostles that Lazarus's death could be explained as follows,

John 11:1-44 New Living Translation (NLT)

The Raising of Lazarus

11 A man named Lazarus was sick. He lived in Bethany with his sisters, Mary and Martha. 2 This is the Mary who later poured the expensive perfume on

the Lord's feet and wiped them with her hair. [a] Her brother, Lazarus, was sick. 3 So the two sisters sent a message to Jesus telling him, "Lord, your dear friend is very sick."

4 But when Jesus heard about it he said, "Lazarus's sickness will not end in death. No, it happened for the glory of God so that the Son of God will receive glory from this."5 So although Jesus loved Martha, Mary, and Lazarus, 6 he stayed where he was for the next two days. 7 Finally, he said to his disciples, "Let's go back to Judea."

Christ's ultimate betrayal by Judas

Another example is Judas's betrayal of Jesus, wherein at the last supper just before Judas leaves to play out Christ's betrayal, Jesus, as a sign to his Apostles of who would be his betrayer, hands Judas a morsel of bread, and immediately Satan is said to have entered into Judas.

◀John 13:27▶

New International Version

As soon as Judas took the bread, Satan entered into him. So Jesus told him, "What you are about to do, do quickly."

In other words, Judas was not going to betray Christ left to his own will. Jesus knew that Satan would enter into Judas and lead him to betray him. But it was all destined that way so that Christ would be arrested and crucified and this would allow God to resurrect him. Of course, this final sequence of events would be the key stage play act that would launch the Christian Faith.

These are all examples of where the scriptures themselves lay evidence to the fact that biblical history has been managed in this illusory world of ours to deliver profound and long lasting lessons for us all. The world is truly a stage, as Shakespeare would say, but it's God's stage; and we are the unsuspecting actors; living, laughing, crying, enduring, dying and hopefully learning along the way.

As that beautiful Aboriginal proverb says,

"We are all visitors to this time, this place. We are just passing through. Our purpose here is to observe, to learn, to grow, to love... and then we return home."

The Story of the Tree of Knowledge of Good and Evil

I would like to finish this section that deals with Holy Scriptural support for the argument that Life is a School, with where in the Old Testament, this worldly material Life starts; i.e. in the Genesis account and the story of the Tree of Knowledge of Good and Evil.

The well-known, so called, "Fall" of Mankind from the Garden of Eden is an account not only of the Christian Faith, but also of the Jewish Faith, the Islamic Faith and is also found in a Tamil poem (and part of the Hindu Faith) called the "Tala Vilasam", which recounts a legend of the tree that parallels the Biblical account. In it, the Creator, Brahma, finally allows the people access to the tree; which in this account, is the Palmyra palm tree.

In Islam the story of what happened to Adam and Eve in the Garden occurs four times in the Qur'an 2:30-39; 7:10-27; 15:28-42; 20:115-127).

For example:

God places Adam and Eve in the garden and tells them that they are free to enjoy of its fruits except not to come near a certain tree: (Qur'an 2:35)

"We said: "O Adam! dwell thou and thy wife in the Garden; and eat of the bountiful things therein as (where and when) ye will; but approach not this tree, or ye run into harm and transgression."

Satan then deceives Adam and Eve into eating of the fruits of the tree: (2:36)

"Then did Satan make them slip from the (garden), and get them out of the state (of felicity) in which they had been. We said: "Get ye down, all (ye people), with some of you having enmity towards others. On earth will be your dwelling-place and your means of livelihood - for a time."

Adam and Eve feel a lot of remorse for their actions, but God turns to Adam in mercy and consoles him: (2:37)

"Then learnt Adam from his Lord words of inspiration, and his Lord Turned towards him; for He is Oft-Returning, Most Merciful."

God then informs Adam that God will send his guidance to Adam and his progeny: (2:38)

"We said: "Get down all of you from this place (the garden), then whenever there comes to you Guidance from Me, and whoever follows My Guidance, there shall be no fear on them, nor shall they grieve."

Islamcan.com notes:

"According to the Qur'an, God's plan was to educate our first parents in paradise, **"then send them into the world for a limited time to resist Satan, the enemy. They were sent to earth as part of God's plan for them; not as a way of preventing them access to the tree of life, but as a test to distinguish those deserving of everlasting enjoyment in God's paradise."["My emphasis"]"**

In the well-known Christian account, God banishes Adam and Eve for disobeying his command that they not eat of the fruit from the Tree of Knowledge of Good and Evil. In this account, not too dissimilar to the Islamic version, God says to Adam and Eve (Genesis 2:17)

"But you must not eat from the tree of the knowledge of good and evil, for when you eat from it you will certainly die." Contrary to this command, the Serpent tells them to eat of the tree in order to become wise and to "be as gods, knowing good and evil". And when Eve saw the tree as "a tree to be desired to make one wise" she took of the fruit and ate and gave also to Adam.

To me, at least, it is very clear what has happened here, even though it all needs to be allegorically interpreted.

The Tree is indeed a source of knowledge and wisdom of the meaning of Good and Evil. Eating of the tree meant that mankind started its school training in what Good and Evil is all about. It meant that we commenced a training program to both ENJOY (experience the Good) and ENDURE (experience the Evil and suffering) of life as we know it. We, from that point on, started "dying" in the sense that we commenced a process of physical embodiment (the Kabbalist notion of our divine sparks being trapped in physical bodies), as well as a process of death and reincarnation in order to reform ourselves.

In other words, it was the start of the illusory material world (our School of Life as used in this work), wherein we are now experiencing in our life, and multiple lives at that, a great variety of experiences designed to teach us the difference between good and evil.

We were given, both "bodies" as well as an "illusory material world", with which to be trained; and to learn that we will never be truly happy unless we reconnect with God and purify ourselves of ungodly desires to enable us to ultimately re-enter his kingdom. And, to use an Islamic notion as mentioned above, **"as a test to distinguish those deserving of everlasting enjoyment in God's paradise"**.

The grant of material bodies is supported in Genesis wherein it notes that,

"Unto Adam and also to his wife did the Lord God make coats of skin, and clothed them". (Genesis 3:21)

Origen of Alexandria, arguably the greatest Christian theologian, believed in this allegorical interpretation.

How can this Genesis account not be compelling scriptural support for the fact our present life is one of gaining knowledge and wisdom by experiencing good and evil throughout our lives?

Of course, such a reading as Genesis needs to be read allegorically as both Origen and Augustine clearly noted. What it naturally represents is that original Mankind (represented by Adam) was purely spiritual in nature and lived in God's presence, but was tempted away from that love by the pursuit of desires, including importantly, the desire to be more powerful and more knowledgeable than God had created him, even if in contradiction to God's wishes.

As I said at the outset, I'm not seeking to use scripture as evidence for my hypothesis. However, the hypothesis needs to be in conformity with the scriptures, for if the hypothesis was indeed true, then since it states that life is a lifelong schooling process and that our teachers are the founders of the Holy Scriptures of the key religious movements, then it needs to be broadly in conformity with what is said therein, otherwise it be unsustainable.

From what we have covered above, it is plain to see that Sacred Scripture does indeed so far support the hypothesis.

Chapter Seven

Progressivism and Universality

Consistent with what I noted earlier, the hypothesis requires evidence that over time individuals or groups are showing advancement in spiritual progress. It also I think requires evidence that mankind overall is progressing. Although for reasons covered later, you will see that this later point becomes somewhat ambivalent, and subservient to the maintenance of a challenging school environment.

And finally, it requires evidence that the opportunity to advance is open to all souls not just to a select few. That is, it must be universal. No God that is all loving and all powerful could design a system without this attribute.

The progress of mankind overall and the universal nature of salvation are however intertwined and we will deal with this later.

Progressivism

When we talk of progression we must talk of this in two contexts. First, the progression of each individual soul and second, the progression of mankind overall. Why so?

The idea that an individual can be reunited with God requires that the soul itself be learning and progressing, but this would not make sense if, over time, some souls progressed but, on the whole, mankind overall was not progressing or, worse still, was going backwards.

So we'd expect to see, as you would in any cohort of students, both individual students progressing, some excelling in an outstanding fashion whilst others maybe falling behind, but overall as the cohort progressed through various stages of learning, you would expect to see a discernible advancement in the overall intelligence and virtues of the cohort as a collective. Surely, that is what a supposed world class learning program would produce. Especially one that was gradually aimed at perfecting all mankind to the point of godly unification.

So where is the evidence for this?

Before we can look for evidence we need to first define what we'd expect progress to look like for both individuals, and collectives thereof, and second, for mankind as a whole.

So what is progress, or in other words how would we define success, first for an individual or small group thereof?

Here let's recall a key aspect of the original hypothesis. God made us to know and love him, and for us to in turn be loved. Moreover, our so-called fall from grace was due to our detachment or forgetfulness of him, and our attachment to idle fancies and other temptations that tempted us away from both him and a virtuous existence with him. By definition, had we remained attached to him and led the life of a soul consistent with his likeness, we would have led a virtuous existence given his all knowing, all loving, compassionate and just essence.

So the definition of a successful redemptive education for us is - to instil in us a realisation that we can never be truly happy without knowing and lovingly (as opposed to slavishly) worshiping God; and that we need to detach ourselves from a focus or reliance on idle fancies such as wealth, power, bodily pleasures, addictions and other distractions and ego, and to appreciate that having a connection with God is incredibly rewarding and that it assists us in our journey through life, as well as our ultimate reunion with him.

By this later point, I don't mean that we need to wait for eons for our soul to reunite with God before we feel a sense of the great pleasure and reward from connecting with him. Rather, I mean that in our present day lives, we should be able to gain some semblance of pleasure and reward by establishing a connection with him, even as we continue to gradually struggle towards detachment from other things, and move progressively to the remembrance and intimate dedication to him, as well as to the love and wellbeing of others. This daily connection is a major assist in our enjoyment of our present lifetime experience.

So where is the evidence of so-called "student souls" moving toward such a state, some either individually or in groups, excelling at times and others progressing more gradually, even faltering at times?

Let's start with what I had earlier called his emissaries or teachers. Of these we know without question that they included Moses, Jesus Christ, Mohammad, the Buddha, Krishna and others including Bahaullah who is lesser known, and possibly Zoroaster, and forgive me if I've left out some which I no doubt have.

Let's start with Christ (or the Christian movement) because we know for sure, outside of biblical scriptures, that Christ existed and with the aid of scriptures and other non-conical writings, we have a good idea of his life, ministry and the development of Christianity after his death.

Even if you put aside all the so-called miracles recounted in the scriptures, including, of course, Christ's own death and resurrection, you have to rationally admit that after his death, Christianity took off in an unprecedented manner; fuelled by the feverish dedication and passion of Saint Paul and the other apostles, and subsequently other martyrs of the Christian cause.

Something exceptional fuelled and drove these people and their followers to drop their concerns with their worldly routine and normal life and start a missionary life of pain, persecution, poverty and in many cases, ultimate martyrdom. These people did indeed give up idle lifestyle desires for a dedication to God and his cause, aimed at bringing others into the light and connecting them with God.

The early Christian communities were unique

in how they lived differently from so-called pagan communities. Even disparaging Roman writers in those early years would acknowledge how virtuous such Christians were. For example, if a plague visited a village, the Christians would not flee and abandon their fellow Christians but would stay behind to nurse and tend to them and their families; and would seem to somehow fair better in resisting the plague than many others. They were close knit and more loving and virtuous people than the norm.

The apostles, the early martyrs of the Christian church, and from what I can tell, many of the Church's designated Saints, were all exceptional souls who lived to the full the high standard we set out earlier of detachment from worldly distractions and dedication to God and his cause. In the illusory school of life, they became assistant teachers and school prefects who led by example, many in return for poverty, persecution, tortuous experiences and often death.

Of course, they all seemed to demonstrate a connection with, and such love of, the Divine that it gave them that present day reward and pleasure we talked of earlier; and that enabled them, indeed drove them, to endure their sacrifices.

Moreover, there are numerous reports of miraculous deeds that took place in connection with their ministries and struggles that cannot easily be dismissed. Indeed, you could surmise that it was God's evident existence through the power of the Holy Spirit so obviously made evident in such miracles, healings and demonic exorcisms that also gave Christ's early followers sufficient rational evidence and confidence to have Faith in the religion.

On the importance of such miracles, we also need to recall that Paul himself said that the single most important fact that underpins Christianity, is the fact of Christ's incarnation and resurrection; and that without that, Christianity would be totally undermined. For a man so contemporaneously placed to the time of such an event, and to have mingled with the apostles of the day, it is inconceivable that he would be driven to undertake the sacrifices and missionary work that he did without an unflinching belief in such a miracle, as well as his own miraculous conversion experience.

And, of course, the same goes for Christ's other apostles who apparently spent time with the risen Christ after his death, including doubting Thomas who wanted to touch and feel Christ's body before believing.

These are real people that made untold sacrifices for what they believed. Many of them, particularly the scholars and mystics, are some of the brightest and most sincere minds that ever walked on the planet.

Moreover, they won over the hearts and minds of many followers and devotees.

These are facts; not religious fabrications and cannot be ignored as evidence of what we are seeking.

The same, of course, applies to subsequent religions which are somewhat more modern than Christianity and therefore of which we also have historical records. Today the Christian faith, broadly defined, numbers some two billion people. The Muslim faith, some one and a half billion.

Can it be doubted that Mohammed and his followers and successors were also virtuous in the sense of wanting to put aside worldly pleasures in return for a focus on God?

The so-called five pillars of Islam are a testament to keeping God top of mind; namely, avoiding the great sin of his forgetfulness and the abstinence from life's fancies to a focus on prayer, pilgrimage, fasting and alms giving.

If we look at the Christian bifurcated Protestant religion, especially its Puritan version, we see the same focus on a Spartan lifestyle focussed on prayer and faith and detachment from earthly pleasures.

It's very instructive to look at the inception of these religious movements to really see them in their pure and unadulterated states. As each religion, or sect thereof, becomes mature and then old, man-made layers of doctrines and dogmas pollute the original source teaching; often to the point of it becoming hardly recognisable, as happened with the Pharisees in the Jewish faith during biblical times.

Whereas when one goes back to its inception, or its revitalisation (e.g. the Protestant revolution for Christianity) one can see the real source faith at its purest.

The Mystics were also another example of devoted believers whose Faith was evidenced, not only by strong beliefs and good works, but also by experiential practices that evinced a connection with the Divine in the present life.

The factually recorded spiritual and ecstatic experiences of people such as Bonaventura, Saint Teresa of Avila, Saint John of the Cross, the stigmata of Saint Francis and Saint Padre Pio, are all examples of this. Again these are real facts to be reckoned with, not religious imaginings, and the individuals involved were dedicated to the religious cause beyond doubt.

One modern example I would like to give is Dadi Shanki, who notes the following:

"Old or young, when I have knowledge of the true self I can become truthful and wise. This also enables me to become sensible and mature.

When I am approaching Life from the standpoint of ego, with my sense of who I am tied up with the body and its relations and connections with the world, I am over sensitive about what goes on around me, getting upset over small things all the time like a small child. With the understanding that comes with purity, I don't get disturbed. This saves an enormous amount of energy.

The essence or the seed of the knowledge that purifies and renews us is: don't look at the past, or at others; look at God, the true Mother and Father, and then look at yourself. Be patient. Remain peaceful. With that true effort, you'll have God's love inside you.

When the Bestower of Knowledge is your companion, at every step He's telling you how things really are. This truth then makes you perform pure, clean, elevated, noble actions. Those actions give power, until you become one who shows truth to the world. Such a diamond will sparkle from a distance.

The stage of awareness in which I am inside myself, silent and bodiless, sitting with God, makes good things happen outside. It's fixed: there is the awareness that the One who had to get it done is there all the time, and I am just an instrument in between.

God is waiting for each of us to become so pure that we can be true instruments in sharing these qualities with all souls.

Purity enables me to be detached, and detachment enables me to remain positive, loving and wise.

When I remain in the awareness that I am a spirit, the light and beauty of that spirituality spreads far and wide. When I connect to God's supreme power, it is as if a powerful current flows to where it is most needed."

Achieving a mystical state of awareness as spirit means we have transcended beyond the sense of being detached individuals, and in that moment we join with the supreme consciousness so that the flow of current that runs through us truly has the power to transform us by elevating our "enlightenment" calibration. It seems that meditating on the divine has the power to do this.

I also particularly like the reference in the above quote to us becoming "instruments" of God and part of his overall plan to enlighten others and Mankind generally. The notion of being an "instrument" ties into what I heard Pope Francis say, on a rare and beautiful occasion, that I was fortunate to experience when I saw him live in a Saint Peters Square address.

He said,

"We not only can experience God's mercy but can also be instruments of his mercy for others."

To me this goes a long way to answering the long puzzlingly question I've had about why Scriptures often refer to us, in general, as God's "servants". Having wondered for years why God would need any servants, I finally understand the context. And that is in this sense.

As Dadi Shanki said earlier,

"When the Bestower of Knowledge is your companion, at every step He's telling you how things really are. This truth then makes you perform pure, clean, elevated, noble actions. Those actions give power, until you become one who shows truth to the world. Such a diamond will sparkle from a distance."

In other words, the connection with God, not only permanently improves your soul essence and therefore leads you to a better way of living, but you also serve God's overall plan of setting an example by showing truth to the world for others to follow. Indeed, we should all strive, for both our benefit and the benefit of mankind at large, to be elevated to being God's "servants".

From what is said above, one can see the clear fact that there are numerous well documented examples of both individuals and groups thereof, that throughout history have dedicated themselves to the abandonment of ordinary life pursuits and, to instead, a focus on a life of worldly detachment and purification, and on knowing God and lovingly worshipping him, as well as the pursuit of good works in his service.

History unequivocally evidences both great teachers and great and illustrious students, many of whom have given birth to new movements and sects, and who have refreshed the previous aging and stagnating religious groups that have gone before them.

Worship, Praise, Unconditional Love and Deification - The End Game

Ok then, so what is the End Game?

So far I have argued that this Illusory School of Life is meant to teach us to be detached from minor worldly fears and desires, and to aim for a love of God and fellow souls; and in so doing, we will perfect ourselves (ourselves here of course being our spiritual soul essences), and that we will then eventually be connected with God in some "complete" sense; be eternally free of the reincarnative process and live in bliss forever.

But let's think logically, putting aside all religious teachings for now, what is the nature and purpose of this End State. Let's revisit the question of WHY does this supposed All Knowing, All Powerful and All Loving force desire such an end state of affairs?

We noted at the very start of this work that there would be little point in being All Loving and All Powerful and yet having hardly anyone to love. Moreover, an All Loving and All Powerful God would not wish to be restrictive in his ability to do good works or benefice others. Surely this is only logical. For instance, if you were All Loving in character and had immense resources that could help and benefice others, would you keep those resources locked up useless to anyone, or would you devote them to good works?

Furthermore, if you were so fortunate to have immense resources and you had no children, would you not wish to have, or at least adopt, children of your own that could benefit from such beneficence available to you? This would only be a logical human tendency and we admire people who adopt or foster children with such intentions.

Logically therefore, it is entirely plausible that God either created us from scratch, or moulded us from existing spiritual essences, for the purpose of enabling him to realize his All Loving nature, and to benefit us by enabling us to ultimately develop into some form of divine unity with him eternally.

Whether this is tantamount to our spirit essences achieving a Godly quality, or something akin to that, is obviously hard to say, but quite likely this is the case. In short, God created us out of his loving beneficence and to exhibit his charitable love.

In addition, the total sum of our End State aggregated experience and creativity will merge with him and, to this extent, you could say that his (as well as our collective) divine nature also benefits and is, indeed, regenerated and enhanced by this End State outcome.

In other words, that just as God is All Loving and wishes to create an End State environment of Love for us and himself in some unified world, he is also All Knowing and Wise, and so the accumulation and expansion of Knowledge and Wisdom is also a key End State objective.

Just as an All Loving outcome is achieved by perfecting our ability and propensity to Love, an All Knowledge and Wisdom outcome is achieved by perfecting our Creative abilities.

That creativity, and in particular the benefit of adding to the pool of total creative consciousness, may well be a key reason for our creation is supported by the logical musings of some well-known philosophers. Moreover, as can be seen from the philosophic quotes below, the link between Creativity and Freedom is intertwined and not to be easily passed over.

We may not only need to "toil" our way out of Plato's Prison of the Cave using our constantly developing Freedom Fighter prowess, but in the process we are increasing the creative pool of universal consciousness. Or put another way, as we work our way through all the lessons and learnings from participating in the School of Life, the intellectual property created from such training enriches the permanent and ever growing pool of creative consciousness that will in turn benefit all concerned, including God.

Refer the following comments from renown philosophers on the subject:

"Creativeness is liberation from slavery. Man is free when he finds himself in a state of creative activity. Creativeness leads to ecstasy of the moment. The products of creativeness are within time, but the creative act itself lies outside time."

Nikolai Berdyaev (1874-1948), Russian Philosopher.

"Freedom is only to be found where there is burden to be shouldered. In creative achievements this burden always represents an imperative and a need that weighs heavily upon man's mood, so that he comes to be in a mood of melancholy. All creative action resides in a mood of melancholy, whether we are clearly aware of the fact or not, whether we speak at length about it or not. All creative action resides in a mood of melancholy, but this is not to say that everyone in a melancholy mood is creative."

Martin Heidegger (1889 –1976), German philosopher.

Finally, if we were moulded by him from existing uncreated essences, then perhaps another reason for God putting us through a boot camp through which some of us (with the rest perishing) hopefully ending up as All Loving souls, is to ensure that we do not end up in a poorer malevolent or evil state; in much the same way we might adopt children who are in a poor quality environment, in order to give them a better chance at life.

Moreover, for the reasons set out earlier, it's clear to me that this eventual End Game we are striving for has to be achieved "with effort" from ourselves and not just left to God's grace with no choice on our part. The reason for this is that if no effort is required on our part, as some Pre-destinationalists argue, then we will feel unworthy to eventually enjoy God's immense love and joys that he has install for us. This may have in fact contributed to our original fall from grace. This effort on our part would naturally give us a tendency to "boast" as Saint Paul suggested, but if we have truly perfected ourselves then, of course, we will not boast even if we were tempted to. After all, that is the very purpose of our training; namely, to learn amongst other things, to resist temptation, including overt pride and the temptation to boast.

If I am correct in this End Game analysis, then surely there is some support for this in the Holy Scriptures, since I have argued all along that the Teachers of the Holy Scriptures are sent to us from this same God to train and guide us.

I have found that whilst these scriptures are supportive, they appear, at least on their face, to be somewhat limited in what they say the "End Game" shall be; or for what ultimate end purpose God created us, and so to what end we are to devote our eventual immortal existence with him.

Some key examples are as follows:

Bible verses related to *Why God Created Man* from the King James Version (KJV)

Isaiah 43:7 - [Even] every one that is called by my name: for I have created him **for my glory, I have formed him**; yea, I have made him.

Revelation 4:11 - Thou art worthy, O Lord, to receive glory and honour and power: **for thou hast created all things, and for thy pleasure they are and were created**.

1 Peter 5:6-7 - Humble yourselves therefore under the mighty hand of God, **that he may exalt you in due time**:

Isaiah 43:21 - This people have I formed for

myself; **they shall shew forth my praise**.

John 3:16-17 - For God so loved the world, that he gave his only begotten Son, that **whosoever believeth in him should not perish, but have everlasting life**.

From the Quran.

"Quran Hud 11:7. (To test which of you is best in conduct ; and to worship Me)

7. It is He who created the heavens and the earth in six days-and His Throne was upon the waters-**in order to test you-which of you is best in conduct**. And if you were to say, "You will be resurrected after death," those who disbelieve would say, "This is nothing but plain witchcraft."

17. Is he who possesses a clear proof from his Lord, recited by a witness from Him, and before it the Book of Moses, a guide and a mercy? These believe in it. But whoever defies it from among the various factions, the Fire is his promise.

19 Those who hinder others from the path of God, and seek to make it crooked; and regarding the Hereafter, they are in denial. 20. These will not escape on earth, and they have no protectors besides God. The punishment will be doubled for them. They have failed to hear, and they have failed to see. 21. Those are the ones who lost their souls, and what they had invented has strayed away from them. 22. Without a doubt, in the Hereafter, they will be the biggest losers. 23. As for those who believe and do good deeds, and humble themselves before their

Lord-these are the inhabitants of Paradise, where they will abide forever.

Quran The spreaders

56. I did not create the jinn and the humans **except to worship Me**.

57. I need no livelihood from them, nor do I need them to feed Me. 58. God is the Provider, the One with Power, the Strong. 59. Those who do wrong will have their turn, like the turn of their counterparts, so let them not rush Me. 60. So woe to those who disbelieve because of that Day of theirs which they are promised.

67. Sovereignty (al-Mulk) In the name of God, the Gracious, the Merciful. 1. Blessed is He in whose hand is the sovereignty, and Who has power over everything. 2. **He who created death and life-to test you-as to which of you is better in conduct**. He is the Almighty, the Forgiving. 3. He who created seven heavens in layers. You see no discrepancy in the creation of the Compassionate. Look again. Can you see any cracks?

4. Then look again, and again, and your sight will return to you dazzled and exhausted. 5. We have adorned the lower heaven with lanterns, and made them missiles against the devils; and We have prepared for them the punishment of the Blaze. 6. For those who reject their Lord, there is the torment of Hell. What an evil destination! 7. When they are thrown into it, they will hear it roaring, as it seethes. 8. It almost bursts with fury. Every time a batch is thrown into it, its keepers will ask them, "Has no

warner come to you?" 9. They will say, "Yes, a warner did come to us, but we disbelieved, and said, 'God did not send down anything; you are very much mistaken.'" 10. And they will say, "Had we listened or reasoned, we would not have been among the inmates of the Blaze." 11. So they will acknowledge their sins. So away with the inmates of the Blaze. 12. As for those who fear their Lord in secret-for them is forgiveness and a great reward. 13. Whether you keep your words secret, or declare them-He is Aware of the inner thoughts. 14. Would He not know, He Who created? He is the Refined, the Expert. 15. It is He who made the earth manageable for you, so travel its regions, and eat of His provisions. To Him is the Resurgence."

From Holy Scriptures such as these therefore, at least superficially, one gets a relatively banal view of *why* God created us. It may be to praise and worship him. It maybe for his pleasure or glory. It maybe to test us and see who performs best under pressure, but even this seems to be for his pleasure, or so that those who survive the gauntlet of life can then praise and worship him. It maybe to give us immortality, but then this is for a reason; presumably, so that we may praise and worship him forever?

However, none of these seem, to me at least, to be valiant end objectives for an All Loving God. Surely, an All Loving All Powerful God doesn't need to be pleasured, praised or worshipped, either temporarily or indefinitely?

If we ignore the scriptures for a moment, it makes perfect sense to me that God would create us out of beneficence as outlined earlier. Although the great Greek philosophers we mentioned earlier concluded logically in a creator God, they do not seem to have addressed logically *why* such an all-powerful being required either a Creation, or creatures, such as us. And equally now, Holy Scriptures give us only seemingly banal reasons for this.

What is really going on here? I think the answer is as follows.

The Power of Love

It is true to say that an All Powerful and All Loving God does not "need" to be praised or worshiped or pleasured, and he certainly does not need us. *However, we should carefully distinguish between, and understand fully, the nature of the beneficence that God intends giving us, as well as the mode of delivery. And, as is so often the case, it seemingly inevitably comes down to, Love.*

The key to this is found in a beautiful Baha'i insight as follows:

"O SON OF BEING! Love Me, that I may love thee. If thou lovest Me not, My love can in no wise reach thee. Know this, O servant."

This notion completes the logical connection between our love of God and his beneficence of us. In other words, it is by the very connection formed from our love of God, and it needs to be faithful unconditional love of him, that he is able to bestow

on us, via his grace, the ability to see things as they really are; and to help us navigate this tough and challenging world we have been given to learn in. It is via this connection that we can hope to eventually become united with him in a blissful everlasting co-existence.

(Bahaullah Hidden Words 5)

Here's how C.S. Lewis puts it in ***Reflections on the Psalms***:

"I had never noticed that all enjoyment spontaneously overflows into praise.... The world rings with praise—lovers praising their mistresses, readers their favourite poet, walkers praising the countryside, players praising their favourite game.... I had not noticed either that just as men spontaneously praise whatever they value, so they spontaneously urge us to join them in praising it: 'Isn't she lovely? Wasn't it glorious? Don't you think that magnificent?' The Psalmists in telling everyone to praise God are doing what all men do when they speak of what they care about. My whole, more general, difficulty about the praise of God depended on my absurdly denying to us, as regards the supremely Valuable, what we delight to do, what indeed we can't help doing, about everything else we value. I think we delight to praise what we enjoy because the praise not merely expresses but completes the enjoyment; it is its appointed consummation. It is not out of compliment that lovers keep on telling one another how beautiful they are; the delight is incomplete till it is expressed."

This expresses the well-known idea that, "If you love someone you will sing their praises"; or "worship the ground they walk on."

It is by the very act of praising and worshipping God (and, of course, it would follow that we would act accordingly and therefore follow his wishes), that we complete our unconditional love of God.

When we do this, we plug into a powerful force that helps perfect us and attain us to a point of godly nature, compared to which our earthly existence, no matter how lavish, would seem to be a state of utter poverty.

This is what Dadi Shanki is saying when she says :

"When I remain in the awareness that I am a spirit, the light and beauty of that spirituality spreads far and wide. When I connect to God's supreme power, it is as if a powerful current flows to where it is most needed."

True and loving praise and worship of God is nothing short of unconditional love of him. Once this level is reached, God's beneficence comes in spades, and the ultimate End Game for each soul is to merge into one blissful coexistence with God. Rightly or wrongly, this has often been referred to as becoming "God like", or deification.

Certainly the Eastern Orthodox Church believed this when it spoke of the notion of Theosis. Refer the following online reference to this.

"Theosis has three stages: first, the purgative way, purification, or katharsis; second, illumination, the illuminative way, the vision of God, or theoria; and third, sainthood, the unitive way, or theosis. Thus the term "theosis" describes the whole process and its objective. By means of purification a person

comes to theoria and then to theosis. Theosis is the participation of the person in the life of God. According to this doctrine, the holy life of God, given in Jesus Christ to the believer through the Holy Spirit, is expressed through the three stages of theosis, beginning in the struggles of this life, increasing in the experience of knowledge of God, and consummated in the resurrection of the believer, when the victory of God over fear, sin, and death, accomplished in the Crucifixion and Resurrection of Jesus Christ, is made manifest in the believer forever.

***Theosis** or deification is a transformative process whose aim is likeness to or union with God, as taught by the Eastern Orthodox Church and Eastern Catholic Churches. As a process of transformation, theosis is brought about by the effects of catharsis (purification of mind and body) and theoria ('illumination' with the 'vision' of God).*

***"According to Eastern Christian teaching, theosis is very much the purpose of human life" ["My emphasis"].** It is considered achievable only through a synergy (or cooperation) between human activity and God's uncreated energies (or operations).*

It is illuminating to see here the connection raised in Eastern Orthodoxy between Theosis and the notion of the Resurrection, as noted above, "....consummated in the resurrection of the believer, when the victory of God over fear, sin, and death, accomplished in the Crucifixion and Resurrection of Jesus Christ, is made manifest in the believer forever."

The notion of Theosis in Easter Christian Orthodoxy appears to be similar, although not identical, to the Roman Catholic notion of the Beatific Vision. Refer to the following on line reference to this.

"In Christian theology, the ***beatific vision*** *(Latin: visio beatifica) is the ultimate direct self-communication of God to the individual person. A person possessing the beatific vision reaches, as a member of redeemed humanity in the communion of saints, perfect salvation in its entirety, i.e. heaven. The notion of vision stresses the intellectual component of salvation, though it encompasses the whole of human experience of joy, happiness coming from seeing God finally face to face and not imperfectly through faith. (1 Cor 13:11–12).*

It is related to the Catholic and Eastern Orthodox belief in theosis, and is seen in most – if not all – church denominations as the reward for Christians in the afterlife."

Monsignor Edward A. Pace in the Catholic Encyclopedia (1907) defined the Beatific Vision:

The immediate knowledge of God which the angelic spirits and the souls of the just enjoy in Heaven. It is called "vision" to distinguish it from the mediate knowledge of God which the human mind may attain in the present life. And since in beholding God face to face the created intelligence finds perfect happiness, the vision is termed "beatific."[9].

In Catholic theology, the intercession of saints is valid because those who have died in the Faith are with God in Heaven and enjoy the Beatific Vision, i.e., unmediated access to God's Presence, actually in Paradise itself, seeing God.

Thomas Aquinas defined the beatific vision as

the human being's "final end" in which one attains to a perfect happiness. Thomas reasons that one is perfectly happy only when all one's desires are perfectly satisfied, to the degree that happiness could not increase and could not be lost. "Man is not perfectly happy, so long as something remains for him to desire and seek." STh I–II, q., 3, a. 8. But this kind of perfect happiness cannot be found in any physical pleasure, any amount of worldly power, any degree of temporal fame or honor, or indeed in any finite reality. It can only be found in something that is infinite and perfect – and this is God. STh I–II, q. 2, a. 8. And since God is not a material thing but is pure spirit, we are united to God by knowing and loving him. Consequently, the most perfect union with God is the most perfect human happiness and the goal of the whole of the human life. But we cannot attain to this happiness by our own natural powers; it is a gift that must be given us by God, who strengthens us by the "light of glory" so that we can see him as he is, without any intermediary. (Thomas quotes Psalm 36:9 on this point: "In your light we shall see light.") STh I, q. 12, a. 4. Further, since every created image or likeness of God (including even the most perfect "ideas" or "images" of God we might generate in our minds) is necessarily finite, it would thus be infinitely less than God himself. STh I, q. 12, a. 2. The only perfect and infinite good, therefore, is God himself, which is why Aquinas argues that our perfect happiness and final end can only be the direct union with God himself and not with any created image of him. This union comes about by a kind of "seeing" perfectly the divine essence itself, a gift given to our intellects when God joins them directly to himself without any intermediary. And since in seeing this perfect vision of what (and who) God is, we grasp also his perfect goodness, this act of "seeing" is at the same time a perfect act of loving God as the highest and infinite goodness.

According to Aquinas, the Beatific Vision surpasses both faith and reason. Rational knowledge does not fully satisfy humankind's innate desire to know God, since reason is primarily concerned with sensible objects and thus can only infer its conclusions about God indirectly. Summa Theologiae

The Theological virtue of faith, too, is incomplete, since Aquinas thinks that it always implies some imperfection in the understanding. The believer does not wish to remain merely on the level of faith but to grasp directly the object of faith, who is God himself. Summa Contra Gentiles

Thus only the fullness of the Beatific Vision satisfies this fundamental desire of the human soul to know God. Quoting St Paul, Aquinas notes "We see now in a glass darkly, but then face to face" (i Cor. 13:12). The Beatific Vision is the final reward for those saints elect by God to partake in and "enjoy the same happiness wherewith God is happy, seeing Him in the way which He sees Himself" in the next life. Summa Contra Gentiles

Pope John XXII and the Beatific Vision controversy

Pope John XXII (1316–1334) caused a controversy

involving the Beatific Vision.[11] He said not as Pope but as a private Theologian that the saved do not attain the Beatific Vision until Judgment Day, a view more consistent with soul sleep.[12]The general understanding at the time was that the saved attained Heaven after being purified and before Judgment Day. He never proclaimed his belief as doctrine but rather as an opinion (see ex cathedra, as defined at the First Vatican Council in 1870).

The Sacred College of Cardinals held a consistory on the problem in January 1334, and Pope John backed away from his novel views to the more standard understanding.

His successor, Pope Benedict XII, declared it doctrine that the saved see Heaven (and thus, God) before Judgment Day."

Platonism

In the philosophy of Plato, the beatific vision is the vision of the Good. In Plato's Allegory of the cave, which appears in the Republic Book 7 (514a – 520a), he writes (speaking, as he does in many of his works, through the character of Socrates):

"My opinion is that in the world of knowledge the idea of good (the Good) appears last of all, and is seen only with an effort; and, when seen, is also inferred to be the universal author of all things beautiful and right, parent of light and of the lord of light in this visible world, and the immediate source of reason and truth in the intellectual." (517b, c).

St. Augustine expressed views similar to Plato's on

this subject, and was familiar with Plato's ideas, most likely via Neoplatonist writings.

Reminiscent of the Eleusinian Mysteries, Socrates' provides a mystic vision of initiation in Plato's Phaedrus:

"There was a time when with the rest of the happy band they saw beauty shining in brightness – we philosophers following in the train of Zeus, others in company with other gods; and then we beheld the beatific vision and were initiated into a mystery which may be truly called most blessed, celebrated by us in our state of innocence before we had any experience of evils to come, when we were admitted to the sight of apparitions innocent and simple and calm and happy, which we beheld shining in pure light". (Phaedrus:250).

Hinduism

The Vedic concept of having a visual perception of the gods and goddesses is generically called darshan. The key difference seems to be that one can also have a darshan when a god or goddess appears while the person is living.

The seeing of blue and yellow colors while in samadhi, which is a state of union with the omnipresent Brahman, who is beyond all duality, is also similar to the idea of beatific vision.

Islam

Sunni Islam also has the idea of beatific vision. The

Qur'an speaks of believers seeing Allah in paradise. In chapter 75, verses 22–23 state "On that day, faces shall be radiant, gazing upon their Lord."

A Hadith of Muhammad (Al-Bukhari, chapter 10 Hadith number 529) says

We were sitting with the Messenger of Allah when he looked at the full moon and observed, "You will see your Lord in the Hereafter as you see this moon having no difficulty in seeing it."

Shia Islam, however, is against this idea. Shiites believe God is absolute, meaning he does not require a form. If God can be seen then God has a form, so God cannot be seen.

Church of Latter Day Saints (Mormons)

In a more modern context the notion of End Game, Theosis or Beatific Vision plays itself out in the concept of Deification espoused by the Mormon Church of Latter Day Saints (LDS).

The LDS is very upfront in that they see the ultimate prize for LDS followers as "Becoming like God".

From the current LDS website, the notion is outlined broadly as follows.

Latter-day Saints see all people as children of God in a full and complete sense; they consider every person divine in origin, nature, and potential. Each has an eternal core and is "a beloved spirit son or daughter of heavenly parents." Each possesses seeds of divinity and must choose whether to live in harmony or tension with that divinity. Through the

Atonement of Jesus Christ, all people may "progress toward perfection and ultimately realize their divine destiny."

In support of their claims they refer to a number of Biblical passages.

"God said, Let us make man in our image, after our likeness. ... So God created man in his own image, in the image of God created he him; male and female created he them."

Once Adam and Eve had eaten the forbidden fruit, God said they had "become as one of us," suggesting that a process of approaching godliness was already underway.

The book of Psalms also declares, "I have said, Ye are gods; and all of you are children of the most High."

When Jesus was accused of blasphemy on the grounds that "thou, being a man, makest thyself God," He responded, echoing Psalms, "Is it not written in your law, I said, Ye are gods?"

In the Sermon on the Mount, Jesus commanded His disciples to become "perfect, even as your Father which is in heaven is perfect."

Moreover, they point out that the earliest Jewish and Christian commentaries on the Creation assumed that God had organized the world out of preexisting materials, emphasizing the goodness of God in shaping such a life-sustaining order. But the incursion of new philosophical ideas in the second century led to the development of a doctrine that God created the universe ex nihilo—"out of nothing."

They note that this ultimately became the

dominant teaching about the Creation within the Christian world. And that in order to emphasize God's power, many theologians reasoned that nothing could have existed for as long as He had. It became important in Christian circles to assert that God had originally been completely alone. **[My insertion: Just on this point, it is worth noting that the greatest question mark hanging over the age old justification of God's existence based on the Aristotelian notion of "first unmoved mover", (which incidentally founded the philosophical beliefs in God's existence as espoused by Augustine and Thomas Aquinas), was the question - why could there not have been more than one "unmoved mover"?; i.e. could there in fact have been more than one eternal being?. If, for example, our soul essences, like God, were uncreated, this in itself may not have prevented God having shaped us, or made us from clay so to speak, to eventually become after much schooling in material bodies through a process of multi lifelong learning, defied like him]**.

They note that creation ex nihilo widened the perceived gulf between God and humans. It became less common to teach either that human souls had existed before the world or that they could inherit and develop the attributes of God in their entirety in the future. Gradually, as the depravity of humankind and the immense distance between Creator and creature were increasingly emphasized, the concept of deification faded from Western Christianity, though it remains a central tenet of Eastern Orthodoxy, one of the three major branches of Christianity.

They also note that their founder, Joseph Smith received revelations wherein he learned that the light or intelligence at the core of each human soul "was not created or made, neither indeed can be." God is the Father of each human spirit, and because only "spirit and element, inseparably connected, receive a fullness of joy," He presented a plan for human beings to receive physical bodies and progress through their mortal experience toward a fullness of joy.

Earthly birth, then, is not the beginning of an individual's life: "Man was also in the beginning with God."

Likewise, Joseph Smith taught that the material world has eternal roots, fully repudiating the concept of creation ex nihilo. "Earth, water &c—all these had their existence in an elementary State from Eternity," he said in an 1839 sermon. God organized the universe out of existing elements. **[My insertion : Here we also need to remember the notion that Jesus is the Logos through which, or by whom, the material world exists; that you will find him under a rock and inside a piece of wood; that God is closer to us than our jugular vein; that in the Hindu faith Vishnu Dreams the Universe into existence. In which case, if the Universe is made though Jesus, Vishnu or God, and all such were eternally present, then perhaps God can indeed be said to have fashioned the material world, and perhaps even us, from eternally existing substances. The "clay" may have always existed, but God, the Omnipotent Creator, perhaps crafted or created us nonetheless from it]**.

Joseph smith noted that human nature was at

its core divine. God "was once as one of us" and "all the spirits that God ever sent into the world" were likewise "susceptible of enlargement." **[My insertion: Does susceptible of enlargement here mean capable of evolving? If so, that is consistent with the notion expressed in this work]**.

He also preached that long before the world was formed, God found "himself in the midst" of these beings and "saw proper to institute laws whereby the rest could have a privilege to advance like himself" and be "exalted" with Him. **[My insertion: Here we have to recall what was said in earlier chapters in this work about the possibility that God evolved into God, if indeed he didn't exist from the start other than in eternal substances of sorts akin to our spiritual essences; and he evolved by the process of Darwinian Evolution of such essences coupled with immense eons of time. Of course, if this was so, it also possible that there are, or at least were at some point, more than one God. Moreover, Smith makes the point that God's purpose in molding us, was out of his beneficence in order to advance us]**.

Smith told his assembly, "You have got to learn how to be a god yourself." In order to do that, people needed to learn godliness, or to be more like God. The process would be ongoing and would require patience, faith, continuing repentance, obedience to the commandments of the gospel, and reliance on Christ. Like ascending a ladder, individuals needed to learn the "first principles of the Gospel" and continue beyond the limits of mortal knowledge until they could "learn the last principles of the Gospel" when the time came. "It is not all to be comprehended in this world," Joseph said. "It will take a long time after the grave to understand the whole." **[My insertion : This of course, is reminiscent of The Ladder of Divine Ascent, except that it also foreshadows a learning process that goes well beyond death, and suggestive of a reincarnative or, at least, a transmigrative soul process, although Mormons do not believe in such notions as far as I can tell. For completeness, in the Icon of The Ladder of Divine Ascent, a ladder stands on the earth and reaches to Heaven. Monks are seen trying to climb the ladder, and winged demons are seen pulling them off. Over the top of the ladder is Christ, emerging from Heaven. At the right side of the scene is shown a monastery building. Standing outside its door is St. John Climacus. His right hand points at the ladder and watching monks stand behind him. In his left hand he holds a scroll on which is written: "Ascend, ascend, Brethren." In the top left corner, opposite the monastery, are angels shown clothed in light-colored garments and having large, strong wings, interceding to endeavour to help those ascending the ladder]**.

Where does all this take us as far as the "End Game" is concerned?

It is clear to me that the God we are talking about is not a God that, of his own necessity, requires praise or worship. He does not want us to praise and worship him primarily for his benefit, but rather for our benefit. This praise and worship that he wishes

from us is vested in Love. He wants us to love him unconditionally to the point where we naturally praise and worship him in the way that C S Lewis used the term praise.

The reason being is that it is ONLY by loving him intensely, that his love and beneficence can reach us, infuse our souls and reform and evolve our innate character so that we may over time, in fact, perhaps over many life times, become like him. This makes perfect logical sense. Remember, if he created us to love him and be loved by him, its only when we reach the point of actually truly and unconditionally loving Him, that we deserve our place alongside him and the great rewards that brings.

It is this connection to Love that truly Resurrects us, and gives us a divine quality of the kind described above, i.e. Theosis or a type of deification.

From a scriptural point of view, I find evidence of this in none other than Jesus himself, as quoted in The Gospel of Thomas, along with two other weighty sources being Saint Paul and The Gospel of John.

See below :

Gospel of Thomas (Will become like me)

108. Jesus said, "Whoever drinks from my mouth will become like me; I myself shall become that person, and the hidden things will be revealed to him."

Gospel of John (We shall be like him)

1 John 3:2-3.

Beloved, we are God's children now, and what we will be has not yet appeared; but we know that when he appears **we shall be like him, because we shall see him as he is**. And everyone who thus hopes in him purifies himself as he is pure.

Saint Paul in Ephesians (So that in the coming ages he might show the immeasurable riches of his grace in kindness toward us in Christ Jesus ; In him you also are being built together into a dwelling place for God by the Spirit)

By Grace Through Faith

2 And you were dead in the trespasses and sins in which you once walked, following the course of this world, following the prince of the power of the air, the spirit that is now at work in the sons of disobedience— among whom we all once lived in the passions of our flesh, carrying out the desires of the body and the mind, and were by nature children of wrath, like the rest of mankind. But God, being rich in mercy, because of the great love with which he loved us, even when we were dead in our trespasses, made us alive together with Christ—by grace you have been saved— and raised us up with him and seated us with him in the heavenly places in Christ Jesus, **so that in the coming ages he might show the immeasurable riches of his grace in kindness toward us in Christ**

Jesus. For by grace you have been saved through faith. And this is not your own doing; it is the gift of God, not a result of works, so that no one may boast. [10] For we are his workmanship, created in Christ Jesus for good works, which God prepared beforehand, that we should walk in them.

One in Christ

Therefore remember that at one time you Gentiles in the flesh, called "the uncircumcision" by what is called the circumcision, which is made in the flesh by hands— [12] remember that you were at that time separated from Christ, alienated from the commonwealth of Israel and strangers to the covenants of promise, having no hope and without God in the world. But now in Christ Jesus you who once were far off have been brought near by the blood of Christ. [14] For he himself is our peace, who has made us both one and has broken down [t]in his flesh the dividing wall of hostility [15] by abolishing the law of commandments expressed in ordinances, that he might create in himself one new man in place of the two, so making peace, [16] and might reconcile us both to God in one body through the cross, thereby killing the hostility. [17] And he came and preached peace to you who were far off and peace to those who were near. [18] For through him we both have access in [c]one Spirit to the Father. [19] So then you are no longer strangers and aliens, but you are fellow citizens with the saints and members of the household of God, [20] built on the foundation of the apostles and prophets, Christ Jesus himself being the cornerstone, in whom the whole structure, being joined together, grows into 'a holy temple in the Lord. **In him you also are being built together into a dwelling place for God by the Spirit."**

Re 22

This verse contains, again, the declaration (as in Ephesians 2:18) of the union of Christians with each Person of THE HOLY TRINITY. The soul made one with THE SON becomes a temple for the indwelling of THE FATHER in the gift of THE HOLY SPIRIT. (See John 14:23.

John 14:23 Jesus replied, "Anyone who loves me will obey my teaching. My Father will love them, **and we will come to them and make our home with them**.

Saint Paul in Corinthians on the importance of Love (...and if I have a faith that can move mountains, but do not have love, I am nothing ; When completeness comes)

"1 Corinthians 13

13 If I speak in the tongues[a] of men or of angels, but do not have love, I am only a resounding gong or a clanging cymbal. **2** If I have the gift of prophecy and can fathom all mysteries and all knowledge, **and if I have a faith that can move mountains, but do not have love, I am nothing**. **3** If I give all I possess to the poor and give over my body to hardship that I may boast, [b] but do not have love, I gain nothing.

4 Love is patient, love is kind. It does not envy, it does not boast, it is not proud. **5** It does not dishonor others, it is not self-seeking, it is not easily angered, it keeps no record of wrongs. **6** Love does not delight in evil but rejoices with the truth. **7** It always protects, always trusts, always hopes, always perseveres.

8 Love never fails. But where there are prophecies, they will cease; where there are tongues, they will be stilled; where there is knowledge, it will pass away. **9 For we know in part and we prophesy in part, 10 *but when completeness comes,*** what is in part disappears. **11** When I was a child, I talked like a child, I thought like a child, I reasoned like a child. When I became a man, I put the ways of childhood behind me. **12** For now we see only a reflection as in a mirror; then we shall see face to face. **Now I know in part; then I shall know fully, even as I am fully known**.

13 And now these three remain: faith, hope and love. But the greatest of these is love."

The Gospel of Mathew also talks of a divine inheritance, potentially in the context of a Prince inheriting a Kingship, and so becoming King.

Matthew 25:34

"Then the King will say to those on his right, 'Come, you who are blessed by my Father; take your inheritance, the kingdom prepared for you since the creation of the world."

Hindu

In the Hindu faith we also see the connection between devotion, worship and love followed by the "attainment of God"; for example:

"To those who are constantly devoted and worship Me with love, I give the understanding by which they can come to Me.

-Bhagavad Gita 10.10

Out of Compassion for them, I, dwelling in their hearts, destroy with the shining lamp of knowledge the darkness born of ignorance.

-Bhagavad Gita 10.11

O Arjun, the scorcher of your foes, it is by single minded devotion alone that I can be known, seen in reality, and also entered into. O Son of Pandu, he who performs actions for Me, who considers Me as the Supreme Goal, who is My devotee, and is devoid of attachments; who is without animosity towards all living beings, he alone attains Me.

-Bhagavad Gita 11.54 and 11.55"

In short, we need Faith to be able to connect with God, (or what some might refer to as a universal cosmic consciousness) in our life and to become self-aware, receive better guidance and overcome worldly attachments; we need Hope to be confident about the future and stay the course on the path of righteousness; and most importantly, we need to Love God and our fellow souls to fully realize the potentially we have within us in our present life, and ultimately to be Resurrected and become of a divine nature and enjoy "the immeasurable riches of his grace".

To me, it also makes complete logical sense that God would want us to become God like. Recall the very logic we discussed at the start of this work; that if you were going to be loved by someone, you'd ideally like that person to be of similar nature to you rather than of an inferior specie. As much as I like animals, I'd rather have a human lover than an animal lover. Remember also that we are told clearly that we were made in his image.

So the notion of "Becoming God Like "as the End Game, makes perfect logical sense. Moreover, the above discussion and references provide Holy Scriptural support for such.

But how can this make sense from a scientific or broader common sense perspective? Even if we accept the fact that we are yet to learn all there is about how life works scientifically, is there any scientific basis that we can envisage, given our current level of knowledge, that suggests that the notion of Theosis, or even Deification, by Love (or otherwise, for that matter) is possible?

Scientific Advances: on Souls, Quantum Physics, Consciousness and Love

We saw in our earlier discussion on Reincarnation that the notion of reincarnation requires some "remnant" of a person to survive physical death; and for this remnant to then reincorporate itself back into a future earthly bodily existence. For want of a better term, we have historically referred to such a remnant as a "soul or spirit essence".

The notion of souls has been with us since antiquity.

Plato noted that:

"When the soul makes use of the senses and

attends to perceptibles, "it strays and is confused and dizzy, as if it were drunk" (79c). By contrast, when it remains "itself by itself" and investigates intelligibles, its straying comes to an end, and it achieves stability and wisdom."

Whilst it has been the basis of both much philosophical thought and, of course, religious presumption and acceptance, scientific proof of souls has alluded us. And yet there have been many examples where mankind has intuitively known of some truth that was, at that time, incapable of proving. Black holes were thought to exist before they were conclusively proven. The Heliocentric notion of the solar system was predicted by Copernicus and Galileo well before Newton proved it mathematically.

Many Hindus and Buddhists, indeed billions of people, believe in Reincarnation which has its foundation in soul survival, without the need for scientific proof of such. Billions more, such as Christians and Muslims, believe in a non-reincarnated soul, without the need for conclusive scientific proof. The risk to all of them of not believing something so intuitive to them, without having to wait for years or even centuries, for Science to catch up, would be catastrophic to their spiritual wellbeing.

But science is now finally starting to show glimpses of catching up, despite the fact that it can at this stage account to understanding only 4% of the *known* universe.

We saw the great work done by Dr Stevenson and his successor Dr Jim Tucker on reincarnation evidentiary trails.

Recently, we have seen the gradual ascension of Quantum Physics as the predominant driving force of scientific explanation of our universe, both at the macro and micro level. And more recently, we have even seen the development of a quantum understanding of a form of "indestructible knowledge" that survives a person's physical death. This notion hints directly to a scientific explanation of the existence of souls.

Refer the following succinct, but informative, online article on the subject.

"Scientists offer quantum theory of soul's existence

(Online News Australia article)

October 31, 2012

A PAIR of world-renowned quantum scientists say they can prove the existence of the soul.

American Dr Stuart Hameroff and British physicist Sir Roger Penrose developed a quantum theory of consciousness asserting that our souls are contained inside structures called microtubules which live within our brain cells.

Their idea stems from the notion of the brain as a biological computer, "with 100 billion neurons and their axonal firings and synaptic connections acting as information networks".

Dr Hameroff, Professor Emeritus at the Departments of Anesthesiology and Psychology and Director of the Centre of Consciousness Studies at the University of Arizona, and Sir Roger have been working on the theory since 1996.

They argue that our experience of consciousness is the result of quantum gravity effects inside these microtubules - a process they call orchestrated objective reduction (Orch-OR).

In a near-death experience the microtubules lose their quantum state, but the information within them is not destroyed. Or in layman's terms, the soul does not die but returns to the universe.

Dr Hameroff explained the theory at length in the Morgan Freeman-narrated documentary Through the Wormhole, which was recently aired in the US by the Science Channel.

The quantum soul theory is now trending worldwide, thanks to stories published this week by The Huffington Post and the Daily Mail, which have generated thousands of readers' comments and social media shares.

"Let's say the heart stops beating, the blood stops flowing, the microtubules lose their quantum state," Dr Hameroff said.

"The quantum information within the micro-tubules is not destroyed, it can't be destroyed, it just distributes and dissipates to the universe at large.

'If the patient is resuscitated, revived, this quantum information can go back into the microtubules and the patient says "I had a near death experience".'

In the event of the patient's death, it was "possible that this quantum information can exist outside the body indefinitely - as a soul".

Dr Hameroff believes new findings about the role quantum physics plays in biological processes, such as the navigation of birds, adds weight to the theory."

Originally published as "Scientists offer 'proof' soul exists ".

In a recent (2016) Documentary, entitled "The Story of God – Beyond Death" (accessible via YouTube) well known actor Morgan Freeman interviews a New York based expert on Near Death Experiences. The expert notes that science is now capable of confirming that Consciousness continues beyond the point when the brain stops functioning. He is even uses the term "Soul" to describe such Consciousness and its capability of continuing beyond death.

The expert **Dr Sam Parnia** is a British[1] Assistant professor of Medicine at the Stony Brook University School of Medicine where he also is director of research into cardiopulmonary resuscitation, and he is director of the Human Consciousness Project at the University of Southampton. Parnia is known for his work on near-death experiences and cardiopulmonary resuscitation.

In the Documentary Morgan poses the following question to Parnia:

Q (MF): Is there any scientific support for the idea of a "Soul"?

Answer (Dr SP): "Today we call the Soul, "Consciousness" in science. And so we can test this theory to see if Consciousness continues after death, or does it stop. The evidence we have is that when a person dies, that part of us that makes us who we are; the Soul, the Consciousness, the Mind, the Psyche or whatever you want to call it; (pointing to himself) Me; it does not become annihilated; it doesn't just disappear into thin air. It continues at least in the early period of death."

(MF–somewhat surprised): "Really!"

(Dr SP): Yes. It continues when the brain is not expected to be functioning and when a person has gone through death."

[End of interview quote]

Interestingly, this notion of "indestructible knowledge or energy" was the foundation for the well-known notion of "eternal return", or "eternal recurrence", as mentioned by Nietzsche in the 19th century. Nietzsche propounded the doctrine for its psychological and philosophical import. Section 1063 of his posthumous notebooks "The Will To Power" states,

"The law of conservation of energy *demands* eternal recurrence."

Wikipedia addresses the notion as follows,

"Eternal return (also known as **"eternal recurrence"**) is a concept that the universe and all existence and energy has been recurring, and will continue to recur, in a self-similar form an infinite number of times across infinite time or space. The concept is found in Indian philosophy and in ancient Egypt and was subsequently taken up by the Pythagoreans and Stoics. With the decline of antiquity and the spread of Christianity, the concept fell into disuse in the Western world, with the exception of Friedrich Nietzsche, who connected the thought to many of his other concepts, including *amor fati [the love of fate].*

In addition, the philosophical concept of eternal recurrence was addressed by Arthur Schopenhauer. It is a purely physical concept, involving no supernatural reincarnation, but the return of beings in the same bodies. Time is viewed as being not linear but cyclical."

Pursuant to Modern Cosmology, whilst the big bang theory in the framework of relativistic cosmology seems to be at odds with eternal return, there are now many different speculative big bang scenarios in quantum cosmology which actually imply eternal return - although based on other assumptions than Nietzsche's.[19] So there are competing models and hypotheses with a temporal, spatial or spatio-temporal eternal return of everything in all variations as Nietzsche has envisaged.

It's clear that with the advancement of Quantum Physics, that science has commenced to bridge the gap on understanding the complexity of Consciousness, and importantly, the notion that such a thing can in fact exist beyond any individual human body or brain. This is despite that fact that science cannot yet explain *how* Consciousness works, even if it were confined to the human brain.

If we accept that recent research of the kind noted above, does start to move towards proving the existence of a Conscious Remnant, or Soul that survives physical death, then the following excerpt by S B Groves provides an interesting and, indeed, intuitively logical insight into how attaching ourselves to God's Love can elevate the finer essences that pertain to our souls, to a point of eventual immortality; perhaps even Deification.

"S B Groves.

Despite the innumerable negativities and heavy states that contaminate our being, the

theme we must make ourselves follow is that of transformation, rebirth, and unending advancement into Greater Life. This is no idle wish but is the very pattern of human life, and it was created to function in this manner. We are not merely another animal species obliged to live out our existence with only death and annihilation as the end of life. Planetary existence provides the energies, interests, stimuli, friction and experience to arrive at an understanding of our very great possibilities, and learn how to actualize, develop and extend those possibilities into fully realized states. While there is much that resists our growth there is very much more to promote and aid our growth towards an unending spiritual life of cosmic usefulness.

The soul of a thing is its subjective spiritual force. The greater this central force, the nearer perfect is the internal organization and the nearer immortal is the individual soul. As we rise in the scale of biological being, from simple to more complex organisms, life becomes more centralized and individualized into individual souls. The soul becomes monarch by acquiring self-consciousness which possesses and dominates the entire frame of the individual. It must subject and subordinate all of its organs and imbue all of its members with its own nucleated soul-substance. ***The mysterious, indivisible organization - that insoluble something we call the soul - struggles to survive the dissolution of death. In cases of extreme limitation or depravity, caused by neglect or overt acts of spiritual suicide, the soul may not be able to recover from the material and***

***psychological shocks in death, and take up again the conscious life with sufficient force to collect together a new system or to organize a new body from finer substances through which it may reign as life giving power*. Such an individual may only survive merely as one of the constituents of such a system in a subordinate way, with no independent conscious individuality, filling eternity with its mighty deeds. Immortality is not an automatic gift, nor heritage, but is a special acquisition. The soul in its essence is indestructible and will survive in some form; yet the soul, as a self-conscious, integrated unit may suffer diffusion and death from sheer neglect**.

To gain personal immortality the individual must grow into a sense of all-inclusive charity. The locked-in sense of self-contained privacy and the refusal or inability to communicate love and feeling must be superseded by the sense of universality afforded by the presence of God. This all-embracing state must be built into the individual life as one of its principal components. At his maximum the individual is at one with the greatest and widest forms of life, and senses the immensity of Divine omniscience and omnipresence. **In losing the narrowness of ego-bound experience the soul gains the larger and lasting good of shared universal life. The conscious immortalization of life through soul-growth establishes the possibility of a fresh forward and upward movement in transfinite realms**.

Hope of immortality is a universal intuition. This hope is an undying spring of action. It is a motive and an inspiration in all living creation. It rises from within as an elemental force of intuitional power because it wells up from the depths of essential supersistential being. **"The universe is filled with Divine Providence which incessantly provides the invitation to grow, to become conscious, to love, to be wise, and to exercise charitable and creative usefulness. Our acceptance of this invitation leads to Life more abundant." ["my emphasis"]"**

This beautifully succinct passage resolves logically a number of issues touched on in this work. It does so with the explanation that a soul has various gradations, or levels of strength, none of which may be as low as to destroy either the soul or the information inherent in it, but which however go to the level of "consciousness" or identity, the soul may have.

For example, a highly elevated soul may be fully conscious and approaching a saintly or divine nature. On the hand, a low grade soul (caused by an inability to detach oneself from worldly addictions, or a total lack of love for God or humanity generally; perhaps even caused from an abundance of evil), may lose the ability to be "conscious" or, in Groves' words, "...Such an individual may only survive merely as one of the constituents of such a system in a subordinate way, with no independent conscious individuality...".

In other words, a soul who has elevated itself, has the potential to move to greater heights and achieve Theosis or Deification. One that is so low in the scale of things, whilst the energies associated with it may not be capable of annihilation or extinguishment, the individual personality or consciousness of that spiritual individual is terminated.

This logically now accounts for how souls can allegorically be, to use a Biblical term, "burnt in hell". This logic can be used to confirm the earlier discussion about whether those who fail the School of Life, become eventually terminated as life giving conscious souls. It also accounts for how in the end, as the scriptures say, "All will be in All"; and yet even the souls "burnt in hell", will form part of this "All", but will not be in a conscious life giving form.

So in the age old Origin debate about whether or not even Satan himself could be saved by God's grace, the answer might be that his soul would be so depraved as to be incapable of being saved, but its constituent parts might nonetheless form part of the "All in All". This makes sense since energy, even bad malevolent energy, cannot be destroyed under present scientific principles; and yet the "lives" of all malevolent beings are nonetheless perished at Judgement Day.

You will recall that earlier we saw something similar in the Mormon beliefs when we noted that,

"In 1832, Joseph Smith and Sidney Rigdon experienced a vision of the afterlife. In the vision, they learned that the just and unjust alike would receive immortality through a universal resurrection, but only those "who overcome by faith, and are sealed by the Holy Spirit of promise" would receive the fullness of God's glory and be "gods, even the sons of God."[28]

In other words, "All energies" will be part of the Universal Resurrection, but only those energies that have connected with God through faithful loving devotion, will truly benefit from God's eternal benefice.

In a similar vein, Groves also makes the point that, **"To gain personal immortality the individual must grow into a sense of all-inclusive charity [meaning Love]**. The locked-in sense of self-contained privacy and the refusal or inability to communicate love and feeling must be superseded by the sense of universality afforded by the presence of God".

Again, we see the power of Love and its ability to elevate the soul essences to withering heights, reminiscent of what we said earlier that, through the Love of God and his resultant worship and praise, is how we elevate our soul essences to a closeness and connection with him such that our lives are forever changed and advantaged.

Indeed, the importance of Love is recognized in our society in a pervasive way. John Lennon's song, "All you need is love", at least to my mind, if read carefully in the context of what we have covered in this work, could be said to be divinely inspired; especially the notion that, through God's illusory school of life there's, "No one you can save that can't be saved. Nothing you can do, but you can learn [through the School of Life] how to be you [i.e. the real divine you] in time."

All You Need Is Love
Some of the Lyrics.
"No one you can save that can't be saved
Nothing you can do, but you can learn how to be you in time

It's easy
All you need is love, all you need is love..........
There's nothing you can know that isn't known
Nothing you can see that isn't shown
There's nowhere you can be that isn't where you're meant to be
It's easy
All you need is love, all you need is love."

Even though Lennon was said to be non-religious, especially given his song "Imagine", this was not the case. Lennon described his own belief in God by quoting the Bishop of Woolwich, saying, "... not as an old man in the sky. I believe that what people call God is something in all of us."

In an interview conducted in September 1980, Lennon told *Playboy* journalist David Sheff,

"People always got the image I was an anti-Christ or anti religion. I'm not. I'm a most religious fellow."

The notion that "God is something in all of us" referred to above by Lennon is a common theme in this work. We were, under my hypothesis, with God at the start, made by him as spiritual essences (albeit perhaps from uncreated "clay" as the Mormons and others might argue), and importantly, were made in his image (meaning with divine essences), to eventually to be like him; to learn from the school of hard knocks over many lifetimes and perhaps in various dimensions, to become perfect divine beings and be his inheritors.

As Jesus in the Gospel of Thomas mentioned, those

divine essences were implanted so that, over time, we would grow into fully developed divine beings.

Gospel of Thomas

(96) Jesus [says]:

(1) "The kingdom of the Father is like [a] woman. (2) She took a little bit of yeast. [She] hid it in dough (and) made it into huge loaves of bread. (3) Whoever has ears should hear."

But how crazy and unbelievable a notion is this? Imagine a Powerful Being either creating us, or moulding us from existing uncreated matter, then putting us in material bodies in an illusory material world, like some sort of animal being placed in a zoo, just so the animal and all its kind can be trained over eons of time to become as Powerful and Majestic as the Being itself?

That is precisely what I'm suggesting. How crazy is that notion?

Well it may seem particularly crazy to some when looked at like from one perspective, but it was illuminating for me to recently watch an episode of Neil Tyson's TV documentary series entitled, "The Inconceivable Universe". After that, the concept didn't seem so crazy at all.

As is generally known, Neil Degrasse Tyson does not espouse a belief in a creator God, and perhaps not a God at all. And so the basis for his views are purely scientific and logically founded.

In this particular episode Tyson notes that our DNA differs from the DNA of chimpanzees by less than 1%. He then notes that such a small difference nonetheless makes a huge difference to what we as humans have been able to learn and achieve over time, compared to our chimpanzee cousins.

He then postulates that if there was other intelligent life in the universe, could it be possible that their DNA is 1% or more superior to ours? And if so, could they already know of our existence? Moreover, he asks the question, "Well since WE have put chimpanzees in Zoos, how do we know that this superior form of alien life has not already placed US in a so-called Zoo?" And I would add, "And is watching and guiding us from near, or afar, as to our development?"

In my view, this is exactly what's happened.

It seems that our modern scientific atheist brothers and sisters seem to be readily accepting of the possibility of a superior form of alien life existing in the universe, and possibly even one that is manipulating our human world, but they seem to have difficulty accepting that such alien life could be God, or God like.

One further point on the Power of Love to elevate souls to the stage of Deification is that it is, of course, all consistent with Darwin's Evolutionary Theory; the very theory that atheists would have us believe undermines a belief in God. As souls progress through their evolutionary stages, over countless lives, those that adapt and elevate their soul essences will survive and prosper. Those that are incapable of doing so will, as S B Groves so eloquently explains, remain at a level that will ultimately see them vanish, not entirely as energy sources as such since energy may per se be indestructible, but certainly as individual soul essences. In other words, the School of Life is indeed a Darwinian school of evolution. You either adapt, learn, grow and love, or otherwise you fade into insignificance. We cover this further below under the topic of Immortality and Judgement Day.

What remains for us to examine then is, what evidence is there that mankind as a whole has advanced spiritually; for despite the obvious advancement of individual persons or groups, or religious movements or sects, if mankind as a whole is floundering or regressing, then the expected notion of a gradual progression towards a higher godly existence as required by our hypothesis, may in fact, be lacking.

For reasons that will become obvious, this issue is intrinsically intertwined with the question of Universal Salvation, so let's examine both concepts together.

Chapter Eight

Universal Salvation and the onward progress of Mankind's Spirituality and Unification with God

This is a complex topic but a crucial one to explore. It also has many facets and they are all interlaced.

For example, is everyone ultimately saved and reunited with God? How does one account for those souls who lived incarnate on earth before the teachings of Moses, Christ, Mohammed and other teachers I mentioned above etc.? How do you explain the variety of different religions and the incessant conflict, both amongst themselves and within themselves? When is it that a unification of all peoples of different Faiths, and ultimately with God, will take place? Is there evidence of such a trend towards unification, and so is there any evidence that mankind as a whole is progressing in spiritual and virtuous development?

The starting point is that if we accept the concept of Reincarnation, then souls who continually reincarnate throughout the ages will gradually have the benefit of all the teachers that God has sent down to us. They therefore do not simply live one life without the benefit of all the great guidance and learning God has supplied us over the ages, and then vanish into oblivion. It cannot make sense that God would allow this to happen in the context of our earlier discussion of him providing a learning environment for us to perfect ourselves and re-enter paradise.

Under my hypothesis therefore, there is no struggle with the question of what happens to such souls. They reincarnate or transmigrate from one existence to the next, and gradually are exposed to various, if not all, faiths and all sacred teachings. Of course, they may indeed find their connection with God through the exposure to just one Faith and that's all it may take.

The next point to make is that history shows us that there is a form of *progressive* revelation, often both within a particular religious faith, as well as amongst them all.

The notion of progressive revelation can mean various things to different readers. It's clear, for example, that God has progressively revealed his faith to the Jewish race in a phased approach starting with Abraham and then again, reaching another milestone with the advent of Moses, and perhaps stages in between (e.g. Noah).

Some, namely Christians, would say that the next stage of that development was the coming of Christ and the growth of Christianity. However, even if you took this to be an entirely new religious movement, the notion of progressive revelation also has meaning in this context because, to pick up the Baha'i notion of progressive revelation, God is sending a series of

Messengers to educate and guide Mankind at various stages of its development.

It is this Baha'i notion of progressive revelation that I think best explains what we have seen play out in history, and which is perfectly consistent with the hypothesis we are considering.

Moreover, the revelation is not in my view just progressive in a time sense, but also has a geographical component to it.

The great religions of the East such as Zoroastrian, Hindu and Buddhism are not only diverse from the so-called religions of "the Book" (Judaism, Christianity and Islam) by time, although there's is overlap of course, but also geographically.

If you wanted to run a school of education to teach the World over, you could not reasonably do it with just one key teacher (i.e. one Messenger). That is, you realistically could not have only one teacher that would touch and interact with the whole world. You would rationally need different schools in different parts of the world with their own charismatic teachers.

You would set the world ablaze with learning, not by trying to start one fire and hoping it would spread everywhere, but instead by lighting smaller fires across the globe and expecting that overtime, they would join up and create a unifying inferno of change and transformation.

The Baha'i Faith (and I should say that whilst I believe the Baha'i Faith is a great world religion, I am not a Baha'i myself even though I empathize with almost all of their beliefs), is the only Faith that acknowledges the validity of the key world religions, and the spiritual authority of their messengers (Zoroaster, Buddha, Moses, Christ, Mohammed, Krishna).

At their temple services on Sunday's and holy days, they read scripture from all these teachers, including their own holy prophets and messengers (the Bab and Bahaullah). Their scriptures also acknowledge and reference directly the holiness of the teachers (i.e. messengers) of these other faiths.

The Baha'is explain, in a rational way, that the apparent differences between various religions can be generally explained by differences that reflect the different time stages and cultural environments in which each messenger came. Just as you would expect different schools to differ in cultural and ritual aspects, so do the religions initiated by God.

Theses religions however should not be defined by their differences, but rather by their similarities. When you do this then it becomes apparent that they were ignited by the same Divine source and are headed towards convergence, despite the apparent opposition and competition that exists between them.

Indeed, the competitive forces inherent in their apparent differences has driven Mankind to change and improve, just as competition generally does in both economics and history, and in our daily lives.

For example, it was the zeal of missionary conversion alongside the competitive forces of different religious options that drove much of the proselytization of the various faiths. As a result, many more souls became exposed to the teachings than would otherwise have occurred.

The Jewish faith on the other hand, lacked a need for competitive growth outside Jewish nationality, and so remained small in global devotees compared to the great (competitive and therefore) missionary religions.

Yes, it's absolutely true that religious competitiveness has led to countless bloodshed, even though much of this is due to egotistical power seeking individuals using religion as their cover for conquest. Nonetheless, you may still ask, how can an all loving all powerful and all-knowing God allow religious competitiveness to occur, and knowing the bloodshed and strife such power hungry individuals would create in religion's name?

The fact is that all religious movements, or any initiative for that matter, will run out of steam and stagnate unless it is constantly refreshed.

Moreover, in order to properly refresh it, it is often easier, if not necessary, to start a new movement from scratch rather than convert or remodel an already stagnant faith. Stagnant faiths generally tend to be highly layered with man-made doctrines, dogmas and corrupt practices.

Constant renewal is necessary for a world class educational program.

In modern day terms, we use the notion of "disruption" to bring about fundamental change to processes, habits and routines that are open to change but won't change of their own accord. Accordingly, a new start-up catalyst force is needed to enliven change. In the process, "old firms" and institutions maybe hurt and possibly torn down, with much human dislocation in the process. But that is the price for human advancement.

As has been said in scripture, you cannot "pour new wine into old skins". You need a totally fresh and disruptive approach which achieves a leap of advancement, not possible by attempting to remodel the existing paradigm.

Each new religious movement, with its separate teachers, including movements within religions, such as Luther's Reformation of Christian thinking as well as the Mormon Faith, as Christian reform examples, bring about such disruptive change; or to use an often quoted economic saying, "creative destruction". These changes tend, by nature, to be genuinely creative, being inspired of course by the Divine creative force, as well as having destructive impacts in the change process they are meant to bring about.

An important key point here is that when you boil down the fundamental tenants of all these religions I have mentioned, they basically extract themselves down to two or three key themes.

First, that man should detach himself from, or temper his reliance on, the temptations and vanities of worldly desires. He must gird his loins with his own innate power to evolve a resistance to temptation.

Second, that he should devote himself to the loving worship of, and connection to, God or a form of supernatural consciousness.

Third, that he should treat others in a manner commensurate with how he himself would wish to be ideally treated. On this aspect, refer the following sayings,

"Hurt not others in ways you yourself would find hurtful (Buddhism)

What is hateful to you do not do to your fellow man (Judaism)

Do onto others as you would have them do onto you (Christianity)

No one of you is a believer until he desires for his brother that which he desires for himself (Islam)

Blessed is he who preferreth his brother before himself (Baha'i)"

These are the elements common to all the disparate fires that have been ignited, both across the global and throughout history.

They are the common DNA of such movements that will ultimately ensure that all such fires eventually unite to set the world (or perhaps the universe) fully ablaze in a common unifying inferno, and from which Man's husks are burnt away to reveal the true inner golden self, which is what is worthy of reunification with God.

At that point, all souls (or at least those proven worthy) will remember all the lessons of their past bodily and spiritual lives, and will have developed themselves to the point where being tempted away from God's loving realm will no longer be a risk. Then death will be conquered as the cycle of death and transmigration of souls will become unnecessary. That will effectively be the arrival of God's kingdom on earth, when All will be in All once more.

Is there evidence that mankind is in fact progressing

down such a path of gradual improvement of both self and global society in general?

On one hand you might say, of course there is. For example, we are light years ahead in today's society with our acceptance of Human rights, equality of races and genders and all that Diversity and Inclusiveness movements entail, compared to where we were when slavery and serfdom was well accepted; or when native and indigenous people were being massacred, abused and children stolen; or when white and black peoples were segregated.

Global institutions such as the United Nations and related human rights organisations reflect how far mankind has advanced, even in a relatively short period of time since the revolutionary age of the late 18 th century. Today the world comes together to protect the accepted human rights of people's to life and liberty like no other time in our intelligible history.

Therefore, you could say that Mankind has not just progressed by virtue of technological advancement but even more impressively by virtue of its acceptance of human rights and dignities which underpin the notion of "love of ones neighbour."

On the other hand, you might point to the fact that Civility per se seems to ebb and flow throughout the centuries. For example, surely the Greeks were more civilized than the barbarous hoards that roamed Europe in the dark ages after the fall of the Roman Empire; and surely more civilized than the brutal savages of the Arabian desert who would bury alive their daughters and threaten their wives with death if they bore them daughters; which incidentally Mohammad conquered and imposed on them the then incredibly human and civilizing edicts of the Quran.

So what are we to make of this point that, when looked at over the time span of centuries or millennia reverting as far back to the Egyptians for example, there may in fact be an unconvincing case to say that Mankind as a whole is showing evidence of civilized and humanitarian progression? Indeed, you might say that the Nazi Holocaust must be one of the low points in human progression, and so how can one say that over time Mankind is on a progressive path?

I think the key point we can make here is this. One thing that is clear from all the factual historical evidence, is that there are bright moments in history where Mankind does certainly lift itself a peg in terms of progression in humanitarian traits. These bright moments, although not all discernible as such, seem to be intertwined with the arrival of a known messenger from God.

Certainly, we find that whenever a new messenger appears. His immediate impact is to provide a betterment to human behavioural knowledge. For example, Zoroaster and Moses gave us Monotheism (focus on one God only) and the Ten Commandments in a barbarous and polytheistic world; Christ the message of love and compassion for both God and ones neighbour; Mohammed the need to remember God through regular prayer and to take care of ones community through respect for women, children and alms giving; the Buddha via detachment from desires and peaceful existence; and more recently, Bahaullah via increased focus on education and rights for women and children, and of course the powerful notion of Progressive Revelation and the Oneness of religious origin overall.

Of course, there are also periods in history we can point to where the world seems to have received a great burst of enlightenment, but for which we cannot easily point to the arrival of a divine messenger. For example, we see this certainly with the Egyptians. Even though we know relatively little of their spiritual theology, we certainly know that they believed in an afterlife (including reincarnation) and of the need to please the gods during their life lifetime.

The great Greek philosophers of Pythagoras, Socrates and Plato and some of their predecessors believed in the concept of an afterlife and reincarnation as part of the cycle of life. Indeed, it is thought that they learned much of this from Egyptian influences.

Whilst neither the Egyptians, nor Greek philosophers are seen (at least not in the Baha'i Faith, although certainly Zoroaster is) as religious messengers, their platonic thinking was incorporated into Christian philosophy by Plotinus who was, in turn, very influential in the thinking and theology of Saint Augustine and therefore in the formulation of western philosophy in general.

The reality is that we just do not know enough about these earlier times to be able to identify a messenger or prophet who might have initiated a period of enlightenment. However, we do know that such messengers of God need not be confined simply to those well known as religious founders, or those mentioned by the Baha'i Faith.

Indeed, it seems to me that people like Socrates, Plato, Aristotle and perhaps even Pythagoras, may have been of that ilk, but of course I cannot prove it. Indeed, a contrarian may say that Socrates, Plato and Aristotle are examples of non-religious people who clearly led to an enlightenment of the world (and probably on more than one occasion if one includes the Renaissance enlightenment sourced in the rediscovery of their works by the Western world). And so it is not the case that only religious people enlighten the world. This maybe of course true, but certainly anyone who understands the theories of these Greek giants of enlightenment will know that they were truly spiritual, in that they all believed in a form of overarching God (i.e. The Good and the Nous - see later discussion on this below). Even Einstein believed in Spinoza's creator god, although not an anthropomorphic god.

In short, whilst we struggle to find evidence of the progress of humanity as a whole over time, we certainly can see that every messenger enlightens our world and refreshes our moral standards.

This seems to be particularly understood by Hindus who believe that sometimes a "god" (of which they have many, but also believe in one true ultimate God - i.e. Brahman), will appear on the earth in living form.

Such an appearance is called an avatar. Perhaps

the best English translation of avatar is 'incarnation'. However avatar also conveys the belief that God has the ability to take any form and will descend to earth at times when there has been a decline in goodness, and evil is influencing human actions.

> "For whenever the law of righteousness (dharma)
> Withers away, and lawlessness (adharma) raises its head,
> Then do I generate myself on earth
> For the protection of the good,
> For the destruction of evildoers
> For the setting up of righteousness
> I come into being, age after age."
> Bhagavad Gita, 4: 7 - 8

And so, perhaps the progress that mankind enjoys is more of the maintenance of a status quo, with ebbs and flows; or as Eckhart Tolle called it in his joint presentation with Deepak Chopra, "a sort of loopy progression, with highs and lows overlapping each other but ever slowly upward tilting".

It may well be the case that if man, left to his own devices and human nature being what it is, (being what it was in fact designed to be for schooling purposes, i.e. loaded with envy, greed and desire) that mankind will, by nature, implode upon itself but for the constant hand of God in sending us guides and teachers.

In other words, the evil inherent in the world is a kind of gravitational pull that will naturally lead to a universe imploding back on itself, but for

God's constant injection of enlightenment to keep the structure stable; akin in a way to Einstein's cosmological constant as an analogy. And perhaps, like Einstein's constant, this steady state of world affairs is what best provides for a stable school environment, just as it does for a stable universe in the physical world.

Taking this perspective then, we should not therefore expect to see a gradual progress of humanitarianism with time, but rather the mere fact that we are not spiralling down to an immoral and barbarous abyss driven by envy, greed and self-centred ego, could itself be clear evidence that the world is being nurtured by a divine force.

Mankind certainly has a long way to go to achieve the desired reunification with God, especially given that such a heinous crime as the Holocaust only happened recently. And so it is probably no surprise that God is nurturing his worldly school along at a pace that gives individual souls sufficient time to learn the lessons of godliness.

The important point here is that this apparently stagnant process does not prevent individuals from connecting to God in the interim. Indeed, the School of Life (being our material world and our lives played through it) needs to be constantly replete with evil and envy in order for it to be a proper school. If it were to reach a point where evil and envy were minimal in nature, the world would hardly provide the challenging learning environment needed to perfect its students.

Imagine a school where, as you progressed, the challenges posed became softer rather than harder. Surely, in a world class schooling environment, the challenges should become harder since students should be individually progressing and better able to cope with arduous challenges. For this reason, it makes some sense that we see such a heinous crime as the Holocaust occur so recently in our timeframe.

Finally, to cover the opposite perspective, we should also not discount the possibility that perhaps mankind *is, in fact, advancing* as a whole when one looks at progress in humanitarianism over a broader time and geographical span.

I think if you look at the world of the Greeks, although you could say that they were incredibly advanced in so many ways compared to later epochs, I suspect they lived in a broader world much more primitive and barbarous than what we have today. And so whilst one might find pockets of advanced groups in ancient times, just as you would find today pockets of barbarous groups in modern times (e.g. Isis or Boko Haram) overall, you would say that today's world is a much more caring and humanitarian world than ancient or medieval times.

And you certainly could not ignore the "uptick" in human understanding and introspection that occurred in the period circa 800BC to 200BC, that Karl Jaspers entitled "The Axial Age". In that period, across the globe, there seemed to be a wave of human sages focussing on the importance of showing respect and love to fellow human beings, as well as on knowledge, enlightenment and the metaphysical:

i.e. the realisation that the world we see is not true reality.

In that relatively short period the foundations of all of the key religions of today were laid. Moses and the Old Testament Prophets laid the foundations for "the Religions of the Book" being Judaism, Christianity and ultimately Islam. At roughly the same time, the Buddha, Mahavira and Confucius lit the flames of Buddhism, Jainism and Confucianism, respectively. And Hinduism took a step turn with the advent of the Upanishads and the Bhagavad-Gita. This is also when Socrates, Plato and Aristotle introduced into the Western World metaphysical notions of Souls, Reincarnation and Eudemonia (i.e. Love of Friendship and Human Companionship).

And, of course, the world experienced another two major "upticks" with the arrival of Jesus Christ, and then Mohammad some 600 years later.

So one could readily mount the argument for progressiveness of mankind over time. Although, for the reasons given earlier, perhaps this is not an appropriate tenant to test for in proving up our hypothesis.

Perhaps a better way of putting all this is to say that, whilst mankind can be said overall to be on a progressive pathway, the world we live in must continue to provide trials and challenges worthy of the educational value which these are intended to present us.

Whilst the world, replete with all its suffering and evil, as well as its amazingly contrasting pockets

of sublime joy and compassion for the human condition, is often said not to be a perfect world, in my humble opinion, it is indeed, *absolutely perfect*; namely, perfect for what it was created to achieve; namely, an intense testing and learning forum for us all.

Let's recall what we said earlier herein from the Quran:

"Have the people thought that they would be left to say "We Believe" without them being tested? 29:2

[29:3] We have tested those before them, for God must distinguish those who are truthful, and He must expose the liars.

also:

[2:155] We will surely test you through some fear, hunger, and loss of money, lives, and crops. Give good news to the steadfast."

Chapter Nine

Summary and Conclusion

Let's try to summarize what we have covered.

We started with the notion, not uncommon to rational thinkers, that if you could develop a hypothesis that seemed to answer rationally a series of difficult conundrums about spirituality and life; for example, could a God actually exist; and if so, how can there be an all loving all powerful God that would allow the horrors of the Holocaust? or enable young innocent children to suffer fatal illnesses?, or why would God rely on a notion of Faith rather than come out and prove himself to all beyond doubt?, how do you reconcile beliefs on matters such as the existence of souls with science?; what to make of obvious inconsistencies between the notion of reincarnation versus bodily resurrection etc.; and if that hypothesis seemed to be capable of being corroborated by actual scientific and historical facts overtime, and even better, if it was capable of being interpreted consistently with holy scriptures that spoke of such a God, then should we not accept that hypothesis as the best working hypothesis of a certain spiritual milieu, at least until a better one came along to displace it?

Let's restate the hypothesis.

God created us because he wanted someone to love and benefice; and possibly to be himself loved by; and, as we also touched on, to eventually himself grow and benefice from the ultimate reunification of us, as creative and multi long-life experienced beings, with Him.

He wanted the highest form of love and so he gave us freewill.

We exercised that freewill and turned away from him, tempted by idle fancies and potentially the desire to be greater than how God had made us (i.e. to be more like God himself).

He developed a world class education program to teach us that resisting such temptations, and having a loving devotion towards him and each other, would give us the only true happiness. The program would achieve this by giving us both joyful and distasteful experiences (i.e. expose us to both good and evil) outside of God's realm; all of which would educate us to understand that long lastingly true happiness only existed within his loving realm.

This education process would make us realise that attachment to worldly ego driven desires, fears and related frustrations and anger, all lead to suffering and a lack of true purpose and life satisfaction, as well as forgetfulness of who we truly are in essence, and that our goal in life is ultimate perfection of self, worthy enough to be united with God.

It would also make us more creative, more loving, better experienced and compassionate souls, and so more worthy of unification with Him (i.e. a "better" Adam, as Thomas Aquinas would say, having benefited from God's Supernatural Grace, as was the case with the prodigal son in the Parable of the Lost Son, which we will touch on later in this work).

The program involves us, being our true selves in the form of souls or spirit essences, gaining and retaining knowledge of self, through countless worldly (and other potentially non worldly) lives via reincarnation (and transmigration).

That the soul also retains bodily features or traits, which means that we retain, in some form of aggregate, every physical person we've ever been; and this becomes inherent in our soul essence.

That whilst we can come to know God and connect with him and the angelic and broader spiritual world whilst we are at school, (i.e. in the illusory material world), we will, if successful in our schooling, one day eventually achieve a level of connectivity and spiritual godliness as to be able to reunite with him; indeed, not only to be reinstated to our original unblemished selves, but to be elevated to an even higher status becoming, or bordering on becoming, God like.

In the meantime, we go through a school learning curriculum governed by experiencing joy, pain, good and evil. In an allegorical sense, we truly ate of the "Tree of Knowledge of Good and Evil" when we Fell away from God. And we undergo countless Karmic lifetime experiences from which we, and others affected by our behaviour, gain valuable lessons and are tested.

As we do this, we advance as individuals and possibly as mankind as a whole, instructed by teachers sent to us at varying phases and geographies of our evolutionary development.

It's possible that this advancement and connection with God can only take place whilst we are incarnate spirits. And so we need to endeavour to find God during our incarnate lifetime, otherwise in the spirit world we will never do so. More on this point later.

We have also discussed why there could be good reasons why mankind may not be *seemingly* advancing itself as a whole; primarily to ensure that the earthly learning environment remains a challenging one for its students.

We then tested this hypothesis against worldly facts and historical knowledge.

Specifically, we tested, and in my humble view, validated this hypothesis against four tenets that really reduced down to two; namely, is there evidence of a World Class Educational System (i.e. The Illusory School of Life) evincing Love, Compassion and Mercy; and second, is there evidence that this education is available Universally and that Progress has been made at both the level of certain individuals, as well as mankind as a whole.

In the process of doing so we also made a number of insightful observations.

For example, we saw that modern science is in some respects so backward as to be able to explain only 4% of the known universe, and yet has advanced enough in the areas of quantum physics as to tell us that the most weirdest and fantastic concepts imaginable in life are indeed possible, including the possible existence of souls and a disembodied consciousness. So events such as multi universes and multiple simultaneous lives, let alone miracles, cannot easily be dismissed. And in the area of reincarnation research, that reincarnation is a provable concept even to the point where physical bodily attributes can be carried over from one life to the next.

We saw that the modern understanding of evolution through eons of time can indeed account for the evolution of a god, i.e. if evolution is so powerful to create the Intricate Watch, then why not also the Masterly Watchmaker?

We saw a series of religious teachers come into the world; all essentially espousing the importance of belittling worldly pleasures in return for relishing virtuous concepts, such as the love of God and ones fellow human beings; and their devoted pupils (apostles, saints and followers generally) regularly living lives of pain, suffering and often martyrdom in total belief and devotion to a Faith or spiritual cause.

We saw the possible need for regular teachers constantly having to refresh the basic divine messages, since religious movements become decayed, ridged and corrupt overtime.

We saw the importance in such a system for the successful students' reliance on "Faith" in an uncertain spiritual divinity, in order to be tested and succeed; as opposed to having an otherwise unhelpful construct wherein God's existence was so unequivocal that it would turn all the unholy and unworthy also into believers, without effecting an underlying character change to their soul.

Faith is needed as part of the purification process to go from unholy to holy. It is part of the Test. God's unequivocal existence through scientific proof does not engender a learning process of soul purification and devotion to God. Unequivocal proof of God simply just makes unworthy souls become believers without the benefit of character reformation.

We saw how mankind has advanced gradually from stage to stage with the varying teachings divinely provided; and how the notion of progressive revelation has phased in the learnings needed in a digestible way for gradually maturing individual souls, as well as mankind as a whole.

Although we also recognised that whilst mankind's progress as a whole is debatable, this might nonetheless be consistent with God's plan to maintain a constantly challenging school environment.

Finally, we then examined how this hypothesis, seemingly corroborated by reference to facts, science and history, is also consistent with those Holy Scriptures which cover the religious teachings at their purest. For example, how the notion of "starving" one's self from the pleasures of the world to devote oneself to the higher purposes of the love of God (or a god like consciousness) and the love of ones fellow souls, transcends all the key Faiths. And how the Power of Love is a pervasive element across all such Faiths, as well as a connector for us as individuals with God on our way, if worthy graduates, to ultimate deification.

Why this method of schooling?

The one question we have not asked yet is this. If my hypothesis is correct, and Life is part of an illusory learning world for our souls to reconnect with God, and if this may take an enormous long time to play out, WHY is God using such a Schooling technique as this?

In other words, if we originally were with God and then Fell away from him; and if he wants us to learn the lesson that he alone can be our sole source of true happiness, why then doesn't he just reprogram us so that, instantly, we learn the lesson rather than having to go through this very long and arduous learning process involving a myriad lives and countless suffering?

The best explanation I can give to this is that *God wants "us" to redeem ourselves by ourselves*; and to do so using our own innate God given abilities, rather than be reprogrammed like robots.

He eventually wants us to stand with him in his realm as equals, or quasi-godly in nature, with the knowledge that we redeemed ourselves by choosing to follow the arduous pathway up the mountain, rather than be helicoptered up by him from having originally fallen off the mountain top.

Our own innate nature tells us that we are much more respectful of a self-made person compared to one who inherited everything from his or her parents.

God wishes us ultimately to climb that mountain back up to him by ourselves, albeit with his guidance along the way; and as a result, and very importantly, to feel worthy of his love and benefaction, rather than simply be a receiver of it without having earned it.

He wants us to be "Warrior Servants" having freed ourselves from temptations and the shackles of desire and fear, and to have climbed out of Plato's Cave on our own merit; rather than be "Daddy's Boys and Girls" having been rescued without the need for a fighting effort on our part.

As Plato says,

"But, whether true or false, my opinion is that in the world of knowledge the idea of good appears last of all, and is seen only with an effort".

In fact, in Kabbalist thinking, it was Adam's shame in being a constant receiver of God's love and benefaction without having earned it in any arduous way that led Adam to want to be more godlike, and so led to his eventual Fall.

Whilst this climb back up the mountain may seem to us like taking a long time involving many lifetimes; in the context of us being akin to immortal souls and therefore living virtually for eternity, the time taken to climb back is, of course, but a flicker of a butterfly's wings.

Another reason I believe God has chosen this illusory world environment to school us back to our senses, is that as an all loving and merciful God, he would not wish to hurt or harm our "real selves"; that is, our spirit essences or souls.

The illusory world enables such souls (i.e. us) to learn from an incredible variety of experiences involving joy, pain, fears, anxieties (i.e. good and evil) and importantly, to do so, all without harm to our real selves.

Moreover, it greatly expands the type of experiences we can have compared to the spirit world. For example, to appreciate life one must learn the pain of having lost a loved one. But if in fact, we are all virtually immortal spirits, we can never, at least in in our spirit world, experience what it is like to lose a loved one; or to be ill or diseased. We can never experience envy for what another has if in the spiritual world there are no possessions we need for our existence, etc.

This is why we can really only "learn" in our non-spirit form (i.e. in our material or incarnate form). And so our learnings and soul evolutionary improvement, and ultimate reconnection with God, must come while we "live" in a material and bodily sense. This is why life is so precious. If we don't become conscious and self-aware, and therefore spiritually elevated, whilst we are "alive" in this material world, we never will.

Immortality and Judgement Day

I have said throughout the course of this work that our real selves are our souls or spirit essences; and that in the spirit form, we have lived since God created us in an immortal, or virtually immortal form.

Whilst I believe this to be true, I do believe that that immortality has a limit, or a cut-off date; i.e. the school bell will at some stage ring and those who have truly connected with God will "graduate" and board the school bus to a blissful eternity with him. The rest will likely never be rehabilitated and so may be extinguished, or perhaps (but unlikely in my view) be forever left to suffer in a never ending environment (colloquially referred to as Hell).

It makes no logical sense for us to be forever immortal if, after numerous chances, we refuse or fail to detach ourselves from worldly desires and devote ourselves to God; unless, of course, we are meant to suffer indefinitely thereafter in punishment.

Moreover, it makes no sense for us to "All be saved"; i.e. all eventually to graduate. A schooling system that keeps recycling failed students forever until they eventually pass, has no real freewill inherent in it.

If eventually everyone is saved, then we cannot stand in God's kingdom feeling as though we "earned" our place in God's home and worthy of his love and benefaction. (Note, this notion does not sit well with Christianity's belief that we have no real say in our salvation since all is predestined. For the reasons set out earlier, I believe this is nonsense and has no foundation in anything that the great teachers mentioned earlier, including Jesus, have said in Holy Scripture. The corrupted notion of Predestination has, in my view, its roots largely in the disbelief of reincarnation for the reasons set out earlier, as well as the fact that it did not suit the Church's power structure for people to think they had more than one chance to be saved).

Only if we genuinely run the risk of failure, can we feel righteous in our eventual achievement in climbing the arduous path back to God's realm. Without this, the cycle of temptation and Fall from God will commence once again; since not having really earned our way back to God's realm, we will feel the same shame we felt in Adam's day when we could not stomach enjoying constantly God's great love and benefaction, without trying to give him something in return; and to do so, we first wanted to become more like him, which led to our downfall.

If we keep "falling" in the knowledge that God will always redeem us back into paradise, where is the genuine evolutionary improvement in our soul essence? For the educational schema to make sense, we must be capable of failing school and never reconnecting with God. For this reason, it is not surprising to find in Holy Scripture (Christian and Jewish) the notion of "Judgement Day" or the "Day of Reckoning" in the Quran; with similar notions in Hinduism and Buddhism, albeit all with slight differences.

At some point, our chances of redemption will cease and a "reckoning" of our efforts will be had; and from that point, we will either enter God's kingdom and have everlasting life, (presumably at that point, being permitted to eat from the "Tree of Life"); or to alternatively, be banished forever, or forever extinguished.

A notable New Testament passage that throws

some insight into this, is one we have encountered before in our discussion of the notion of Faith. This passage also raises the question of what is meant by "living" and "dying"; as well as the notion of immortality of the soul.

Christ's words in John's Gospel:

John 11:25 to 26 ▶

Parallel Verses

New International Version

Jesus said to her [Martha], "I am the resurrection and the life. The one who believes in me will live, even though they die; and whoever lives by believing in me will never die."

New Living Translation

Jesus told her, "I am the resurrection and the life. Anyone who believes in me will live, even after dying; and everyone *who lives in me and believes in me* will never ever die."

These passages, at least to me, provide some telling insights.

First, "dying", when first mentioned means physical death. So Jesus is saying, even though you may physically die, if you had Faith, you will surely reincarnate (or transmigrate) and have another opportunity to reach a level of purity and holiness as to fully connect with God. That means that all believers, even though they may still have much progress to go in fully connecting with God, will progress to other "classes in school" to enable them to advance further. By definition, non-believers cannot be guaranteed this. And so as the day of reckoning approaches, the non-believers cannot be guaranteed that they will be given another "life", or school class year, in order to find God.

The second time the notion of "dying" is used, I think it is meant to convey not merely physical death, but also spiritual death. In other words, once an individual progresses to a high level of connectivity with God, he then turns himself so conclusively towards him and "lives in" him to the point where his spirit will truly become forever immortal. It will be at that point that his soul has completed its "resurrection" and attained eternal life. ("I am the Resurrection and the Life").

This has echoes of the Neoplatonic notion of the Father being the central hub (i.e. The One); Christ or the Word / Logos being the inner circle around the hub; and the mass of individual souls surrounding the Logos looking away from the centre and focussed on external desires.

Then once an individual soul in the outer ring "turns" back towards God, (i.e. loses his "stiff neck" as in the earlier quote from Deuteronomy) and therefore merges itself into the inner circle (i.e. "lives in me"), then it re-enters God's circle of influence and love.

At some point, all those souls who continue to look away from God and fail to purify themselves from desires and temptation, will be extinguished (on Judgement Day) and what is left will comingle with God being the One, so that "All will be in All".

Like Zoroastrianism, Muslims believe that on Judgement Day all souls will pass over a bridge over hell (As-Sirāt in Islam, Chinvat Bridge in Zorastrianism) which those destined for hell will find too narrow and fall below into their new abode.

According to one hadith, out of every one thousand people entering into the afterlife, nine hundred and ninety-nine of them will end up in the fire. Another states that women make up the majority of the population of Jahannam. Although it should also be mentioned that in another hadith the majority of people in heaven are women.

At least two verses in the Quran (6:128[110] and 11:107[111]) emphasise that consignment to hell is horrible and eternal, with the caveat "except as God (or your Lord) wills it".

Quran 6.128

128. On the Day when He gathers them all together: "O assembly of jinn, you have exploited multitudes of humans." Their adherents among mankind will say, "Our Lord, we have profited from one another, but we have reached the term that you have assigned for us." He will say, "The Fire is your dwelling, wherein you will remain, except as God wills. Your Lord is Wise and Informed. 129. Thus We make some of the wrongdoers befriend one another, because of what they used to do.

130. "O assembly of jinn and humans, did there not come to you messengers from among you, relating to you My revelations, and warning you of the meeting of this Day of yours?" They will say, "We testify against ourselves." The life of the world seduced them. They will testify against themselves that they were disbelievers.

Quran 11:96

96. And We sent Moses with Our signs and a clear mandate. 97. To Pharaoh and his nobles, but they followed the command of Pharaoh, and the command of Pharaoh was not wise. 98. He will precede his people on the Day of Resurrection, and will lead them into the Fire. Miserable is the place he placed them in. 99. They were followed by a curse in this, and on the Day of Resurrection. Miserable is the path they followed. 100. These are of the reports of the towns-We relate them to you. Some are still standing, and some have withered away. 101. We did not wrong them, but they wronged themselves. Their gods, whom they invoked besides God, availed them nothing when the command of your Lord arrived. In fact, they added only to their ruin. 102. Such is the grip of your Lord when He seizes the towns in the midst of their sins. His grip is most painful, most severe. 103. In that is a sign for whoever fears the punishment of the Hereafter. That is a Day for which humanity will be gathered together-that is a Day to be witnessed. 104. We only postpone it until a predetermined time. 105. On the Day when it arrives, no soul will speak without His permission. Some will be miserable, and some will be happy. 106. As for those who are miserable, they will be in the Fire. They will have therein sighing and wailing. 107. Remaining therein for as long as the heavens and the earth endure, except as your Lord wills. Your Lord is Doer of whatever He wills. 108. And as for those who are happy, they will be in Paradise, remaining therein for as long as the heavens and the earth endure, except as your Lord wills-a reward without end."

Why now? What's changed?

If I'm correct in my theory as outlined above, why would such a hypothesis and its evidentiary corroboration be discoverable (or more appropriately in my case be relayed to me from on High) now rather than have been the subject of writing by any of the great theologians and philosophers of the past?

Please note that I am not suggesting I alone have written about such a notion. Unbeknownst to me, others may well have. My question however is regardless of who discovered such a theological notion, why should it surface now rather than in a much earlier time period?

What might have changed or what paradigms might have shifted that could have led to a more enlightened worldly view of the meaning of life now?

In no particular order, first there is the recent scientific research into reincarnation by the pioneering Doctors Ian Stevenson and Jim Tucker that certainly was meaningful to me, especially in light of my own personal experiences with the concept of reincarnation.

Consistent with this is the realisation that bodily traits can also be transmigrated and this confirms the soul's ability to retain knowledge and therefore lessons and experiences from the past. It also means that the well-known Abrahamic notion of bodily resurrection is potentially consistent with reincarnation.

As I mentioned earlier, even though greats like Socrates, Plato and Origen all believed in reincarnation, the notion got washed out of western philosophy due to the influence of the Catholic Church and so, great as they were, Augustine and Aquinas never openly contemplated the notion in their writings.

The advent of the enlightenment with its focus on scientific proof then permanently disconnected the notion of reincarnation from western philosophical thinking. The enlightenment, coupled with a not very well thought out notion of Darwinian evolutionary thinking, also wiped out the ability to sustain the notion of a creator god in western thinking.

We also saw that the notion of the recurring learning experiences of souls, coupled with eons of evolutionary time, can be extrapolated to the evolution of a god (i.e. an Evolved god) even if one did not accept the existence of such from the outset.

We are also now realising, through the uncertainty created by Quantum Physics, that the world we see is not necessarily all there is and that a broad consciousness seems to exist independently of our individual brain constrained minds. Even Einstein, who had reservations about aspects of Quantum Physics in the early days of its development, referred to Quantum Entanglement (the notion that information between two "entangled" Quanta seemed to travel between them at a speed fast than the unsurpassable speed of light) as "Spooky Action at a Distance".

The advent of the Baha'i Faith has also given rise to a view of Progressive Revelation, and one that encompasses the world's key faiths. It also emphasises the Schooling notion of Life, with all its past great religious teachers and guides.

Its teachings have also made me aware of the unique relevance and importance of the notion of Faith per se for a true connection with God, as opposed to reliance on scientific proof for belief in God.

The Baha'i faith has also sprung up in a modern technology connected world, when individuals across the globe have the technical ability on mass to be aware of, and better understand, the range of religious faiths across the globe; and so to better appreciate the Schooling milieu that has occurred over the centuries. Not many of the great philosophers and theologians spoke about the possibility of Progressive Revelation in this context, but perhaps partly because they did not appreciate all the diverse faiths across the globe with the benefit of historical hindsight.

The relatively recent archaeological discoveries in the mid 1940's of the Dead Sea Scrolls and the Nag Hammadi Gospels, alongside other scriptures, all lend weight to a better understanding of ancient theology which also assists our current thinking.

Finally, the world is only now starting to open up to a global movement of Diversity and Inclusiveness (that encompasses gender, race, sexual preferences as well as increasingly religious Faiths), and which seems to herald a general awakening of mankind to the importance of treating ones neighbour, and the so-called "other" with respect. Perhaps this gives some credence to the notion of the "Age of

Confluence" that many tell us we are now in.

For all these reasons, I believe the world is now better placed to understand the importance of the Illusory School of Life that God has given us, and the Divine purpose he has in mind for us.

One word of caution though.

We are moving into an Age wherein much of the different religious beliefs seem to be synergising into a common set of themes; and many of these themes are no longer just the domain of religious orders but are finding their way into the secular domain; for example, the recognition of international Human Rights and the many Diversity and Inclusiveness movements at both a corporate employer and every day news media level. As a result, the teachings we have referred to herein are becoming readily available for all to hear and see. The age of the internet and modern media communications has made learning and social behavioural norms accessible to virtually all the world instantaneously.

Moreover, the master teacher Christ, both as man and logos in the form of Jesus, has come and gone. And when he was alive he preached that the apocalyptic end of the world was near at hand. Of course many would laugh at this now because more than 2000 years have since past and Judgement Day so called has not yet arrived. But what is 2000 years in the cosmic time calendar? Some 4 seconds as we saw earlier over a 15 billion age old universe.

It is therefore possible that the reason why we are seeing a more holistic synergy between not only the separate Faiths, but also between Faith and secular society, as well as between Faith and Science, is that the End of Days is in fact fast approaching.

Remember that the whole notion of Faith as outlined earlier was that it required a belief in something that was not obvious or provable. Indeed, we saw that if God's existence as an all loving, all rewarding and all powerful God was made evident to all the masses, then all the prisoners of the Plato's Cave would simply accept that they lived in an illusory world and would seek to move to the outside world, but without having undergone the soul changing transformational change that is required as a precondition to moving into God's heavenly realm.

As science therefore gradually moves to solving the true mysteries of the universe, for example by the recent advent of Quantum Physics which shows that the universe is more akin to a living conscious organism rather than the mechanistic model of classical physics, we may get close to realising and being able to prove the existence of an All Loving, All Knowing, All Powerful God scientifically. Once this is achieved, there can no longer be any room for "Faith". If, as many religions believe, Faith in a deity or godly consciousness of sorts is a prerequisite to salvation, then at that point there is no longer any room for salvation.

That point becomes the logical time for the End of Days and for Judgement Day to arrive.

Chapter Ten

Sense Check against what Jesus said Life was all about

As a final sense check of what we've covered so far, I believe comparing the hypothesis to Christ's sayings in the Gospel of Thomas is a valuable exercise for a number of reasons.

First, if the hypothesis is correct then, as I mentioned earlier, it should be capable of being corroborated against holy scripture even though it is not dependant on scripture. If indeed God has been sending Teachers and Guides to us for millennia, then surely their teachings would be consistent with the hypothesis posed.

Second, the Gospel of Thomas (unlike the Canonical gospels which focus on what our soul's mission should be, i.e. the love of God and fellow human souls) covers some of the methods by which God is teaching us, and provides insights into what was said in Isaiah.

"For my thoughts are not your thoughts, neither are your ways my ways, says the LORD. For as the heavens are higher than the earth, so are my ways higher than your ways and my thoughts than your thoughts" (Isaiah 55:8-9).

In other words, Thomas provides insights into the

knowledge schema that God has ordained for us, and so it is the logical Gospel to compare the hypothesis against.

Third, even though we could compare against certain other holy scriptures, e.g. the Quran, Baha'i scriptures etc., comparing against what Jesus said is probably the most appropriate. I believe that Jesus was a most special messenger, unlike any before him or after. If he wasn't God in the sense of an emanation of God, as in part of the Trinitarian notion (and he may well be such), then he certainly was, in any event, a most powerful being in the sense described by Saint Paul; and so powerful in fact, as to be The Logos mentioned in the Gospel of John (i.e. the Word, or Wisdom).

Saint Paul refers to Jesus as follows

"Corinthians 8:6, "Yet for us there is but one God, the Father, from whom are all things and we exist for Him; and one Lord, Jesus Christ, *"by whom are all things, and we exist through Him". ["My emphasis"]"*

Paul regards Jesus as more than just a messenger. Indeed, in the context of our hypothesis, he regards him as the keeper and sustainer of the illusory world aimed at teaching and redeeming us (i.e. the School of Life). So sense checking the hypothesis against what Jesus said is very important, because if it does not make sense in that comparison, then the hypothesis is a flawed one.

You may well ask the question, how reliable anyway is the Gospel of Thomas as a compendium of what Jesus taught? For that I must defer to the experts and I quote the following authority,

"Significantly, Professor Helmut Koester of Harvard University, speaking as President of the

Society of Biblical Literature (U.S.A.), has declared that "nearly all biblical scholars in the United States agree that Thomas is as authentic as the New Testament Gospels."

You can do your own research on this point, but the Gospel of Thomas, although shunned by the Church for millennia (and why this is so will become evident when we see some of the insights Jesus gives us in The Gospel, some of which do not fit with longstanding Church teachings), has been widely accepted by scholars as authentic Holy Scripture.

Let's look at the sayings in the Gospel of Thomas, and I will only comment on those that are relevant to what we have been discussing and on which I feel I can contribute something insightful.

"These are the hidden words that the living Jesus spoke. And Didymos Judas Thomas wrote them down.

(1) And he said: "Whoever finds the meaning of these words will not taste death."

(2) Jesus says:

(1) "The one who seeks should not cease seeking until he finds.

(2) And when he finds, he will be dismayed.

(3) And when he is dismayed, he will be astonished.

(4) And he will be king over the All."

This, in my view, reflects the search I have personally gone through. After a personal black patch in my life, I started to search for meaning in my life and life in general. As I did that, I became incessant at searching. As I discovered the concept of reincarnation and tried to make sense of it in a

Christian context, and so discovered Origen and the teachings of the early Alexandrian Fathers, I certainly did become both dismayed and then astonished.

Now that I'm confident in what I have rationally concluded and corroborated by my own personal experience and reading, I feel that I understand God's schema, and I feel a strong sense of both life's purpose and my repose with it. I feel like I finally get it, and that I can ask for God's help with any aspect of it.

(3) Jesus says:

(1) "If those who lead you say to you: 'Look, the kingdom is in the sky!' then the birds of the sky will precede you.

(2) If they say to you: 'It is in the sea,' then the fishes will precede you.

(3) Rather, the kingdom is inside of you and outside of you."

(4) "When you come to know yourselves, then you will be known, and you will realize that you are the children of the living Father.

(5) But if you do not come to know yourselves, then you exist in poverty, and you are poverty."

This is exactly what my hypothesis seeks to do. Namely, to explain who we are, and to hopefully help each individual to know oneself; not only that we are God's children, but that the true WE (our spiritual selves represented by the soul / light within us) are potentially immortal; and that God has a long term reunification plan for us. And along the way he has "hearts to love us and eyes to watch over us" (Bahaullah) and we can, through prayer, meditation and the love of others, connect with him and those watching over us. And that without such awareness we exist in a state of "poverty", being ignorant of the great potential we have within us and being constantly busy with useless worldly fancies, all played out in an illusory world.

In listening recently to a lecture by Eckhart Tolle (Awakening to your Consciousness) I believe he espouses similar notions; especially when he talks of looking inward to find oneself and to connect with a form of Cosmic Consciousness, which seems akin to God. Indeed, I noted that he defines this Consciousness as the Creator of all things.

(4) Jesus says:

(1) "The person old in his days will not hesitate to ask a child seven days old about the place of life, and he will live.

That's because the seven day old child is a body whose soul has only recently entered it, and the body seems to take a while to make the soul forgetful of who it really is, and where it comes from. That's why in the reincarnation research work done by Doctors Stevenson and Tucker, they always interviewed young child generally under the age of seven or eight years old.

(2) For many who are first will become last, (3) and they will become a single one."

(5) Jesus says:

(1) "Come to know what is in front of you, and that which is hidden from you will become clear to you.

(2) For there is nothing hidden that will not become manifest."

Once you realise that what we see is just a God

created illusionary world, aimed at teaching our souls many lessons, then those hidden aspects of God's schema will become evident as we seek to learn more.

As the prisoner in Plato's Cave realises that he is watching an illusory movie in front of him, he will start to look for the true reality and that's when God's grace comes to his assistance to make Truth "manifest".

(6)

(1) His disciples questioned him, (and) they said to him: "Do you want us to fast? And how should we pray and give alms? And what diet should we observe?"

(2) Jesus says: "Do not lie. (3) And do not do what you hate.

(4) For everything is disclosed in view of <the truth>.

(5) For there is nothing hidden that will not become revealed.

(6) And there is nothing covered that will remain undisclosed."

Here Jesus is telling his disciples not to practice religious rituals such as fasting and praying and alms giving in a pretentious way for God knows what's really in men hearts. Jesus is not, however, in my humble view, saying do not do these thing in a genuine way.

(7) Jesus says:

(1) "Blessed is the lion that a person will eat and the lion will become human.

(2) And anathema is the person whom a lion will eat and the lion will become human."

Here the lion represents our rapacious worldly desires and fears that are incessantly never satisfied. If we control our fears and desires by "Governing the

Will" then we tame the wild beast and attain to our true human nature which is made in God's image.

On the other hand, if the lion devours us and so our true godly / human nature is overcome by such ravenous fears and desires, then we have little hope and are an anathema.

(8)

(1) And he says: "The human being is like a sensible fisherman who cast his net into the sea and drew it up from the sea filled with little fish.

(2) Among them the sensible fisherman found a large, fine fish.

(3) He threw all the little fish back into the sea, (and) he chose the large fish effortlessly.

(4) Whoever has ears to hear should hear?"

Jesus is saying that if a person, in the course of fishing (or searching) for meanings in life (i.e. all the fish drawn up in the net), was to find among them the truest and most significant meaning of life (a large fine fish), and to therefore realise that the greatest happiness in life comes from love and devotion to God and fellow souls, then surely he would choose that meaning and abandon all other lesser pleasures; and do so effortlessly.

(9) Jesus says:

(1) "Look, a sower went out. He filled his hands (with seeds), (and) he scattered (them).

(2) Some fell on the path, and the birds came and pecked them up.

(3) Others fell on the rock, and did not take root in the soil, and they did not put forth ears.

(4) And others fell among the thorns, they choked the seeds, and worms ate them.

(5) And others fell on good soil, and it produced good fruit. It yielded sixty per measure and one hundred twenty per measure."

(10) Jesus says:

"I have cast fire upon the world, and see, I am guarding it until it blazes."

Here Jesus seems to be confirming that the method he is using to teach us all, is by throwing us all in the deep end and those who, in the process toil and survive, will be saved. He has, from the start of the material world, lit a furnace of pain, suffering, division and discontent across the globe. And through that, albeit with guidance and watchful eyes, he expects that the dross we have over us (which makes us cling to fears and desires) will slowly be burnt away so as to ultimately reveal the inner gold of our true selves. This furnace is the process of continuous reincarnation (and transmigration) of our souls into continuous lifelong learning experiences, and painful ones at that. Until we realise that there is only one route to the greatest happiness (i.e. only one big fish) and therefore, until we resolve to pursue God's love as the true path for ourselves.

(11) Jesus says:

(1) "This heaven will pass away, and the (heaven) above it will pass away.

(2) And the dead are not alive, and the living will not die.

(3) In the days when you consumed what was dead, you made it alive. When you are in the light, what will you do?

(4) On the day when you were one, you became two. But when you become two, what will you do?"

The immense passing of time leads to the worlds we know expiring. As immortal souls we will witness this. If we recognise ourselves and connect with God, we will be alive and aware and come into the light and open ourselves to it. Once we have achieved this connection, then we are "living" and will never die. Without that connection, although we are physically alive we are still dead (not alive) spiritually.

We were once in the light when we were all one soul (the original Adam), but after the Fall we divided, and now Jesus asks, what will we do now? Will we stay out of the light as dead, or seek to re-join it and become truly alive?

(12)

(1) The disciples said to Jesus: "We know that you will depart from us. Who (then) will rule over us?"

(2) Jesus said to them: "No matter where you came from, you should go to James the Just, for whose sake heaven and earth came into being."

(13)

(1) Jesus said to his disciples: "Compare me, and tell me whom I am like."

(2) Simon Peter said to him: "You are like a just messenger."

(3) Matthew said to him: "You are like an (especially) wise philosopher."

(4) Thomas said to him: "Teacher, my mouth cannot bear at all to say whom you are like."

(5) Jesus said: "I am not your teacher. For you

have drunk, you have become intoxicated at the bubbling spring that I have measured out."

(6) And he took him, (and) withdrew, (and) he said three words to him.

(7) But when Thomas came back to his companions, they asked him: "What did Jesus say to you?"

(8) Thomas said to them: "If I tell you one of the words he said to me, you will pick up stones and throw them at me, and fire will come out of the stones (and) burn you up."

Jesus was originally their teacher but once they drank from his bubbling spring of knowledge, grace, love and faith they became living spirits similar to Jesus, and Jesus obviously had secret insights that he could share with some (such as with Thomas who better understood him) but not others.

(14) Jesus said to them:

(1)"If you fast, you will bring forth sin for yourselves.

(2) And if you pray, you will be condemned.

(3) And if you give alms, you will do harm to your spirits.

(4) And if you go into any land and wander from place to place, (and) if they take you in,

(then) eat what they will set before you. Heal the sick among them!

(5) For what goes into your mouth will not defile you. Rather, what comes out of your mouth will defile you."

Jesus is saying that his disciples should not focus on a life of asceticism but rather interact with non-believers. Go into their towns, take whatever is given them (even if not kosher) and heal their sick, and do good deeds and preach the Word of God.

(15) Jesus says:

"When you see one who was not born of woman, fall on your face (and) worship him. That one is your Father."

(16) Jesus says:

(1) "Perhaps people think that I have come to cast peace upon the earth.

(2) But they do not know that I have come to cast dissension upon the earth: fire, sword, war.

(3) For there will be five in one house: there will be three against two and two against three, father against son and son against father.

(4) And they will stand as solitary ones."

Consistent with logion 10, Jesus is saying the world is a furnace of pain and suffering. Importantly, that it was God's design as such, and those who divorce themselves from it, and stand alone with God as their only focus, will be rewarded.

(17) Jesus says:

"I will give you what no eye has seen, and what no ear has heard, and what no hand has touched, and what has not occurred to the human mind."

(18)

(1) The disciples said to Jesus: "Tell us how our end will be."

(2) Jesus said: "Have you already discovered the beginning that you are now asking about the end? For where the beginning is, there the end will be too.

(3) Blessed is he who will stand at the beginning. And he will know the end, and he will not taste death."

Jesus is acknowledging that the End Game will be to take those fallen souls who reform themselves back to God's kingdom. That is, to where they originated from. Those who truly understand that this is God's plan and who "stand at the beginning" that is, have reformed their souls to their original state, will be blessed and be saved from forever tasting death.

(19) Jesus says:

(1) "Blessed is he who was, before he came into being.

(2) If you become disciples of mine (and) listen to my words, these stones will serve you.

(3) For you have five trees in Paradise that do not change during summer (and) winter, and their leaves do not fall.

(4) Whoever comes to know them will not taste death."

(20)

(1) The disciples said to Jesus: "Tell us whom the kingdom of heaven is like!"

(2) He said to them: "It is like a mustard seed.

(3) <It> is the smallest of all seeds.

(4) But when it falls on cultivated soil, it produces a large branch (and) becomes shelter for the birds of the sky."

God's kingdom is like a very tiny thing that's hard to see and many would ignore it as a result. But if seen by someone who recognises it's potential and embraces it (like cultivated soil), it brings rich rewards. But note that the soil must be cultivated, i.e. a man must have already learnt through successive lives that happiness can only come from embracing God's word.

Here the tiny mustard seed is God's implanted Divine Light in us already. It is just surrounded by despoiled soil rather than cultivated soil. Once the despoiled soil is purified by detachment from worldly distractions and watered with love of the divine, the seed can flourish.

This reminds me of a beautiful Baha'i teaching and song, as follows:

"O MY BROTHER! Hearken to the delightsome words of My honeyed tongue, and quaff the stream of mystic holiness from My sugar-shedding lips. Sow the seeds of My divine wisdom in the pure soil of thy heart, and water them with the water of certitude, that the hyacinths of My knowledge and wisdom may spring up fresh and green in the sacred city of thy heart."

The Hidden Words of Baha'u'llah (33)

(21) (1) Mary said to Jesus: "Whom are your disciples like?"

(2) He said: "They are like servants who are entrusted with a field that is not theirs.

(3) When the owners of the field arrive, they will say: 'Let us have our field.'

(4) (But) they are naked in their presence so as to let them have it, (and thus) to give them their field."

(5) "That is why I say: When the master of the house learns that the thief is about to come, he will be on guard before he comes (and) will not let him break into his house, his domain, to carry away his possessions.

(6) (But) you, be on guard against the world!

(7) Gird your loins with great strength, so that the robbers will not find a way to get to you."

(8) "For the necessities for which you wait (with longing) will be found.

(9) There ought to be a wise person among you!

(10) When the fruit was ripe, he came quickly with his sickle in his hand, (and) he harvested it.

(11)Whoever has ears to hear should hear"

The field is the hearts and minds of men in the illusory world created for us; which world Jesus administers in order for us to become educated and redeemed.

Men's hearts and minds are currently replete with idle desires, envy, greed and malice (as Jesus says elsewhere, he came into the world and found mankind intoxicated with ungodly fancies and no one hungry for God's love). The hearts and minds of men are therefore the domain of the evil doers who currently inhabit and "own" the field.

Jesus wishes his disciples to be God's servants and tender to the field once he is gone. Their job will be to spread God's word so that men's lives are God's domain. The disciples are to win over ownership of the field from the evildoers. The fruits of the field will come from spreading the Word and converting men to God's love.

Because the disciples (yet to become Apostles) have yet to receive the strength and wisdom of the Holy Spirit, they are weak and unable to properly guard the field from the evildoers who will return and demand control of the field again.

Jesus uses this example to, in turn, warn us "to guard against the world" (i.e. the place of evil and evildoers) so that when we are confronted by idle fancies, envy, greed and malice, we are able to resist it because we have "girded our loins" by connecting with God in advance, and have invited him and the Holy Spirit in to deliver us from Evil (as is reflected in the Lord's Prayer).

When the apostles become enabled by the Holy Spirit they will be readily able to harvest men's souls quickly (like the man with the sickle) when such souls are ready to receive God's Word – ie when the fruit is ripe.

(22)

(1) Jesus saw infants being suckled.

(2) He said to his disciples: "These little ones being suckled are like those who enter the kingdom."

(3) They said to him: "Then will we enter the kingdom as little ones?"

(4) Jesus said to them: "When you make the two into one, and when you make the inside like the outside and the outside like the inside and the above like the below —

(5) that is, to make the male and the female into a single one, so that the male will not be male and the female will not be female —

(6) and when you make eyes instead of an eye and a hand instead of a hand and a foot instead of a foot, an image instead of an image, (7) then you will enter [the kingdom]."

Origen talks in a similar way in his essay on Heraclites. Here the concept is that each man has an outer man, being flesh, and an inner man of soul or spirit. Each has eyes and ears and human traits but they play different roles. For example, the outer eyes see material things and our outer ears hear worldly things, but our inner eyes and ears can see and hear things from the incorporeal world.

Once we have transformed ourselves to be holy and so driven by our inner selves, (i.e. our higher selves), then we will connect with God. In such a state, we will neutralise our male female tendencies and be indifferent to sexual proclivities and other divisive tendencies just as new born infants are.

(23) Jesus says:

(1) "I will choose you, one from a thousand and two from ten thousand.

(2) And they will stand as a single one."

Jesus here is saying that he expects only a relatively few souls will ultimately be saved, and those that are, will not only be chosen, but also that the chosen will be reunified into the new Adam to join God's kingdom. The rest may indeed perish. That's why perhaps not all will be saved in the end - but perhaps from what is left (i.e. the chosen ones), then they will stand as a single unified (indeed a reunified) soul (i.e. the new Adam).

Interestingly, as we saw earlier from Islamic scripture, and consistent with this logion, according to one hadith, out of every one thousand people entering into the afterlife, nine hundred and ninety-nine of them will end up in the fire.

(24)

(1) His disciples said: "Show us the place where you are, because it is necessary for us to seek it.

(2) He said to them: "Whoever has ears should hear!

(3) Light exists inside a person of light, and he shines on the whole world. If he does not shine, there is darkness."

This confirms that once a person becomes awakened and becomes a person of light, then the divine dwells within him and this person emanates light onto others.

(25) Jesus says:

(1) "Love your brother like your life!

(2) Protect him like the apple of your eye!"

This, of course, is an important commandment and echoes one of the only two critical canonical commandments Jesus gave us; namely, to love God with all our heart mind and soul, and to love our neighbour as ourselves.

This also ties into the notion of "service" and "good works". For how can we truly love our brothers and sisters "like your life" and "the apple of your eye" without doing good works in their favour?

In many respects, the ability of us to follow Jesus' first commandment being: To love God with all our heart, mind, soul and strength, is inextricably linked with his second commandment: To love our neighbour as ourselves.

This is particularly seen in a passage in the Gospel of Mathew as follows,

"Matthew 25:31-46

(NIV)

31 "When the Son of Man comes in his glory, and all the angels with him, he will sit on his glorious

throne. [32] All the nations will be gathered before him,
and he will separate the people one from another as
a shepherd separates the sheep from the goats. [33] He
will put the sheep on his right and the goats on his
left.

[34] "Then the King will say to those on his right,
'Come, you who are blessed by my Father; take your
inheritance, the kingdom prepared for you since the
creation of the world. [35] For I was hungry and you
gave me something to eat, I was thirsty and you gave
me something to drink, I was a stranger and you
invited me in, [36] I needed clothes and you clothed me,
I was sick and you looked after me, I was in prison
and you came to visit me.'

[37] "Then the righteous will answer him, 'Lord,
when did we see you hungry and feed you, or thirsty
and give you something to drink? [38] When did we see
you a stranger and invite you in, or needing clothes
and clothe you? [39] When did we see you sick or in
prison and go to visit you?'

[40] "The King will reply, 'Truly I tell you, whatever
you did for one of the least of these brothers and
sisters of mine, you did for me.'

[41] "Then he will say to those on his left, 'Depart
from me, you who are cursed, into the eternal fire
prepared for the devil and his angels. [42] For I was
hungry and you gave me nothing to eat, I was thirsty
and you gave me nothing to drink, [43] I was a stranger
and you did not invite me in, I needed clothes and
you did not clothe me, I was sick and in prison and
you did not look after me.'

[44] "They also will answer, 'Lord, when did we see

you hungry or thirsty or a stranger or needing clothes or sick or in prison, and did not help you?'

45 "He will reply, 'Truly I tell you, whatever you did not do for one of the least of these, you did not do for me.'

46 "Then they will go away to eternal punishment, but the righteous to eternal life."

In other words, loving God with all your heart, mind, soul and strength is not just about going to Church, the Synagogue, Mosque and the Temple or anywhere for that matter and praying, mediating, singing spiritual songs in the name of praise and worship. It's also about HELPING OTHERS. Some call it Service, Good Works, Charity, Giving, Acts of Kindness etc. Whatever one calls it, its essence is found in lovingly helping others.

(26) Jesus says:

(1) "You see the splinter that is in your brother's eye, but you do not see the beam that is in your (own) eye.

(2) When you remove the beam from your (own) eye, then you will see clearly (enough) to remove the splinter from your brother's eye."

(27)

(1) "If you do not abstain from the world, you will not find the kingdom.

(2) If you do not make the Sabbath into a Sabbath, you will not see the Father."

No logia makes it clearer than this, that FASTING or ABSTAINING from worldly temptations is the pathway to God. In order to train and prepare us for returning to God's kingdom in a sustainable way, we need to be able to resist temptation which led us to the Fall in the first place. To do this we must harden and discipline ourselves to resist worldly pleasures and evil temptations; we must gird our loins and be ready for battle.

This should not take the form of a monkish isolationist approach to life. Rather God wants us to be able to walk amongst temptations, perhaps even savour them in some moderate way, without being consumed by them, or forgetful of our love for him and fellow souls by prioritising them.

Jesus defeated evil not just by his resurrection, but by resisting the devil's temptation of him as he prayed and meditated in the desert. There's nothing more that the devil would have wanted than to dissuade Jesus from dying on the cross, and so turning God's own son away from him. Jesus's resistance of this and the completion of his mission is why God was so pleased with him and elevated him even more so.

The world has toyed with asceticism for millennia and philosophers such as Kant, Kierkegaard and Schopenhauer have written about why, in some forms, it is good for us. Nietzsche noted that we should not abstain from the passions of life but rather to savour them in a manner that did not consume us.

Clearly Jesus, unlike it seems John the Baptist, did not isolate himself from women, or wine, or fine oils and those things that can lead to addictions. He could walk amongst the addictive temptations of life, but maintain nonetheless his focus on the love of God and Humanity. THAT is true strength and devotion. It is what Nietzsche says is commendable in one who can discipline his desires.

Note - some interpretations also translate the second part of this logion as meaning that fasting from the world should take place seven days a week not just on the Sabbath.

(28) Jesus says:

(1) "I stood in the middle of the world, and in flesh I appeared to them.

(2) I found all of them drunk. None of them did I find thirsty.

(3) And my soul ached for the children of humanity, because they are blind in their heart, and they cannot see; for they came into the world empty, (and) they also seek to depart from the world empty.

(4) But now they are drunk. (But) when they shake off their wine, then they will change their mind."

When he says,

"I stood in the middle of the world, and in flesh I appeared to them." it is implicit in this first, that he had the power to stand in the midst of the world. Second, that he chose to appear in the flesh, and so has the power to decide how he shows himself to us. And finally when he says "And my soul ached for the children of humanity," it's clear that the real Jesus is the Soul within; i.e., interestingly, it's not his human heart that ached, but his soul.

Jesus incarnated and came into the world of illusion designed to teach souls godliness. It's the very world he created, with His Father's blessing, and which he administers as "School Principal" and Master Teacher.

Despite the lessons of earlier Messengers (Moses

and others), having incarnated as a man inside his own illusory world, he found mankind dominated by desires for worldly things. It was intoxicated with Satan's worldly temptations. Mankind could not see the true reality, namely, that it is of Divine origin and yet living in a cesspool of ungodly temptations; and just as Mankind had come naked into the world, it would, without changing, leave the world blind and naked.

Mankind showed no thirst for searching for a better Life Purpose (i.e. in Plato's Cave allegory, no thirst to break the chains, lose the stiff neck and look for the True and Divine Life outside). It is only by ensuring that the illusory world makes life painful for Mankind, like when a drunk goes through rehab in order to "shake off his wine", that mankind can hope to become truly aware (truly conscious), change its habits, and ultimately be redeemed.

We here again see the need for painful experiences in order to bring about evolutionary changes. Life is purposely full of obstacles and challenges so that we learn to overcome them by evolutionary changes. These changes are then embedded permanently in our souls on a path to ultimate reunification with the Godhead.

(29) Jesus says:

(1) "If the flesh came into being because of the spirit, it is a wonder.

(2) But if the spirit (came into being) because of the body, it is a wonder of wonders.

(3) Yet I marvel at how this great wealth has taken up residence in this poverty."

This logion is quite revealing. Jesus is saying that it's amazing enough that God, being a spirit or consciousness personified, created man and the material world (i.e. flesh came into being due to spirit, perhaps through the spirit of Christ himself).

But it's even more amazing to see how this illusory fleshy world can be used to train and evolve the soul and restore it (the spirit) to its original state. That is, the spirit comes into being because of the body; meaning that it is truly marvellous how the learning environment of physical bodies and the material world of temptations, can ultimately fashion a unclean soul into a divine spirit worthy of deification.

He also acknowledges the wonder of how the great potential we have within us (that is, the divine sparks as children of God), can have been inserted in such a desolate place as the world of flesh and material desires and fears.

(30) Jesus says:

(1) "Where there are three gods, they are gods.

(2) Where there are two or one, I am with him."

(31) Jesus says:

(1) "No prophet is accepted in his (own) village.

(2) A physician does not heal those who know him."

(32) Jesus says:

"A city built upon a high mountain (and) fortified cannot fall, nor can it be hidden."

A soul that is representing a person's higher self, and which has been purified of temptations and therefore fortified from Satan's allures, can no longer fall to Satan's debasing temptations.

Moreover, the bright light within it, now no longer held captive by dark and murky inhibitors, shines brightly for all to see and be guided by.(33) Jesus says:

(1) "What you will hear with your ear {with the other ear} proclaim from your rooftops.

(2) For no one lights a lamp (and) puts it under a bushel, nor does he put it in a hidden place.

(3) Rather, he puts it on a lampstand, so that everyone who comes in and goes out will see its light."

Importantly, Jesus here says that those souls who are fortunate enough to have heard God's Word and message, (having heard it not by their physical ears, but from the mind's eye or inner ear, as they awakened to true reality and to Life's Purpose) should not keep it to themselves. They should proclaim and share it with the rest of humanity so that all may have an opportunity to find it. This underlies the entire Missionary zeal of most religious movements.

Indeed, this is why I have felt so compelled to make this work public and readily accessible, even though when I commenced it, I was writing it only for myself and those close to me (whom I hope, one day might read it when they are ready).(34) Jesus says:

"If a blind (person) leads a blind (person), both will fall into a pit."

If your teachers, or mentors, or those whom you look to for guidance, are not of the light and therefore blind, they will do you no good. Only teachers who have their eyes open through an awakening, or who otherwise are from the world of light, can give you good guidance.

(35) Jesus says:

(1) "It is not possible for someone to enter the house of a strong (person) (and) take it by force unless he binds his hands.

(2) Then he will loot his house."

Evil cannot steal away the soul of a holy person unless it first restricts his ability to defend himself by, for example, enticing him into temptation and addiction, and thereby limiting his ability to respond to a threat via the use of his love and knowledge of God and Mankind.

The "binding of hands" is reminiscent of the prisoners chained to their seats in Plato's Allegory of the Cave. For this reason, Satan, Temptation and vices and addictions are all necessary training tools to enable souls to learn resistance and become "freedom fighters" and learn the Art of how to liberate themselves (or otherwise ultimately perish, and live in pain in the meantime).

(36) Jesus says:

"Do not worry from morning to evening and from evening to morning about what you will wear."

If you place your life and future in God's hands then your daily concerns will be taken care of. This is a very powerful teaching for all those people enmeshed in trying to accumulate material wealth and all its trappings. As a result, they are blind to the Truth and the power of God's love.

(37)

(1) His disciples said: "When will you appear to us, and when will we see you?"

(2) Jesus said: "When you undress without being ashamed and take your clothes (and) put them under

your feet like little children (and) trample on them,

(3) Then [you] will see the son of the Living One, and you will not be afraid."

When you give up what you have and show that you no longer care for worldly matters and have conquered your fears, you will truly see God.

In the Gospel of Phillip there is also a reference to removing ones earthly clothes - although there, one needs to put on the spiritual clothes in order to become truly immortal. In Thomas, the Logion speaks simply of being naked and being comfortable with our nakedness which represents the true spiritual selves in us; devoid of earthly covering. Once the Light preventing dross is removed, we will then remain comfortably naked.

(38) Jesus says:

(1) "Many times have you desired to hear these words, these that I am speaking to you, and you have no one else from whom to hear them.

(2) There will be days when you will seek me (and) you will not find me."

(39) Jesus says:

(1) "The Pharisees and the scribes have received the keys of knowledge, (but) they have hidden them.

(2) Neither have they entered, nor have they allowed to enter those who wish to.

(3) You, however, be as shrewd as serpents and as innocent as doves!"

The religious rulers entrusted to teach and guide the people have failed them. They have become subsumed in their own power and corruption, and the layers of man-made dross have absconded the keys of knowledge; and so the entryway to the kingdom is not to be found through them.

This, of course, happens to all religious movements overtime; and renewal is required either through a painful revolution or reformation of the existing religion, or through the introduction of a new religious faith.

(40) Jesus says:

(1) "A grapevine was planted outside (the vineyard) of the Father.

(2) And since it is not supported, it will be pulled up by its roots (and) will perish."

(41) Jesus says:

(1) "Whoever has (something) in his hand, (something more) will be given to him.

(2) And whoever has nothing, even the little he has will be taken from him."

(42) Jesus says:

"Be passers-by."

Become disinterested in this life except to learn from it. Understand that you are here temporarily and make the most of the learning experience, but do not crave for the world as it is not your real and ultimate home, but an illusion meant to teach you from varied experiences.

This is reminiscent of a well-known Aboriginal quote,

"We are all visitors to this time, this place. We are just passing through. Our purpose here is to observe, to learn, to grow, to love... and then we return home."

How succinct and powerful is this simple

Aboriginal teaching? It makes the key points that we are here to "learn" (i.e. from the School of Life); and to thereby "grow" (i.e. elevate our soul calibration to a higher level); and to "love" (i.e. God and Mankind thereby releasing the Power of Love we noted earlier in this work to help us approach Deification); and ultimately "we return home" (i.e. to our spiritual home with God or the God Consciousness).

(43)

(1) His disciples said to him: "Who are you to say this to us?"

(2) "Do you not realized from what I say to you who I am?

(3) But you have become like the Jews! They love the tree, (but) they hate its fruit. Or they love the fruit, (but) they hate the tree."

(44) Jesus says:

(1) "Whoever blasphemes against the Father, it will be forgiven him.

(2) And whoever blasphemes against the Son, it will be forgiven him.

(3) But whoever blasphemes against the Holy Spirit, it will not be forgiven him, neither on earth nor in heaven."

(45) Jesus says:

(1) "Grapes are not harvested from thorns, nor are figs picked from thistles, for they do not produce fruit.

(2) A good person brings forth good from his treasure.

(3) A bad person brings (forth) evil from the bad treasure that is in his heart, and (in fact) he speaks evil.

(4) For out of the abundance of the heart he brings forth evil."

(46) Jesus says:

(1) "From Adam to John the Baptist, among those born of women there is no one who surpasses John the Baptist so that his (i.e., John's) eyes need not be downcast."

(2) "But I have also said: Whoever among you becomes little will know the kingdom, and will surpass John."

(47) Jesus says:

(1) "It is impossible for a person to mount two horses and to stretch two bows.

(2) And it is impossible for a servant to serve two masters. Else he will honor the one and insult the other.

(3) No person drinks old wine and immediately desires to drink new wine.

(4) And new wine is not put into old wineskins, so that they do not burst; nor is old wine put into (a) new wineskin, so that it does not spoil it.

(5) An old patch is not sewn onto a new garment, because a tear will result."

Renewal requires an abandonment of old ways and a fresh start. For this reason, new teachers and religious movements have to appear and people need to walk away from the old to properly embrace the new; since you cannot adhere to two sets of beliefs, especially if the old is polluted and decayed.

This Logion clearly gives support to the notion of Progressive Revelation.

(48) Jesus says:

"If two make peace with one another in one and the same house, (then) they will say to the mountain: 'Move away,' and it will move away."

(49) Jesus says:

(1) "Blessed are the solitary ones, the elect. For you will find the kingdom.

(2) For you come from it (and) will return to it."

Again, it seems that those souls who disavow the world and become solitary (but not in my view meaning monkish or isolated from the world, but rather can exercise discipline within it) will find God and life's true purpose; and will accordingly be reunited to the heavenly place they originated from. These are the, so-called, "elect", but this does not mean elect only in this life, but only after many lives; i.e. only those left standing as elevated souls (the "school graduates" you might say) when the eventual cycle of reincarnation and transmigration comes to a halt.

(50) Jesus says:

(1) "If they say to you: 'Where do you come from?' (then) say to them: 'We have come from the light, the place where the light has come into being by itself, has established [itself] and has appeared in their image.'

(2) If they say to you: 'Is it you?' (then) say: 'We are his children, and we are the elect of the living Father.'

(3) If they ask you: 'What is the sign of your Father among you?' (then) say to them: 'It is movement and repose.'"

From this logion it could not be clearer that

we are God's children and we came from the Light and the Light is independent; that is, uncreated, or perhaps self-created. This may lend support to the Mormon notion that both God and our own divine souls are all uncreated.

It also has some connectivity with Login (29) where Jesus hints at the possibility of the Spirit coming into existence out of a non-spiritual environment, wherein Jesus says,

"(2) But if the spirit (came into being) because of the body, it is a wonder of wonders.(3) Yet I marvel at how this great wealth has taken up residence in this poverty"

His comment on "repose" is interesting as it suggests to me that we exhibit a Godly quality when we pray in certain ways, or meditate.

(51)

(1) His disciples said to him: "When will the <resurrection> of the dead take place, and when will the new world come?"

(2) He said to them: "That (resurrection) which you are awaiting has (already) come, but you do not recognize it."

This seems to contradict the well-known orthodox Christian expectation of a Judgement Day when the saved will be resurrected and the rest dammed for eternity. No doubt another reason why the Church tried to bury The Gospel of Thomas.

On the other hand, the notion of a "now" Resurrection is entirely consistent with our hypothesis in that, at the time of the Fall, wherein we succumbed to Evil, God created a School of Life for us through which we could progress, and have an opportunity to "arise" to a state of perfection or Godliness, in order to re-enter God's kingdom.

The so-called "Resurrection" that this logion speaks of, is our own journey of rising through the School of Life to God's Kingdom. Jesus is acknowledging that such a Resurrection has already commenced. Indeed, as was mentioned earlier, a reference in the Gospel of Phillip para 90, suggests that the Resurrection we need (i.e. our own awakening and reconnection with God) must come during our time in our illusory world of the flesh.

In other words, that ***only during our schooling days*** can we transform ourselves from fallen souls to risen souls? ***Only during schooling*** can we jettison the fleshy clothes we put on after the Fall, and walk the pathway to God in order to realise our spiritual selves and elevate ourselves to our true consciousness. It appears we cannot do this whilst in spirit. This makes sense of course, since if we could achieve this whilst in spirit, we would not need a school involving an illusory material world and fleshly bodies to learn from.

In the Gospel of Phillip, the author talks of jettisoning our earthly clothes and putting on incorruptible clothes. The Gospel of Thomas simply talks of jettisoning earthly clothes and going comfortably naked. And so that is why finding God, whilst we are in the material world, should be a priority for us; as we do not know when the School bell will ring, and therefore when the time to redeem ourselves is forever lost.

Moreover, it's not clear how many opportunities we will be given to incarnate, or transmigrate, in order to keep learning. ***We need to be fast learners.***

When at some point the School bell does ring, there will be a Judgement Day because the School can not last forever and so at that point, those who have progressed sufficiently will be saved from future reincarnations and transmigrations by being given eternal rest in God's kingdom. The others will be forever dammed, or perhaps just extinguished in a living soul sense (as suggested by S B Groves earlier); and if extinguished, then those remaining survivors may be reunited with God so that All (as in all that's left) will be in All. When Judgement day comes no one knows, and so Jesus elsewhere in this Gospel, and other Gospels, warns us to be ever ready.

(52)

(1) His disciples said to him: "Twenty-four prophets have spoken in Israel, and all (of them) have spoken through you."

(2) He said to them: "You have pushed away the living (one) from yourselves, and you have begun to speak of those who are dead."

(53)

(1) His disciples said to him: "Is circumcision beneficial, or not?"

(2) He said to them: "If it were beneficial, their father would beget them circumcised from their mother.

(3) But the true circumcision in the spirit has prevailed over everything."

Again this talk of circumcision is a reference to detaching the spirit or soul from the fetters of worldly desires and fears. It resonates with the Deuteronomy quote, mentioned earlier in this work, asking Jewish believers to "circumcise their hearts", and devote them to the Lord.

(54) Jesus says:

"Blessed are the poor. For the kingdom of heaven belongs to you."

The reference to poor here doesn't just simply mean that because you have very little materially, you will enter God's kingdom. Since there are many poor that desire much materially and pay little attention to their spiritual wealth, or lack of it.

It means blessed are those who care little for worldly goods and vanities, because they have realised that devotion to God and the love of ones neighbour, is paramount.

(55) Jesus says:

(1) "Whoever does not hate his father and his mother cannot become a disciple of mine.

(2) And whoever does not hate his brothers and his sisters (and) will not take up his cross as I do, will not be worthy of me."

It's not clear to me that the word hate here means hate as in vengeful intent. It may simply mean that one must recognise that devotion to God, and love of ones neighbour, is paramount to blind devotion to one's family ties.

(56) Jesus says:

"Whoever has come to know the world has found a corpse.

And whoever has found (this) corpse, of him the world is not worthy."

Again, this is consistent with the hypothesis idea that we live in an otherwise illusory fake and dead world; that our real world is of the spirit not the flesh, and once you recognize this, you gradually progress to the stage where you are ready for another stage of your schooling by perhaps transmigrating to another world closer to God's kingdom, or achieving a state of enlightenment where ongoing reincarnations or transmigrations are no longer necessary.

(57) Jesus says:

(1) "The kingdom of the Father is like a person who had (good) seed.

(2) His enemy came by night. He sowed darnel among the good seed.

(3) The person did not allow (the servants) to pull up the darnel.

He said to them: 'Lest you go to pull up the darnel (and then) pull up the wheat along with it.'

(4) For on the day of the harvest the darnel will be apparent and it will be pulled up (and) burned."

Consistent with our hypothesis, we came from "good seed" but through Satan's temptations (His enemy) and our freewill to choose evil, we were all infested with evil. God could have wiped us all out and burnt the lot of us. But out of his love and mercy he created a schooling environment for us so we would have an opportunity to cleanse ourselves. At some point, Judgement Day, those who are clean (the Wheat) will be harvested and those who do not graduate from God's, tough but merciful, School will perish (i.e. be burned in hell, perhaps by virtue of their lowly elevated soul energies unable to sustain a living identity as S B Groves eloquently described earlier, and therefore will cease to be immortal).

(58) Jesus says:

"Blessed is the person who has struggled. He has found life."

God has created a world of pain and suffering so that our souls experience ups and downs; and when we are down we realise that worldly pleasures and addictions do not bring happiness, and often we crack under that downward pressure. When we crack, to use a Leonard Cohen phrase "that's how the light gets in".

The Kabbalist belief is that God's light is ever present and always shining on us, and whether we allow God's light into our soul depends on whether we can open ourselves up to properly receive it. It is through life's struggles and the resultant "cracks" in us from the pain and pressures we experience, that the light eventually gets in. So struggles in life maximize our chances of success. By the way, we do not have to go looking for such struggles as life is intentionally full of them and they are tailor made to suit each of us.

However, when they do come, and pain and suffering follows, then we must try to use the occasion to connect with God, or to be faithful to Him. These occasions are given to us as "Tests" (Quran) to test our Faith and belief system, and/or as opportunities to effect a "Turn to God" and awaken to his calling.

In the Platonic Allegory of the Cave, it is the chained prisoner who struggles to liberate himself from the bonds of desire and fear, who then is no longer "stiff necked" (Deuteronomy) and can turn towards the Light of the cave exit to find Truth outside the cave.

(59) Jesus says:

"Look for the Living One while you are alive, so that you will not die (and) then seek to see him. And you will not be able to see (him)."

This makes it clear, that we MUST find ourselves and God during the Schooling process, whilst we have the chance, and our chances are limited. Again, consistent with Logia 51 and 57, we must do this during our years at School and, when we do, our lives will be forever changed.

Those who think that they can put this off and continue to enjoy their earthly material life, may not only end up disappointed in this life, but may forego forever their chance at eternal bliss in God's kingdom, since you never know if you will be given a new school term.

This is reminiscent of a Baha'i saying, from the Persian Hidden Words, Part II,

"40:

O MY SERVANT! Free thyself from the fetters of this world, and loose thy soul from the prison of self. Seize thy chance, for it will come to thee no more."

I think this point should be of particular interest to those of us who have already been given the benefit of this knowledge of God's merciful and

loving School Schema. If you are reading this work, you are by definition such a person. If you do not act on this in your present life, you may never be given another opportunity. I say this because the process of reincarnation and transmigration may possibly only last until a soul has had a clear an obvious opportunity to be shown and realize the Truth, and be given the clear chance to accept it or reject it. If rejected, then it's not clear that that soul will be given another chance at material existence. It may simply have to wait in spirit form for Judgement Day, knowing that it will then perish. For this reason, I say that we need to be fast learners.

(60)

(1) <He saw> a Samaritan who was trying to steal a lamb while he was on his way to Judea.

(2) He said to his disciples: "That (person) is stalking the lamb."

(3) They said to him: "So that he may kill it (and) eat it."

(4) He said to them: "As long as it is alive he will not eat it, but (only) when he has killed it (and) it has become a corpse."

(5) They said to him: "Otherwise he cannot do it."

(6) He said to them: "You, too, look for a place for your repose so that you may not become a corpse (and) get eaten."

Jesus is saying here that we should find our Faith (i.e. find repose), by praying, meditating on God (as per Aristotle's contemplation of the One), follow God's key commandments, and do whatever you can to connect with God, so that your soul may stay connected with God and therefore be "alive". Otherwise without that, you are really dead, a corpse, and can be eaten and extinguished at any time. This is consistent with what was said in Logion 59 and others mentioned therein.

(61)

(1) Jesus said: "Two will rest on a bed. The one will die, the other will live."

(2) Salome said: "(So) who are you, man? You have gotten a place on my couch as a <stranger> and you have eaten from my table."

(3) Jesus said to her: "I am he who comes from the one who is (always) the same. I was given some of that which is my Father's."

(4) "I am your disciple!"

(5) Therefore I say: If someone becomes < like > (God), he will become full of light.

But if he becomes one, separated (from God), he will become full of darkness."

Jesus is acknowledging that he was given his authority and godly powers by God himself- and we too should aim to receive God's grace.

Interestingly, Jesus does not say he is the Father i.e. God - just that he was given some of the Father's essence. This accords with what Origen held, that although Jesus was made of godly fabric, he was lesser than the Father. As this did not accord with orthodox Christian thinking, he was eventually anathematised.

It also instructive to see Jesus mention the notion of someone, becoming "like" God. This ties into what we said earlier about the End Game and Deification as the ultimate outcome for those souls who "Graduate". It may be somewhat tedious to debate whether in such cases one becomes God, or simply becomes "like" God; either way the reward for Graduating is immense and beyond all imaginings.

(62) Jesus says:

(1) "I tell my mysteries to those who [are worthy] of [my] mysteries."

(2) "Whatever you right hand does, your left hand should not know what it is doing."

This probably means that if you are reading all this *and* it resonates with you, then Jesus has deemed you worthy to receive and understand the mysteries of life. Not everyone is ready or worthy to hear them. Just because the right hand is ready, it doesn't mean the left hand is also ready and therefore worthy. This echoes somewhat the logion advising us not to throw pearls to the pigs.

(63) Jesus says:

(1) "There was a rich person who had many possessions.

(2) He said: 'I will use my possessions so that I might sow, reap, plant,

(and) fill my storehouses with fruit so that I will not lack anything.'

(3) This was what he was thinking in his heart. And in that night he died.

(4) Whoever has ears should hear."

Here Jesus points out the futility of worldly possession building. It is instead spiritual wealth that counts; you can take that with you to your next life or world. I believe, but can't of course conclusively prove, that if you build your spiritual wealth then you don't lose it from one life or world to the next. It's spiritual wealth that both counts and lasts, not material wealth.

We know that Soul essences survive death because we know reincarnation is a very real phenomenon from our earlier discussion. We also saw Professors Penrose and Hameroff earlier espouse a theory of non-destructible knowledge that can transcend death. This is the Soul essence I believe stores our spiritual gains in life and preserves them into the next.

(64) Jesus says:

(1) "A person had guests. And when he had prepared the dinner, he sent his servant, so that he might invite the guests.

(2) He came to the first (and) said to him: 'My master invites you.'

(3) He said: 'I have bills for some merchants. They are coming to me this evening. I will go (and) give instructions to them. Excuse me from the dinner.'

(4) He came to another (and) said to him: 'My master has invited you.'

(5) He said to him: 'I have bought a house, and I have been called (away) for a day. I will not have time.'

(6) He went to another (and) said to him: 'My master invites you.'

(7) He said to him: 'My friend is going to marry, and I am the one who is going to prepare the meal. I will not be able to come. Excuse me from the dinner.'

(8) He came up to another (and) said to him: 'My master invites you.'

(9) He said to him: 'I have bought a village. Since I am going to collect the rent, I will not be able to come. Excuse me.'

(10) The servant went away. He said to his master: 'Those whom you invited to the dinner have asked to be excused.'

(11) The master said to his servant: 'Go out on the roads. Bring (back) whomever you find, so that they might have dinner.'

(12) Dealers and merchants (will) not enter the places of my Father."

Again, this emphasises the point that we can easily become consumed by worldly concerns and miss the opportunity to let in God's grace and light; and it's the down and outers in our society, i.e. those that are struggling and have little to grasp onto, that are more easily inclined to accept God's grace when it's offered to them.

This of course accords with the biblical saying that "it is easier for a camel to pass through the eye of a needle than for a rich man to enter God's kingdom". (Matthew 19:24)

(65) He said:

(1) "A [usurer] owned a vineyard. He gave it to some farmers so that they would work it (and) he might receive its fruit from them.

(2) He sent his servant so that the farmers might give him the fruit of the vineyard.

(3) They seized his servant, beat him, (and) almost killed him. The servant went (back and) told his master.

(4) His master said: 'Perhaps <they> did not recognize <him>.'

(5) He sent another servant, (and) the farmers beat that other one as well.

(6) Then the master sent his son (and) said: 'Perhaps they will show respect for my son.'

(7) (But) those farmers, since they knew that he was the heir of the vineyard, seized him (and) killed him.

(8) Whoever has ears should hear."

Here I think Jesus relays the story of how God (who owns the Vineyard) established a rearing ground to train fallen souls and to ultimately recover them at some point, (i.e. "so that they would work it (and) he might receive its fruit from them"). The farmers are the religious leaders who have inherited the charge of the various religious orders from time to time.

Many of the messengers and prophets that God has sent including his own Son (Jesus, John the Baptist, many Saints, the Bab, Bahaullah, and others who I clearly no little about) have met their death at the hands of the so-called "farmers" being leaders of religious orders, or at their insistence.

He would send teachers and prophets from time to time to help collect the harvest, but these would constantly be rejected. Even his own son was so rejected and killed. This of course ties into the logion concerning the constant rejection of God's messengers as well as the next logion 66.

(66) Jesus says:

"Show me the stone that the builders have rejected. It is the cornerstone."

(67) Jesus says:

"Whoever knows all, if he is lacking one thing, he is (already) lacking everything."

Even an incredibly knowledgeable person, who knows all else, but doesn't know God's message of love, knows in fact nothing worthwhile.

(68) Jesus says:

(1) "Blessed are you when (ever) they hate you (and) persecute you.

(2) But they (themselves) will find no place there where they have persecuted you."

(69) Jesus says:

(1) "Blessed are those who have been persecuted in their heart.

They are the ones who have truly come to know the Father."

(2) "Blessed are those who suffer from hunger so that the belly of the one who wishes (it) will be satisfied."

(70) Jesus says:

(1) "If you bring it into being within you, (then) that which you have will save you.

(2) If you do not have it within you, (then) that which you do not have within you [will] kill you."

Without God's light entering your soul you are destined for eternal death.

(71) Jesus says:

"I will [destroy this] house, and no one will be able to build it [again]."

(72)

(1) A [person said] to him: "Tell my brothers that they have to divide my father's possessions with me."

(2) He said to him: "Man, who has made me a divider?"

(3) He turned to his disciples (and) said to them: "I am not a divider, am I?"

(73) Jesus says:

(1) "The harvest is plentiful, but there are few workers.

(2) But beg the Lord that he may send workers into the harvest."

Souls ready to learn and receive the word of God are plentiful, but servants who understand this and stand willing to assist in the conversion are few. The world needs more light workers.

(74) He said:

"Lord, there are many around the well, but there is nothing in the <well>."

(75) Jesus says:

"Many are standing before the door, but it is the solitary ones who will enter the wedding hall."

It's those souls who can stand separate from the world and resist all its fancies that will find true happiness in God's realm. The wedding hall presumably being where God is reunited with the lost souls.

(76) Jesus says:

(1) "The kingdom of the Father is like a merchant who had merchandise and found a pearl.

(2) That merchant is prudent. He sold the goods (and) bought for himself the pearl alone.

(3) You too look for his treasure, which does not perish, (and) which stays where no moth can reach it to eat it, and no worm destroys it."

Like the fishing logion here, the godly man rejects all attachments but his connection with God.

This logion also importantly seems to be saying that such a treasure can be taken with you throughout your worldly reincarnations and transmigrations, and will not be lost or diminished.

You will see later that obtaining the Pearl was also symbolic to being the key to God's Kingdom in the so-called Gnostic Hymn of the Pearl.

(77) Jesus says:

(1) "I am the light that is over all. I am the All. The All came forth out of me. And to me the All has come."

(2) "Split a piece of wood — I am there.

(3) Lift the stone, and you will find me there."

You may recall that I mentioned earlier that Einstein believed in Spinoza's God, being a pantheistic notion that God is indeed everywhere and that we live in him and everything around us is also part of him. Einstein knew all too well how miraculous a world we live in and all the fine cosmic and mathematical nuances that had to be intensely accurately calibrated for our world to exist, and for there to be life on it. He did not believe it was just a freak of nature as most atheists would have us believe, no matter how big the universe might be. Like Spinoza, he therefore believed that we live in a "designed" world and that therefore there must be a cosmic architectural designer (or God of sorts). Although he did not believe that such a God was anthropomorphic in the sense that he was a personal God that you could, for example, dialogue with. In this context, he mirrors Aristotle's believe in God. The Logion above gives credence to this pantheistic notion although, of course, in my view and in the view of the Abrahamic religions, God is also clearly anthropomorphic.

We will see later also that in the Hindu faith one of their "Trinitarian" gods, Vishnu, is said to be "dreaming" or projecting the universe into existence; again a pantheistic notion of existence.

In this Logion Jesus is confirming the Gospel of John notion that he is the Logos or the Word by which the illusory world was made; and because it emanates from his existence, he is in every part of it. It is as if God has entrusted the whole schema of the School of Life and rehabilitation to Jesus, who emanates from the Father, or is a sort of mighty angel, and provides the mechanism for the projection or creation of the world (but not of ourselves as souls which God himself was responsible), as per Saint Paul.

Paul described Jesus as Creator, "Yet for us there is but one God, the Father, from whom are all things and we exist for Him; and one Lord, Jesus Christ, by whom are all things, and we exist through Him." (1 Cor. 8:6).

This of course is reminiscent of the wording in the Gospel of John 14:6

"I am the way and the truth and the life. No one comes to the Father except through me."

At this point you would be right to ask the question - well if as the Roman Catholic Church has for millennia proclaimed that everyone must come through Jesus to be saved (i.e. must be a Christian believer) and if support for this is found in scripture, such as for example in John and in Thomas above, then how could the notion of Progressive Revelation, involving Salvation through any of the key Faiths, be true?

If Christian scripture, indeed, the words of Jesus himself, say that he is the only way to God, then how could any non-Christian possibly connect with God, as our hypothesis anticipates?

This is a complex area but, in short, Jesus is saying that he, through being the Logos and being God's son, was present with God at the outset; (in Genesis 1:16 when God said "Let US make man in our image" Christ was part of the "us"; i.e. Christ was God's instrument in creating the physical world intended to train and school us. He is effectively the school principal and sustainer. And so without getting through the school he set up, and which he continues to maintain, no one gets to connect with God. ***But this doesn't mean he is the sole teacher!***

Whilst Moses, Mohammed, Buddha, Krishna, Bahaullah etc. are all truly great teachers, Christ is a special case; a teacher of teachers, and when he says,

"I am the way and the truth and the life. No one comes to the Father except through me."

He is simply acknowledging the need for all to rise through the School of Life into God's kingdom, rather than each soul having to believe in Jesus, as a Christian would believe, in order to find God.

After the second Vatican Council, the Catholic Church started to accept a notion of Universal salvation in the sense that Christ, incarnated as man, died and was resurrected by God to save ALL mankind, not just Christians.

Refer the fact that during the Council, in 1965, Pope Paul VI proclaimed the Declaration "Nostra Aetate. On the Relation of the Church to non-Christian Religions." The Church now regarded Muslims "with esteem", the Declaration said, highlighting how they "adore the one God" and revere the figures of Jesus and Mary. In a turnaround from earlier views, the Declaration also pointed out how Muslims "value the moral life", and made a call "to forget the past and to work sincerely for mutual understanding" and to work together for "social justice and moral welfare, as well as peace and freedom".

Indeed, both Pope Paul VI and Pope John Paul II, started to talk in terms that regarded other religions, especially monotheistic religions, as on a par with Christianity; refer below to Pope John Paul II's speech to a Muslim youth gathering in Casablanca in 1985.

Pope John Paul II in Casablanca, 1985, at an 85,000 people congregation of Muslim youth noted,

"I believe that we, Christians and Muslims, must recognize with joy the religious values that we have in common, and give thanks to God for them. Both of us believe in one God the only God, who is all Justice and all Mercy; we believe in the importance of prayer, of fasting, of almsgiving, of repentance and of pardon; we believe that God will be a merciful judge to us at the end of time, and we hope that after the resurrection he will be satisfied with us and we know that we will be satisfied with him.

Loyalty demands also that we should recognize and respect our differences. Obviously the most fundamental is the view that we hold on the person and work of Jesus of Nazareth. You know that, for the Christians, this Jesus causes them to enter into an intimate knowledge of the mystery of God and into a filial communion by his gifts, so that they recognize him and proclaim him Lord and Saviour.

Those are important differences, which we can accept with humility and respect, in mutual tolerance; there is a mystery there on which, I am certain, God will one day enlighten us.

Christians and Muslims, in general we have badly understood each other, and sometimes, in the past, we have opposed and even exhausted each other in polemics and in wars.

I believe that, today, God invites us to change our old practices. We must respect each other, and also we must stimulate each other in good works on the path of God.

With me, you know what the reward of spiritual values is. Ideologies and slogans cannot satisfy you nor can they solve the problems of your life. Only the spiritual and moral values can do it, and they have God as their fundament.

Dear young people, I wish that you may be able to help in thus building a world where God may have first place in order to aid and to save mankind. On this path, you are assured of the esteem and the collaboration of your Catholic brothers and sisters whom I represent among you this evening."

I will further discuss this notion of who Jesus is,

and the connection to Progressive Revelation later in this work.

(78) Jesus says:

(1) "Why did you go out to the countryside? To see a reed shaken by the wind,

(2) And to see a person dressed in soft clothing [like your] kings and your great persons?

(3) They are dressed in soft clothing and will not be able to recognize the truth."

(79)

(1) A woman in the crowd said to him: "Hail to the womb that carried you and to the breasts that fed you."

(2) He said to [her]: "Hail to those who have heard the word of the Father (and) have truly kept it.

(3) For there will be days when you will say: 'Hail to the womb that has not conceived and to the breasts that have not given milk.'"

(80) Jesus says:

(1) "Whoever has come to know the world has found the (dead) body.

(2) But whoever has found the (dead) body, of him the world is not worthy."

This echoes the earlier logion 56.

(81) Jesus says:

(1) "Whoever has become rich should be king.

(2) And the one who has power should renounce (it)."

(82) Jesus says:

(1) "The person who is near me is near the fire.

(2) And the person who is far from me is far from the kingdom."

(83) Jesus says:

(1) "The images are visible to humanity, but the light within them is hidden in the image.

(2) The light of the Father will reveal itself, but his image is hidden by his light."

(84) Jesus says:

(1) "When you see your likeness you are full of joy.

(2) But when you see your likenesses that came into existence before you — they neither die nor become manifest — how much will you bear?"

(85) Jesus says:

(1) "Adam came from a great power and a great wealth. But he did not become worthy of you.

(2) For if he had been worthy, (then) [he would] not [have tasted] death."

Jesus points out that the first soul, Adam, had it all, but succumbed to temptation and by being disconnected with God, tasted death. The Jewish Kabbalists believe that after the Fall, Adam (being God's created Soul of Mankind), was exploded into a multitude of smaller souls, and these are the souls that are immortal and comprise our inner selves, and which take on bodies to learn and ultimately progress back to the kingdom of Light from which they came.

Jesus here seems to be suggesting that we have in us the ability to be even greater than Adam; presumably, by going through our multi lifetime's education and redemption program; and as a result, resist temptation better than did Adam.

In a way, it's reminiscent of the prodigal son story, where the son who ultimately returns to the Father and begs his forgiveness, is a better man (more worthy) than the man, who years earlier, had chosen to leave the homestead.

It is also somewhat consistent with what Thomas Aquinas said about the notion of supernatural grace, which comes to us through God and can eventually elevate us to a status even higher than Adam.

(86) Jesus says:

(1) "[Foxes have] their holes and birds have their nest.

(2) But the son of man has no place to lay his head down (and) to rest."

(87) Jesus says:

(1) "Wretched is the body that depends on a body.

(2) And wretched is the soul that depends on these two."

If we are so dependent on our material wealth, or even our families and other bodily companions, then we are forever wretched. We must, as the Buddhists say, detach ourselves from all attachments and be at one with our heavenly host.

(88) Jesus says:

(1) "The messengers and the prophets are coming to you, and they will give you what belongs to you.

(2) And you, in turn, give to them what you have in your hands (and) say to yourselves: 'When will they come (and) take what belongs to them?'"

Here Jesus is acknowledging that what the messengers and prophets give us, i.e. God's word and guidance, is something that belongs to us. It is concrete support, scripture wise at least, for the fact that we are destined to participate in a long term learning process. This program belongs to us because God has ordained it for us, and allocated these great teachers to guide and teach us. In turn, we have in our possession God's hidden light, our spirit souls made in God's image, and if we adhere to God's teachings, we will rehabilitate ourselves and be worthy to go back to both whom and where we belong.

We have this "in our hands", and should offer it up to such teachers and prophets and ask when will it be taken but, of course, no one will take it until it's ready; the baker does not take the bread out of the oven until it has risen.

The other important point in this logion is **that Jesus says that the messengers and prophets "are coming", not "have come"** ; and I believe what he means here is that, after him, not only will he and God send the Holy Spirit, but there are other messengers and prophets to come.

Now in the Christian sense, what other messengers and prophets have there been since Christ? You could speculate about the great Church Fathers, or even some of the Saints, but these are not messengers and prophets in the sense that was, in my humble view, intended by Jesus here; certainly not by comparison to the great messengers and prophets of the past. The one exception may be Saint Paul, although Paul was alive during Jesus's time of course.

The more likely intentional meaning here, is that Jesus is referring to the other truly great messengers and prophets of other religions, such as, Mohammed

(Islam), Joseph Smith (Mormons) and the Bab and Bahaullah (Baha'is) and, perhaps others to follow. In this way, Jesus is saying that God's message, is to be carried to all peoples of the world by various teachers and not only by the Christian Faith, including yet to be established Faiths. Indeed, all those monotheistic Faiths that I mentioned, have that same constant theme we have covered; namely, the theme of one true loving God as well as the need to love ones neighbour.

Those who would challenge this would quote John 14:6,

"Jesus said to him, 'I am the way, the truth, and the life. No one comes to the Father except through me.'"

As a result, they would say that the Islamic or Baha'i faiths could not provide an avenue to God and so the notion of a Unity of Faiths, albeit monotheistic faiths saying all the same key things, is not plausible.

Of course, if one looks at the Faiths I have mentioned, one quickly realises that those faiths are all consistent with each other. This is especially evident in Islam and the Baha'i faith being monotheistic faiths and all giving special reverence to Jesus in any event.

Even if one were to include the eastern faiths of Hinduism and Buddhism, one would see the common notions of detachment from worldly desires, and the goal to lift oneself up to a heavenly level of consciousness approaching love of a heavenly deity, as well as a devotion to love of ones neighbour.

This is what Jesus taught, and so, if one follows

what he taught, it's obvious that John 14:6 is in any event satisfied. More on this latter on.

(89) Jesus says:

(1) "Why do you wash the outside of the cup?

(2) Do you not understand that the one who created the inside is also the one who created the outside?"

(90) Jesus says:

(1) "Come to me, for my yoke is gentle and my lordship is mild.

(2) And you will find repose for yourselves."

Rest and repose is reflective of God's kingdom.

(91)

(1) They said to him: "Tell us who you are so that we may believe in you."

(2) He said to them: "You examine the face of sky and earth, but the one who is before you, you have not recognized, and you do not know how to test this opportunity."

Man spends inordinate amounts of time and energy exploring both space and earth, looking for something worth discovering, but it fails to see the obvious most important discovery that's staring it in the face.

(92) Jesus says:

(1) "Seek and you will find.

(2) But the things you asked me about in past times, and what I did not tell you in that day, now I am willing to tell you, but you do not seek them."

(93)

(1) "Do not give what is holy to the dogs, lest they throw it upon the dunghill.

(2) Do not throw pearls to swine, lest they turn <them> into [mud]."

There's no point sharing the inner mysteries of God's sacred plan for us to those not ready, or willing, to hear them.

(94) Jesus says:

(1) "The one who seeks will find.

(2) [The one who knocks], to that one will it be opened."

When the student is ready (i.e. when he starts seeking), then he will start to find the teachings.

(95) Jesus says:

(1) "If you have money, do not lend (it) out at interest.

(2) Rather, give [it] to the one from whom you will not get it (back)."

Do not hoard your wealth but share it consistent with the notion of loving ones neighbour as oneself.

(96) Jesus says:

(1) "The kingdom of the Father is like [a] woman.

(2) She took a little bit of yeast. [She] hid it in dough (and) made it into huge loaves of bread.

(3) Whoever has ears should hear."

The yeast is God's divine light in us. The dough is our material selves, and the bread is what's worth waiting for (i.e. our rejuvenated divine worthiness), but only after we have been cooked in God's oven furnace of the School of life.

(97) Jesus says:

(1) "The kingdom of the [Father] is like a woman who is carrying a [jar] filled with flour.

(2) While she was walking on [the] way, very

distant (from home), the handle of the jar broke (and) the flour leaked out [on] the path.

(3) (But) she did not know (it); she had not noticed a problem.

(4) When she reached her house, she put the jar down on the floor (and) found it empty."

We all have amazing potential in us. We carry it with us every day; we just don't know it. We have forgotten where we came from and who we are; and we can go through life having totally wasted all that potential by ignoring all the opportunities to see, hear and understand the teachings; or just by being preoccupied with distractions and desires around us. We may not realise what potential we had until it's too late. Indeed, the Islamic Faith emphasises this notion of "forgetfulness" as a great error/sin to be avoided, and so has developed mandatory daily prayers (as also exist in other Faiths e.g. Baha'i faith) to ensure people do not forget who they are and where they came from. The same *forgetfulness* notion can be seen in the Gnostic Hymn of the Pearl.

The Hymn of the Pearl!
(The Hymn of Judas Thomas the Apostle in the Country of the Indians)

Translated by G.R.S. Mead

I.

When, a quite little child, I was dwelling
In the House of my Father's Kingdom,

And in the wealth and the glories
Of my Up-bringers I was delighting,

From the East, our Home, my Parents
Forth-sent me with journey-provision.

Indeed from the wealth of our Treasure,
They bound up for me a load.
Large was it, yet was it so light
That all alone I could bear it.

II.

Gold from the Land of Beth-Ellaya,
Silver from Gazak the Great,
Chalcedonies of India,
Iris-hued [Opals?] from Kãshan.
They girt me with Adamant [also]
That hath power to cut even iron.
My Glorious Robe they took off me
Which in their love they had wrought me,
And my Purple Mantle [also]
Which was woven to match with my stature.

III.

And with me They [then] made a compact;
In my heart wrote it, not to forget it:

"If thou goest down into Egypt,
And thence thou bring'st the one Pearl –
"[The Pearl] that lies in the Sea,

Hard by the loud-breathing Serpent –
"[Then] shalt Thou put on thy Robe
And thy Mantle that goeth upon it,
"And with thy Brother, Our Second,
Shalt thou be Heir in our Kingdom."

IV.

I left the East and went down
With two Couriers [with me];
For the way was hard and dangerous,
For I was young to tread it.
I traversed the borders of Maish~ n,
The mart of the Eastern merchants,
And I reached the Land of Babel,
And entered the walls of Sarbãg.
Down further I went into Egypt;
And from me parted my escorts.

V.

Straightway I went to the Serpent;
Near to his lodging I settled,
To take away my Pearl
While he should sleep and should slumber.
Lone was I there, yea, all lonely;
To my fellow-lodgers a stranger.
However I saw there a noble,
From out of the Dawn-land my kinsman,
A young man fair and well favoured,
Son of Grandees; he came and he joined me.

VI.

I made him my chosen companion,
A comrade, for sharing my wares with.
He warned me against the Egyptians,
'Gainst mixing with the unclean ones.
For I had clothed me as they were,
That they might not guess I had come
From afar to take off the Pearl,
And so rouse the Serpent against me.

VII.

But from some occasion or other
They learned I was not of their country.
With their wiles they made my acquaintance;
Yea, they gave me their victuals to eat.
I forgot that I was a King's son,
And became a slave to their king.
I forgot all concerning the Pearl
For which my Parents had sent me;
And from the weight of their victuals
I sank down into a deep sleep.

VIII.

All this that now was befalling,
My Parents perceived and were anxious.
It was then proclaimed in our Kingdom,
That all should speed to our Gate –
Kings and Chieftains of Parthia,
And of the East all the Princes.
And this is the counsel they came to:

I should not be left down in Egypt.
And for me they wrote out a Letter;
And to it each Noble his Name set:

IX.

"From Us – King of Kings, thy Father,
And thy Mother, Queen of the Dawn-land,
"And from Our Second, thy Brother –
To thee, Son, down in Egypt, Our Greeting!
"Up an arise from thy sleep,
Give ear to the words of Our Letter!
"Remember that thou art a King's son;
See whom thou hast served in thy slavedom.
Bethink thyself of the Pearl
For which thou didst journey to Egypt.

X.

"Remember thy Glorious Robe,
Thy Splendid Mantle remember,
"To put on and wear as adornment,
When thy Name may be read in the Book of the Heroes,
"And with Our Successor, thy Brother,
Thou mayest be Heir in Our Kingdom."
My Letter was [surely] a Letter
The King had sealed up with His Right Hand,
'Gainst the Children of Babel, the wicked,
The tyrannical Daimons of Sarbãg.

XI.

It flew in the form of the Eagle,
Of all the winged tribes the king-bird;
It flew and alighted beside me,
And turned into speech altogether.
At its voice and the sound of its winging,
I waked and arose from my deep sleep.
Unto me I took it and kissed it;
I loosed its seal and I read it.
E'en as it stood in my heart writ,
The words of my Letter were written.

XII.

I remembered that I was a King's son,
And my rank did long for its nature.
I bethought me again of the Pearl,
For which I was sent down to Egypt.
And I began [then] to charm him,
The terrible loud-breathing Serpent.
I lulled him to sleep and to slumber,
Chanting o'er him the Name of my Father,
The Name of our Second, [my Brother],
And [Name] of my Mother, the East-Queen.

XIII.

And [thereon] I snatched up the Pearl,
And turned to the House of my Father.
Their filthy and unclean garments
I stripped off and left in their country.
To the way that I came I betook me,

To the Light of our Home, to the Dawn-land.
On the road I found [there] before me,
My Letter that had aroused me –
As with its voice it had roused me,
So now with its light it did lead me –

XIV.

On fabric of silk, in letter of red [?],
With shining appearance before me [?],
Encouraging me with its guidance,
With its love it was drawing me onward.
I went forth; through Sarbãg I passed;
I left B~ bel-land on my left hand;
And I reached unto Maishan the Great,
The meeting-place of the merchants,
That lieth hard by the Sea-shore.

XV.

My Glorious Robe that I'd stripped off,
And my Mantle with which it was covered,
Down from the Heights of Hyrcania,
Thither my Parents did send me,
By the hands of their Treasure-dispensers
Who trustworthy were with it trusted.
Without my recalling its fashion, –
In the House of my Father my childhood had left it,--
At once, as soon as I saw it,
The Glory looked like my own self.

XVI.

I saw it in all of me,
And saw me all in [all of] it, –
That we were twain in distinction,
And yet again one in one likeness.
I saw, too, the Treasurers also,
Who unto me had down-brought it,
Were twain [and yet] of one likeness;
For one Sign of the King was upon them –
Who through them restored me the Glory,
The Pledge of my Kingship [?].

XVII.

The Glorious Robe all-bespangled
With sparkling splendour of colours:
With Gold and also with Beryls,
Chalcedonies, iris-hued [Opals?],
With Sards of varying colours.
To match its grandeur [?], moreover, it had
been completed:
With adamantine jewels
All of its seams were off-fastened.
[Moreover] the King of Kings' Image
Was depicted entirely all o'er it;
And as with Sapphires above
Was it wrought in a motley of colour.

XVIII.

I saw that moreover all o'er it

The motions of Gnosis abounding;
I saw it further was making
Ready as though for to speak.
I heard the sound of its Music
Which it whispered as it descended [?]:
"Behold him the active in deeds!
For whom I was reared with my Father;
"I too have felt in myself
How that with his works waxed my stature."

XIX.

And [now] with its Kingly motions
Was it pouring itself out towards me,
And made haste in the hands of its Givers,
That I might [take and] receive it.
And me, too, my love urged forward
To run for to meet it, to take it.
And I stretched myself forth to receive it;
With its beauty of colour I decked me,
And my Mantle of sparkling colours
I wrapped entirely all o'er me.

XX.

I clothed me therewith, and ascended
To the Gate of Greeting and Homage.
I bowed my head and did homage
To the Glory of Him who had sent it,
Whose commands I [now] had accomplished,
And who had, too, done what He'd promised.
[And there] at the Gate of His House-sons

I mingled myself with His Princes;
For He had received me with gladness,
And I was with Him in His Kingdom;

XXI.

To whom the whole of His Servants
With sweet-sounding voices sing praises.

* * * * *

He had promised that with him to the Court
Of the King of Kings I should speed,
And taking with me my Pearl
Should with him be seen by our King.

The Hymn of Judas Thomas the Apostle,
which he spake in prison, is ended.

There is no doubt much in the way of metaphor in this beautiful poem which is beyond my ability to fully discern. However one can readily see the commonalities it has with much of the religious world.

Leaving one world behind and going to another in order that one may acquire a "treasure" (i.e. the pearl) that would make one worthy of a Kingly inheritance resonates with Adam's (Adam and Eve together representing the both the higher and lower self of mankind) journey in leaving God's heavenly Kingdom and becoming earth bound in a material world searching for redemption therein; and via supernatural grace (to use a term from Thomas Aquinas) having the ability to redeem himself and return to a heavenly realm. And in fact return as a better person than how he had left it.

It of course also resonates with the New testament story of the Prodigal Son as we shall cover later herein. And as we shall also see later, it has echoes of Plato's Allegory of the Cave and the prisoner's realisation of who he really was (i.e. Plato's recommendation to Mankind "To Understand thy Self") before he could lose himself from his chains and ascend to the world of light.

It also has the Buddhist notion of "awakening" inherent in it (i.e. "I waked and arose from my deep sleep)."

---

(98) Jesus says:

(1) "The kingdom of the Father is like a person who wanted to kill a powerful person.

(2) He drew the sword in his house (and) stabbed it into the wall to test whether his hand would be strong (enough).

(3) Then he killed the powerful one."

Logion 98 to me says it so clearly; i.e. that Life is one big training program or boot camp. We have to train and practice and learn before we can perform any major task. For example, and this is not necessarily what the Logion is limited to, if we want to kill off Satan and ensure we are not seduced away again from God's kingdom, we have to practice and learn how to resist temptations and control our fears, anger and passions. Having practiced through many lifetimes, we can hopefully calibrate our inner selves to ensure we have the strength and courage to do so when Satan (or the satanic forces within us as Carl Jung would say) tries to lead us astray in the future.

(99)

(1) The disciples said to him: "Your brothers and your mother are standing outside."

(2) He said to them: "Those here, who do the will of my Father, they are my brothers and my mother.

(3) They are the ones who will enter the kingdom of my Father."

(100)

(1) They showed Jesus a gold coin and said to him: "Caesar's people demand taxes from us."

(2) He said to them: "Give Caesar (the things) that are Caesar's.

(3) Give God (the things) that are God's.

(4) And what is mine give me."

Caesars image is on the coin and so give it to Caesar.

God's image is on your soul so give that to God.

(101)

(1) "Whoever does not hate his [father] and his mother as I do will not be able to be a [disciple] of mine.

(2) And whoever does [not] love his [father and] his mother as I do will not be able to be a [disciple] of mine.

(3) For my mother [...], but my true [mother] gave me life."

(102) Jesus says:

"Woe to them, the Pharisees, for they are like a dog sleeping in a cattle trough, for it neither eats nor [lets] the cattle eat."

The Pharisees have so overwhelmed the original teachings of Moses, that they make it impossible for souls to find the true original teaching, (as well as the new teachings of Christ which represents mankind's next phase of development, i.e. his next level of schooling). As a result, they prevent religious seekers (the cattle) from "eating" from God's nourishing trough of teachings.

Indeed, the Pharisees have such entrenched rules and are so powerful, as to make it impossible to change without a total new religious movement commencing; in this case it was Christianity.

We, of course, have since witnessed this same historical repetitiveness with Christianity's rigidity after many centuries resolving into the advent of Protestantism and other forms of Christian religions. And so, as was covered earlier, there is a constant need to refresh each Faith.

(103) Jesus says:

"Blessed is the person who knows at which point (of the house) the robbers are going to enter, so that [he] may arise to gather together his [domain] and gird his loins before they enter."

He who understands that Evil is there to challenge and test us (a notion also readily found in the Quran) will be better prepared to see it coming and deal with it (also refer logion 21).

(104)

(1) They said to [Jesus]: "Come, let us pray and fast today!"

(2) Jesus said: "What sin is it that I have committed, or wherein have I been overcome?

(3) But when the bridegroom comes out of the wedding chamber, then let (us) fast and pray."

(105) Jesus says:

"Whoever will come to know father and mother, he will be called son of a whore."

(106) Jesus says:

(1) "When you make the two into one, you will become sons of man.

(2) And when you say 'Mountain, move away,' it will move away."

(107) Jesus says:

(1) "The kingdom is like a shepherd who had a hundred sheep.

(2) One of them went astray, the largest. He left the ninety-nine, (and) he sought the one until he found it.

(3) After he had toiled, he said to the sheep: 'I love you more than the ninety-nine.'"

Like the logion of the big fish, the most prized possession one truly has (i.e. connecting with God) is worthy of forsaking all other lesser possessions for.

(108) Jesus says:

(1) "Whoever will drink from my mouth will become like me.

(2) I myself will become he,

(3) and what is hidden will be revealed to him."

Jesus word and teachings, which fulfil and

complement the earlier lessons of past teachers, is the water that flows from his mouth. Whoever listens and abides by what he says will connect with him, and through him will be revealed all that he needs to know for salvation.

When you truly connect with God it will be by turning away from the Neoplatonic outer world and turning inward towards the divine light emanating from God; being Jesus (The Christ), the Word or the Logos. When you do this, your soul connects so intricately with Christ that you merge with him; i.e. become "like me".

Because Christ provides the bridge between the Father (i.e. the One) and the wayward outer souls, no one can reach the Father except through him. But of course this doesn't mean you need to believe in or worship Jesus to achieve this. You only need to do what Jesus's sole commandments to us were, namely, love God (i.e. The Father) with all your heart, mind and soul; and love your neighbour like yourself. That's why heaven is open to all religious believers. More on this point later.

(109) Jesus says:

(1) "The kingdom is like a person who has a hidden treasure in his field, (of which) he knows nothing.

(2) And [after] he had died, he left it to his [son]. (But) the son did not know (about it either).

He took over that field (and) sold [it].

(3) And the one who had bought it came, and while he was ploughing [he found] the treasure.

He began to lend money at interest to whom he wished."

The light and presence of God in each of us representing our potentiality to become worthy of connection with God is the treasure here. God's potentiality is buried within us and we may go through life without realising this. Successive generations and incarnations may also fail to realise this. It is only the person that is motivated to look for truer meaning (i.e. to plough the field) that stands the chance of finding it and profiting from it.

We must therefore first understand that we all have a buried treasure and we must look for it. We must be seekers. This is something we seem to be able to do only in our incarnate state; that is, as we live in this material world. And so we need to understand how precious it is to be alive since it is only now that we have a field with buried treasure in it.

(110) Jesus says:

"The one who has found the world (and) has become wealthy should renounce the world."

If you have found the world it means you have understood who you are, and that your place in the world is but transitory and your real home is with God. If you have the privilege of having understood this and you have worldly riches or desires, then you must renounce them; otherwise you will not be purified and cannot connect with God (and may never have that opportunity again).

Notice again that once someone has had the opportunity to have been enlightened (i.e. found the world) the obligation on him to purify himself is even greater. *Ignorant souls can be excused but not so enlightened ones*. This, of course, is a huge challenge for any individual, as the Young Rich Ruler found in the earlier mentioned Gospel parabola.

(111) Jesus says:

(1) "The heavens will roll up before you, and the earth.

(2) And whoever is living from the living one will not see death."

(3) Does not Jesus say: "Whoever has found himself, of him the world is not worthy"?

Regarding sentence 1 and 2 - it means that at the end of the schooling period (i.e. end of the cosmic cycle), those souls that have connected with God shall survive but the rest will perish.

Re 3 - this world will no longer be appropriate or worthy enough for the person who has understood the meaning of life and his place in it; and who has connected with God. He will no longer need to return back to this world as a reincarnated soul. That person has already "found himself"; or to use a platonic term, he has heeded the words "know thy self "and done so.

(112) Jesus says:

(1) "Woe to the flesh that depends on the soul.

(2) Woe to the soul that depends on the flesh."

When the flesh is subjugated by the soul, then the bodily desires and addictions that are at the behest of the soul essence succumb to the soul, and so will therefore be tamed and swept aside so that the flesh is not in control of the higher self (and the "lamb" is therefore alive). On the other hand, if the soul essence is at the behest of the bodily desires, then it succumbs to them and the lower self is in control, and the person though not physically dead, his soul is dead.

This is of course reminiscent of the Hindu saying we saw earlier that,

"The will governed, sets the soul at peace ".

(113)

(1) His disciples said to him: "The kingdom — on what day will it come?"

(2) "It will not come by watching (and waiting for) it.

(3) They will not say: 'Look, here!' or 'Look, there!'

(4) Rather, the kingdom of the Father is spread out upon the earth, and people do not see it."

Consistent with earlier logia, Jesus is saying that God's kingdom is already here for the taking by those who understand the importance of loving God and neighbour, and moving towards purification and perfecting themselves to achieve this with full spiritual faith and devotion.

In other words, there are two stages of salvation, or two forms of enjoying God's kingdom. First, is that you can find God in your lifetime; and only find him in your avatar life time it seems, from what was said earlier; and when you do, you will go from being dead to alive (as in the lamb that stays alive, and also in contrast to the saying, 'Let the dead bury their dead'). In this context, his kingdom is spread across the earth already because we are living in the School of Life right now.

The second stage is where, once you have found God and are therefore alive, at some point God will close the School and roll up the heavens and earth (see earlier logion), and if you are then still alive you will enter his kingdom. In this context, the Father's kingdom is yet to come. At that time, if you are still dead you will be eaten like the lamb and burnt out of existence as you will not be living from the living one (logion 111).

This logion is also consistent with the notion that God's kingdom is already here and within us, as per the canonical Gospel of Luke,

"The kingdom of God does not come with observation; nor will they say, 'See here!' or 'See there!' For indeed, the kingdom of God is within you" (Luke 17:20-21)."

(114)

(1) Simon Peter said to them: "Let Mary go away from us, for women are not worthy of life."

(2) Jesus said: "Look, I will draw her in so as to make her male, so that she too may become a living male spirit, similar to you."

(3) (But I say to you): "Every woman who makes herself male will enter the kingdom of heaven."

Where the Mind of Athens and the Heart of Jerusalem Truly Meet

Before we leave this Chapter dealing with Jesus Christ and Christian teachings, I very much wish to include here, appropriately I believe, some learnings I received from my loving mother's local Catholic priest at her small suburban parish church.

Father Dennis once noted in his sermon (or homily) that, it has been said on many occasions,

that the messages inherent in the entire four New Testament canonical Gospels of Mark, Matthew, Luke and John can be fully reflected in two memorable parables; namely, the Parable of the Lost Son (or Prodigal Son), and the Parable of the Good Samaritan. These parables give credence to the key Christian learnings of Forgiveness and Compassion respectively.

Since I have focussed on Jesus's teachings from the Gospel of Thomas, I think it is appropriate to dwell for a moment on how what I have covered so far in this work, my hypothesis in particular, relates to these two iconic parables.

Let's recount them first.

The Parable of the Lost Son

Luke 15:11-32 (NIV)

11 Jesus continued: "There was a man who had two sons. 12 The younger one said to his father, 'Father, give me my share of the estate.' So he divided his property between them.

13 "Not long after that, the younger son got together all he had, set off for a distant country and there squandered his wealth in wild living.14 After he had spent everything, there was a severe famine in that whole country, and he began to be in need. 15 So he went and hired himself out to a citizen of that country, who sent him to his fields to feed pigs. 16 He longed to fill his stomach with the pods that the pigs were eating, but no one gave him anything.

17 "When he came to his senses, he said, 'How

many of my father's hired servants have food to spare, and here I am starving to death! 18 I will set out and go back to my father and say to him: Father, I have sinned against heaven and against you. 19 I am no longer worthy to be called your son; make me like one of your hired servants.' 20 So he got up and went to his father.

"But while he was still a long way off, his father saw him and was filled with compassion for him; he ran to his son, threw his arms around him and kissed him.

21 "The son said to him, 'Father, I have sinned against heaven and against you. I am no longer worthy to be called your son.'

22 "But the father said to his servants, 'Quick! Bring the best robe and put it on him. Put a ring on his finger and sandals on his feet. 23 Bring the fattened calf and kill it. Let's have a feast and celebrate. 24 For this son of mine was dead and is alive again; he was lost and is found.' So they began to celebrate.

25 "Meanwhile, the older son was in the field. When he came near the house, he heard music and dancing. 26 So he called one of the servants and asked him what was going on. 27 'Your brother has come,' he replied, 'and your father has killed the fattened calf because he has him back safe and sound.'

28 "The older brother became angry and refused to go in. So his father went out and pleaded with him. 29 But he answered his father, 'Look! All these years I've been slaving for you and never disobeyed your orders. Yet you never gave me even a young goat so

I could celebrate with my friends. 30 But when this son of yours who has squandered your property with prostitutes comes home, you kill the fattened calf for him!'

31 "'My son,' the father said, 'you are always with me, and everything I have is yours. 32 But we had to celebrate and be glad, because this brother of yours was dead and is alive again; he was lost and is found.'"

To me this parable supports more than just learnings on Forgiveness and Compassion, although it does that for sure. To me this parable confirms much of what is in the Gospel of Thomas, as well as the essence of my Hypothesis.

It also ties into Plato's Allegory of the Cave as explained and illustrated earlier in this work. How does it do this?

The Parable of the Lost Son can be interpreted as follows.

- The lost son and his brother lived with their father in a place of riches and, as can be seen from the character of the father, also what must have been a place of great love, generosity and compassion.

- the lost son grew restless in his environment and wanted to taste and experience allures outside of that realm; just as we did long ago, i.e. the original Adam and Eve.

- he therefore left that realm and entered another world. This world can be viewed as the world of Plato's Cave. A world in which people are controlled by the chains of their own Desires and alluring temptations, but one which is pervaded by fundamental suffering and unrest. This allegorical realm is our material world.

- having tried to negotiate this darker, difficult and painful world, the son concludes (having "come to his senses", and similar to "shaking off their wine" in the earlier Gospel of Thomas Logion) that his previous existence was better and resolves to return to the father to seek reconciliation.

- given that his life in the dark world ended up being harsh, poor and difficult, it was relatively easier for the lost son to reject that world and return home compared to others. This would not easily happen for those who, on the contrary, found the prison world of the cave comfortable and alluring due to their being wealthy, or powerful, or readily able to enjoy bodily, material and other earthly pleasures. For example, take the young man we encountered in the Parable of the Young Rich Ruler, who was not prepared to give up all his wealth to follow Jesus. The chains of Wealth and Comfort were too strong for him to break. For this reason, the harsher and more painful the earthly life of a person, the easier it is to break those prison chains and seek to look for greater meaning in life; i.e. to look for a path out of that cave.

- upon returning to the Father, the Father was overjoyed and did not seek to impose retribution on his son. Indeed, the Father gave the son rewards for returning home beyond anything that the son could expect, just like the Buddhist story of the Burning House. The father in the Lost Son Parable exhibited the divine traits of compassion and genuine unconditional love. This incredibly forgiving and unconditional love of the father is exactly what we should expect to find, if we are able to free ourselves from the allures of the earthly world and, by our own efforts as well as God's grace, seek to make our way out of the Cave to our original heavenly world of light and truth.

- it is also instructive to see, despite the Father's rich status with great resources and servants at his disposal, that before the Son resolves to find his way back home, the Father does not send out his servants to rescue the son, or forcibly return him from the dark world of temptations to which the son went. Rather the son had to return of his own accord. The Father therefore respected his son's right to free determination; his freewill to choose to return home or not. But as soon as the Father heard of his son's decision to find his way back home, he sent his servants to help him return. This gives credence to the fact that our effort to return to God the father must be initiated by us. We must have a degree of Faith (i.e. a belief that there must be more to life than our shackled existence, and that a divine power exists that can give us love and solace); and this Faith must come from within us, unaided by divine intervention (but of course there can be divine guidance or teachers as we covered earlier in this work), before the Father and his helpers (i.e. the Holy Spirit) can reach out and help us. This is because the Father has truly given us a freewill. It's not that he cannot help us; it is rather that, just like the father in the parable of the lost son, God wants us to experience the dark, alluring, hard world of pain and suffering we have chosen so as to improve our character and also convince us of our folly in leaving home. He therefore wants our experience in that world to have the effect of transforming our inherent character in an evolutionary way, before welcoming us back into his realm. And, moreover, WE have to take the first step to move out of that dark prison cave, before his love can reach into our souls and help us out.

Recall the Baha'i reading from Bahaullah as follows,

"O SON OF BEING! Love Me, that I may love thee. If thou lovest Me not, My love can in no wise reach thee."

(The Hidden Words, Arabic no.5)

You may also recall that in a number of healing miracles Jesus performed, and described in the New Testament Gospels, (e.g. the Roman centurion's son; the blind man in the Temple; the woman who touched Jesus's garment and healed) Jesus's healing was typically preceded by confirmation from either the healed person, or their relative who sought Jesus's healing powers, that they had Faith. Even in the raising of Lazarus, Jesus confirms the Faith of Martha before he raises Lazarus.

There are some notable and understandable exceptions to this where God, or perhaps even Jesus post his death, has specifically called individuals to do his work, without that individual seeking first to "turn" towards him. Likely examples of this include Saint Paul and his dramatic conversion whilst on the road to Damascus. Another likely example is Emperor Constantine and his conversion, via a vision that led him to winning a battle; and then adopting Christianity as his own religion, and which ultimately led to it becoming the official Roman religion.

This point raises, appropriately, the concept of Grace and Predestination.

God's gift of freewill to us means we can choose to walk away from his love and he will not force us back. That's why the father in the Lost Son Parable never tried to repatriate his son against his will. WE have to make the first "turn" towards God; we have to take the first step to seek his aid; we need to first cry for his help before he can reach out to us. When we are sitting in chains in Plato's prison of theatrical life, we have to first wrestle against the chains and "turn" our head backwards (i.e. to convert) and cry for help (i.e. we must not only "crack", but we must cry out for his help also before the light can get in). God has placed in that Prison Cave, the Holy Spirit, who is ever wafting around looking to help us, but we need to call that Graceful Attendant over and ask for assistance in unchaining ourselves, and thereby changing our life. When that happens, help will come readily to unshackle us and show us a pathway out, provided we are prepared to listen and have ongoing Faith in what's happening, (i.e. those who seek, will find).

Christian religion has come to believe that no one can find their way to God without the gift of Grace. This may be true but what is unbelievable, if you believe in an all loving God as I do, is that some are predestined for it (and therefore will find God) and others are not (and so will Never find him). This nonsensical belief perhaps comes from Christians historically observing that some individuals never find God in their lives (for example; because they were never exposed to Christian beliefs; or even if they are Christian, they never seem to truly find unconditional love for God). And so Christianity assumed that God did not volunteer his grace to them. Also perhaps from observing some young children dying too early to have found salvation, and so assuming that they were never therefore destined for it, since it did not come through any fault of their own. The fallacy in this sort of thinking arises from various failures, including a failure to accept reincarnation, and therefore a realisation that all souls will have multiple opportunities to find God, and often those opportunities may not arise in the space of just one lifetime. The true gift of freewill given to all souls, means that no soul is predestined for heaven or hell, but that each will receive multiple lifetime chances to "turn" to God and be saved. But WE must first call out to the attendant for help - then Grace will come in spades.

-it is also noteworthy that when the lost son decided to return to his father, his desire was simply to be a "servant" to his father. He did not expect to return as an heir. A mere servant's role would have sufficed. How often do we hear the notion of "becoming God's servant" and wonder what this means. This parable beautifully puts this notion into a meaning context and shows us that aiming to be servants of God is all we really need to aim for; that is a worthy status in itself.

- the reaction of the lost son's brother in the parable is also very instructive. The brother, even though he remained in the father's home in an environment of love, generosity and compassion (judging from the Father's character in the parable), he nonetheless exhibits signs of both envy upon his brother's return, and fear that he might lose some of his own inheritance. Note that the lost son has undergone a character change (or soul mutation), through all the trials and tribulations he has gone through, including his eventual seeking of his father's forgiveness, and his honourable desire to return home content to be a simple servant and not desirous of any more inheritance. *[We should note in passing that coincidentally, Plato mentions that the freed prisoner who leaves the cave and understands the world outside, will gladly offer to be a slave servant in the outside (or Real World) rather than a king in the illusory world of the cave]*. And so it actually appears from all this that the returned son's character has become nobler than the character of the son who never left home. From this, one could surmise a further message in this immensely instructive and insightful parable, that "having experienced the dark alluring world "(i.e. having eaten, albeit painfully, from the Tree of Knowledge of Good and Evil), the lost son has acquired a nobler character than that of his brother.

Perhaps the Father knew this might happen when his son asked for his inheritance at the outset. Perhaps the Father knew that the dark world of illusory desire (Plato's Prison cave) that lured his son away from the outset, would be the very experience that would mould and transform his son's character into an ever nobler person, and also a person who would be much more resistant to temptation in the future. In other words, the returned lost soul is even more divine that the original soul. The original Adam may well have had a divine nature, but the eventually reformed Adam is even closer to God.

This again reminds me of a saying that is found in many parts of the Roman Catholic teachings and regular Church services, namely, "... that the cause of our downfall might become the means of our salvation, through Christ our Lord."

For example, refer below,

"Missal
Preface
A.9.c. Preface of Sundays in Ordinary Time III
The salvation of man by man
V. The Lord be with you.
*R. **And with your spirit.***

V. Lift up your hearts.
*R. **We lift them up to the Lord.***

V. Let us give thanks to the Lord our God.
*R. **It is right and just.***

It is truly right and just, our duty and our salvation,
always and everywhere to give you thanks,
Lord, holy Father, almighty and eternal God.

For we know it belongs to your boundless glory,
that you came to the aid of mortal beings with your divinity
"and even fashioned for us a remedy out of mortality itself,
that the cause of our downfall
might become the means of our salvation,
through Christ our Lord."["My emphasis"]"

Saint Thomas Aquinas's notion of Supernatural grace also attests to this belief that the New Adam is more Godly than the original Adam.This point is further supported in the following Baha'i teaching, which speaks of "converting satanic strength (i.e. the alluring of the Lost Son away with worldly temptations) into heavenly power".

"XCIX: The vitality of men's belief in God is dying

The vitality of men's belief in God is dying out in every land; nothing short of His wholesome medicine can ever restore it. The corrosion of ungodliness is eating into the vitals of human society; what else but the Elixir of His potent Revelation can cleanse and revive it? Is it within human power, O Hakím, to effect in the constituent elements of any of the minute and indivisible particles of matter so complete a transformation as to transmute it into purest gold? *[My Insertion: Note this has echoes of S B Groves's notion of the transmutation of our fine spiritual essences to a higher level]* **"Perplexing and difficult as this may appear, the still greater task of converting satanic strength into heavenly power is one that We have**

been empowered to accomplish."["My emphasis"] The Force capable of such a transformation transcendeth the potency of the Elixir itself. The Word of God, alone, can claim the distinction of being endowed with the capacity required for so great and far-reaching a change."

(Gleanings From the Writings of Bahaullah).

The Parable of the Good Samaritan

Luke 10:25-37(NIV)

25 On one occasion an expert in the law stood up to test Jesus. "Teacher," he asked, "what must I do to inherit eternal life?"

26 "What is written in the Law?" he replied. "How do you read it?"

27 He answered, "'Love the Lord your God with all your heart and with all your soul and with all your strength and with all your mind'[a]; and, 'Love your neighbor as yourself.'[b]"

28 "You have answered correctly," Jesus replied. "Do this and you will live."

29 But he wanted to justify himself, so he asked Jesus, "And who is my neighbor?"

30 In reply Jesus said: "A man was going down from Jerusalem to Jericho, when he was attacked by robbers. They stripped him of his clothes, beat him
and went away, leaving him half dead. 31 A priest
happened to be going down the same road, and when he saw the man, he passed by on the other
side. 32 So too, a Levite, when he came to the place
and saw him, passed by on the other side. 33 But a

Samaritan, as he traveled, came where the man was; and when he saw him, he took pity on him. 34 He went to him and bandaged his wounds, pouring on oil and wine. Then he put the man on his own donkey, brought him to an inn and took care of him. 35 The next day he took out two denarii[c] and gave them to the innkeeper. 'Look after him,' he said, 'and when I return, I will reimburse you for any extra expense you may have.'36 "Which of these three do you think was a neighbor to the man who fell into the hands of robbers?"

37 The expert in the law replied, "The one who had mercy on him."

Jesus told him, "Go and do likewise."

As I have mentioned on several other occasions, life's purpose is to ingrain into our soul a disposition or "hexis" as Aristotle would say, (i.e. A Habit) that liberates our soul from worldly attachments AND teaches us to love God and mankind.

We have seen already from what has been said earlier, how both Plato and Aristotle came to the conclusion, albeit differently, that from a pure logical and non-revelation perspective, having our "eyes fixed" on (Plato) or "contemplating" on (Aristotle) God, is the highest and most rewarding purpose in life.

For the reasons mentioned earlier, this lines up perfectly with the New Testament commandment of Jesus to "love God with all our heart, mind and strength".

The Parable of the Good Samaritan naturally exemplifies the second of Jesus's commandments; namely, to love your neighbour.

What might be surprising to many is that Aristotle reasoned his way, using pure logic, to the same conclusion when after having concluded that contemplation of the divine should be our first objective, that our second priority should be to lead a life of companionship and friendship of the highest order of possible "friendship types".

An anonymous online writer has described Aristotle's views on the nature of friendship as follows:

"In Book VIII of "The Nichomachean Ethics", Aristotle makes reference to three kinds of friendship.

1) The first is friendship based on utility, where both people derive some benefit from each other.

Aristotle describes a friendship of utility as shallow, "easily dissolved" or for the old. He views them as such because this type of friendship is easily broken and based on something that is brought to the relationship by the other person. Aristotle uses the example of trade and argues that friendships of utility are often between opposite people, in order to maximize this trade

2) The second is friendship based on pleasure, where both people are drawn to the other's wit, good looks, or other pleasant qualities. Aristotle says that a friendship of pleasure is normally built between the young as passions and pleasures are great influences in their lives. This type of relationship is characterized by such feelings as passion between lovers, or the feeling of belonging among a likeminded group of friends. It differs from the friendship of utility in that those who seek utility friendships are looking for a business deal or a long term benefit, whereas the friendship of pleasure Aristotle describes is where one seeks something which is pleasant to them presently.

The first two kinds of friendship are only accidental, because in these cases friends are motivated by their own utility and pleasure, not by anything essential to the nature of the friend. Both of these kinds of friendship are short-lived because one's needs and pleasures are apt to change over time.

3) <u>The third is friendship based on goodness,</u> where both people admire the other's goodness and help one another strive for goodness.

Friendships of the good are ones where both friends enjoy each other's characters. Aristotle calls it a "...complete sort of friendship between people who are good and alike in virtue..." ***This is the highest level of Philia, (φιλία), often translated "brotherly love", and one of the highest forms of Love in Aristotle´s "Nichomachean Ethics". [My emphasis]***

Aristotle (384 BC / 322 BC).-

Those involved in a "friendship of the good" must be able to value loving over being loved and as such, their relationship will be based more around loving the other person and wanting what is good for them. Goodness is an enduring quality, so friendships based on goodness tend to be long lasting.

This friendship encompasses the other two, as good friends are useful to one another and please one another. Such friendship is rare and takes time to develop, but it is the best.

As well, Aristotle believes that it is through friendship that cities are held together. Those with the moral virtue to enter virtuous relationships are a major part of this but friendships of utility and pleasure are also needed as friendships of virtue are severely limited in number. It is the friendships of utility and pleasure that keep the city together. However; it takes the character of those in the virtuous friendship for a solid community to exist.

Aristotle states in Book VIII, Chapter 1: "Between friends there is no need for justice, but people who are just still need the quality of friendship; and indeed friendliness is considered to be justice in the fullest sense. It is not only a necessary thing but a splendid one". Aristotle bases his conception of justice on a conception of fair exchange, and does the same for friendship. Friendships are balanced by the fact that each friend gives as much as receives. Hence, justice and friendship are closely connected."

In essence, this writer is aptly saying that Aristotle's notion of friendship, an important ingredient of man leading a "flourishing life", is the same notion of Brotherly Love espoused in the Parable of the Good Samaritan. Some commentators might say that Jesus's notion of Brotherly Love is a higher standard since the Good Samaritan stood to gain nothing from his efforts in taking care of the needy traveller. Whilst Aristotle's notion of friendship, even the highest form thereof, involves some benefit to the giver. In my view they are identical, since the act of giving by one motivated to give out of love always has an immediate reward or sense of satisfaction to the giver.

I again point out that it is no coincidence that the great giants of logic and philosophy, Plato and Aristotle, reasoned their way to concluding that the best things man can do to lead the Greek notion of a "flourishing life", are to love God and love ones' fellow man; and to do so by controlling one's passions and desires from distracting him from such a task.

To me it's clear that the "mind of Athens" here meets up with the "heart of Jerusalem". What the great teachers of religions have been advocating to us; namely, the love of God and fellow souls, is exactly what the Ancient Greek giants of philosophy had concluded was, for Reason alone, a good thing for us to devote our lives towards. As a result, and in contrast to what has often been said, in my view, Athens has everything to do with Jerusalem.

Chapter Eleven

Why bother with the hypothesis anyway?

A series of Questions.

Q - Does it matter whether Life has Purpose?
Would it not be useful to know what Life's Purpose was, if in fact there was such a purpose?

I heard the story of an elderly lady on her death bed who sole regret was that she wished she had led her life with a greater sense of purpose.

In life one can readily have various objectives or purposes in mind, for example, raise my family in a good way; make lots of money; stay healthy; travel the world; give to charity; be good at something e.g. sport, art, business, profession etc.

Now imagine you were invited to play a game of Monopoly and never played it before and did not read the instructions. You might be forgiven for thinking that any one of various objectives was the key objective of the game. For example, having the most cash as compared to the other players, having the most properties or hotels, circumnavigating the board more than anyone else etc. What if only at the very end when the game was ending (or worse still after it had finished) did you come to realize that the objective of the game was to bankrupt all your opponents? You would surely kick yourself for not asking well before then, "What's this all about anyway?"

Well in life do we pause and ask that question? Do we take time out and seek such a purpose? Most of us don't; and then if we do, we don't really want an answer that might be different to what we are currently enjoying about life. We don't want to change what we like doing; and we may not like the change in us that it might require if we were to find a purpose that was different to what we currently prioritize. In short, we do what we like doing (as Nietzsche said) and we rationalize what we do on some arbitrary basis so as to justify continuing to do it.

But what if there really was a key objective that we were meant to achieve in our life? Should we not spend time objectively and free from self-bias to understand what that could be? And in doing so, should we not examine what others had to say about the potential possibilities thereof? And if one of those possibilities was objectively and reasonably the best we could find, then should we not consider it as a serious option?

Nietzsche once wrote, "He who has a why to live for can bear almost any how".

The hypothesis I have put forward, for all the reasons set out earlier, I think fits that criteria. If someone can argue reasonably for a better alternative I will be the first to adopt it.

The hard reality is that there IS a purpose to

life which, for those who get it, is very evident and ever present and many of us are exposed to it but few actually see it.

I recently heard the story of a busker playing a violin outside of Sydney's central railway station. He played for a full day some of the best music he knew. And since he played during both the morning and evening rush period, his music was exposed to thousands of people who walked by. Yet only a few people, less than 20, stopped to listen to him and throughout the whole day he collected only a few dollars.

Virtually all the passers-by who walked straight passed him without paying him any attention, were too busy immersed in their daily work or social preoccupations. Many of those who stopped to listen to him, on the other hand, were jobless or in bereaved financial and social circumstances. They were not distracted by their busy lifestyle preoccupation; but instead, took some solace from the soothing and melodious music he played.

Yet unbeknown to all those who passed by, the busker was himself a great violinist who had only a few days ago played at the Sydney Opera house to a sold out house. The violin he was playing looked a little old but was in fact a Stradivarius violin, worth some millions of dollars and he played some of the most renown and beautiful music ever written.

He could have come out and proclaimed to all the passers-by who he was, as well as the nature of his great music and the unique instrument with which he played it. Had he done so, no doubt many people would have stopped to listen to him. They would have stopped not because "the music sang to them" and they related to it, but rather because of his obvious fame. However, he did not want to attract those types. He just wanted to see who really loved the music. He wanted only to attract those who innately had a deep love for the music, and who placed that love ahead of their work and social preoccupations. He wanted to attract those, who by their nature, were in tune with the music and loved it for what it was; undistracted by worldly goings on, and not for the fame or might of the player or his instrument.

It seems to me, that God is like the Sydney Central Station violin busker. His message is constantly playing for whoever stops to listen to it. And it's played for lovers of the music, not for lovers of fame and pomp. He plays it without overtly advertising himself, and he relies on the innate faith of the listener for establishing an allegiance to him and his message. In his busking plate he asks not for money, but for total faith and allegiance to him. In return, he will play his incredibly beautiful, soothing and life satisfying music to you for as long as that allegiance exists.

Unfortunately, he has found that those preoccupied with daily work, social and other devotions in life, have little interest in his message. It seems it's only those who are divorced from life's treadmill of wealth, social and other preoccupations that seem to more easily hear the beauty of the music best. It's life's "down and outers" that get it best and are therefore best placed to give their allegiance to Him.

Like the message in Logion 64 of the Gospel of Thomas, it's the "down and outers" who readily accept God's invitation to his feast, rather than those invitees who are preoccupied with fame and making money. And so in the end, it is much easier to see why, as Jesus said, "the first" (i.e. those who have wealth, status and fame in this world) will be last, and "the last" (i.e. the down and outers) will be first.

God's message about Life's purpose, is there for all to see. If we pause to listen to it, we find it is mesmerizing, sublime, pervasive and all satisfying. But we must make the effort to stop and listen and search for it. To take the time to seek it. For, as it is said so often, those who seek shall find. Listen for it and you shall hear it. Those who have ears to hear, hear it.

The Quran also gives such a clear message when it says,

"And those who strive in Our (Cause), We will certainly guide them to Our Paths: for verily God is with those who do right.[154]

But to those who receive guidance, He increases the (light of) Guidance ...[155]"

This is well put by Dadi Shanki when she talks of the reward and beauty of finding God.

"When the Bestower of Knowledge is your companion, at every step He's telling you how things really are. This truth then makes you perform pure, clean, elevated, noble actions. Those actions give power, until you become one who shows truth to the world. Such a diamond will sparkle from a distance."

Finally, even if we do not accept the above

mentioned hypothesis put forward as Life's purpose (nor any other alternative for that matter), the karmic and reincarnative forces we go through over many lives, will nonetheless mean that all of us still progress through Life's school of pain and redemptive evolution. You don't have to be a believer in order to get some of the benefits of going to this school. Everyone is attending school whether you like it or not, and you are going to learn things along the way; maybe slowly, maybe painfully, maybe without realizing who you are, or what you are mixed up with; but learn something you will. That is one of the many amazing outcomes of God's brilliant redemptive schema.

But you do have to be a believer in order to progress quickly, with less pain, and with the greatest amount of true joy and happiness (as opposed to "idle fancy" happiness); let alone understanding of what the whole schema is.

In the end, you clearly need to be a believer in order to succeed; but the beauty of God's schema is that he gives us enormous (but not endless) time and experiences (both joyful and painful) in order for us to ultimately become perfected believers; at least for those who are eventually saved.

Q - Could one's addictions and downtrodden state be a blessing?

If a key reason why we are in God's illusory School of Life is so that we learn to resist temptations of the highest order (temptations that the Dark Side, or Satan, can throw at us) then should we not take advantage of the fact that at some stage in our life we will likely become addicted to some form of idle fancy? E.g. sex, money, drugs, alcohol, gambling, power, ego, fame, extreme passions for travel, even collectibles, etc. For then by disciplining ourselves and exorcising such addictions or vices, we are evolving into a more disciplined soul? i.e. we are learning the art of becoming Freedom Fighters and in the process becoming Free! Moreover, the strength needed to exorcise such is often found by a turning towards spirituality (e.g. refer to Alcoholics Anonymous' (AA) twelve step program).

This point about addictions and vices is a key point that is central to both the hypothesis and how life actually works. Remember that there are essentially three things that God wants to teach us through our innate learning experience over many lives. One, that he loves us unconditionally and he would like us to do the same in return. Two, that we should love all others. And finally, that we should steel ourselves (gird our loins) and be capable of resisting all temptations sent to us by the Dark Side that aim to dissuade us from doing One and Two.

This notion of detachment from worldly vices and, at their worst, uncontrollable addictions, is inherent in all the key religions of the world.

So how does God, in his world class teaching school, teach us to resist temptation? As you would expect, it's simple and brilliantly beautiful.

Our soul, just like every other animate thing, is constantly evolving. But, as we know, evolutionary forces work best when there is a crisis that therefore requires change, which in turn forces an evolutionary mutation to take place.

Darwin came to the notion of Evolution by reading Malthus's work on the constant shortages of food in nature. He concluded that a species, over a long period of time, developed mutations which would render some species better at coping with their changing environment. Those that could not cope with change generally died away. So it was the species' ability to change through crisis periods, or periods of dramatic changing environments, that lead to evolutionary change for the betterment of the species.

Man's lower self is that which continually is grasping at worldly desires and constantly attracted to material, rather than spiritual matters. His higher self is that which is attracted to the light, and constantly looking for the higher virtues and goodness in order to be satisfied. Indeed, you could say man himself is bifurcated between the forces of good and evil; light and darkness. (Indeed Carl Jung says as much in his analysis of the Archetypes within the Human Psyche).

A vice, or even stronger, an addiction, is something grasped at by the lower self. The higher self then, in turn, has to "gird its loins" and exercise strong willpower to persuade the individual to detach itself from such a negative practice. If man's higher self is capable of doing so, then it has conditioned itself to resisting temptation.

Plato of course understood this from the time of the Greeks when he spoke about souls falling into bodies as a result of the unruly horses unsettling the rider who was at a constant struggle to control the upper and lower forces.

As we saw earlier, Aristotle also spoke of the importance of "hexis" or habit forming.

An anonymous author has noted the importance of Habit in the following well known riddle, which I noted as recently being lauded as the key to a successful sporting career by one of Australia's most successful AFL sporting coaches, Paul Roos.

Question – Who am I?

"I am your constant companion.

I am your greatest helper or heaviest burden.

I will push you onward or drag you down to failure.

I am completely at your command.

Half the things you do you might just as well turn over to me, and I will be able to do them quickly, correctly.

I am easily managed - you must merely be firm with me. Show me exactly how you want something done, and after a few lessons I will do it automatically.

I am the servant of all great people; and alas, of all failures as well. Those who are failures, I have made failures.

I am not a machine, though I work with all the precision of a machine plus the intelligence of a human being.

You may run me for a profit or turn me for ruin - it makes no difference to me.

Take me, train me, be firm with me, and I will

place the world at your feet.

Be easy with me and I will destroy you.

Who am I?

I AM HABIT"

The stronger the vice or addiction, naturally the harder is the task, and many souls may therefore fail and never reform. But equally, the stronger the task, the greater the reward will be if the negative practice is exorcised. In fact, the dramatic change needed to exorcise the bad habit is so strong that it leaves a permanent mark on the soul. The impression it makes on the soul is so powerful as to make a long lasting mutation to it, which betters it and elevates the soul to a higher calibration.

Individual souls may need to experience many lives to eventually have their souls highly calibrated, and so accustomed or "habituated" to resisting the many forms of vices that exist. That is, for the soul to be totally purified.

Moreover, the dramatic change needed to overcome a major vice or addiction will point the soul to a spiritual solution. It may well be that the individual has hit such a rock bottom state that his only option is to turn to God, or in his mind, some sort of spiritual force, in order to overcome the habit. He therefore, to use a Leonard Cohen phrase, needed to first "crack" under pressure because, "that's how the light get gets in".

The process of overcoming bad habits is intricately tied to Karmic forces. For instance, take an individual who cannot overcome a particular bad habit. It maybe that the person allows others to dominate him without being prepared to fight back or resist oppression. No doubt Satan exercises all sorts of oppressive tactics and God wants us to be capable, innately in our souls and spirit selves, to resist such oppression. If so, the godly influences, through reincarnation and karmic forces, will continually pair us with dominating people in our lives until we are fully capable of dealing with them.

Have you ever noticed how some people always seem to attract people with similar habits, e.g. an oppressed woman might keep attracting men who oppress her, or who are alcoholics or problem gamblers. A loving and caring woman might keep finding men who require her love and care and give little in return. An overly generous man might keep finding women who use him.

Then hopefully, sooner rather than later and ideally in this lifetime, they learn their lesson and become capable of dealing with such individuals, or alternatively learn to walk away from them for a better choice. Their soul has learnt to shun oppression and not be lured into accepting it simply because the individual might fear being left alone, or because they want the other benefits which that oppressive relationship brought them (e.g. money, power, sex, fame, security, etc.).

The ability to turn away from powerful addictions is a life changing force. For example, a man totally hooked on gambling or alcohol may go through countless anguish, to both himself and those around him, to beat the habit. The painful and depressive forces unleashed in the process also make their mark on many who come into that person's path. They, in turn, create their own karmic influences and may be cause for changes in the souls of those individuals.

What does this say about how we should regard those in life burdened with vices and addictions? In one way, whilst being controlled by a vice or addiction is not something one would wish for, sometimes being in such a state can be a blessing in disguise. Why? Because it's our opportunity to undergo a life changing mutation to our soul for betterment. **The complete 'down and outer' can achieve, if successful, what other souls may endure lifetimes trying to achieve**.

A person who is so burdened and depressed with what life has handed him can, by turning to God, at once can accomplish a complete turn to spirituality, place his fate in God, dispense thereby with all his fears, and overcome his addictive habits. He allows into his soul purifying light which cleanses his lower self-desires, permanently mutates his soul and connects him with an allegiance to God in a way that no other life experience could do in such a dramatic and revolutionary way.

Of course if he fails "to turn" to God and cleanse his bad habits, he could remain inflicted by them for life, or even die quickly as a result. But at least such individuals are given a unique opportunity to let God come into their lives.

You might well say to me that it is ridiculous to think that having conflict and depression in your life is better than leading a troubled free life. There are no doubt couples, for instance, who marry and stay married for life and seem to have relatively fewer problems than others.

I recall reading somewhere that the secret to a long marriage was when one of the couple allows the other partner to dominate him or her, so that there are few conflicts in the marriage. From my brief experience with life, this seems to ring true. However, think about whether those individuals really grew or advanced as a result. You might say, well of course they did since they had a relatively long lasting and presumably (since it was long lasting) happy marriage.

But remember that under our hypothesis the real persona is the individual's soul or spirit essence. What advancement was made by the soul who succumbed to the dominant will of the other partner for the entire marriage? That soul is obviously well accustomed to being the subject of oppression and manipulation. It is the perfect kind of soul for Satan to subdue and keep subdued, and such a soul would not likely question or rebel against that oppressive force. This is not an advanced soul that God would be pleased with. Whilst God might ultimately desire a peaceful end state environment for all his "graduated' souls to live in, he certainly does not seek to achieve it by having one group of souls be subservient to, or oppressed by, others. Think of how many fall into this category; slaves, serfs, mistreated servants or workers, oppressed women, oppressed races, oppressed religious believers etc.

Oppression is the work of Satan. God desires total freedom for all of us. It's the very freedom he gave us that led to our downfall of course. But he wants us to rise up now with the benefit of our soul evolutionary experience from Life's School to achieve the point where we can be fully free, but living in harmony with others without any oppression or subjugation of some by others; that is when the Lion will sit down with the Lamb.

Similarly, for the soul of the marriage partner who dominated the long lasting marriage, that soul for similar reasons, is not a soul type that God would regard as "an advanced student". It is one that Satan however would love to have many of.

The point is that life cannot be seen to be successful just because one had a long marriage (and my first marriage incidentally lasted for 28 years). If the two people are not advancing in spiritual qualities, and if the marriage is not assisting in the development of the goodly qualities of character and love, then the marriage is not advancing the betterment of their souls. This produces no soul mutations worthy of having lived another reincarnated life. The students have not advanced. They have, in fact, truly wasted a lifetime opportunity to do so.

It is better to be downtrodden, thrown into a lifetime crisis, having reached a black patch in your life, and then turned to God, rather than lived a long seemingly contented life where no substantive progress has occurred in your soul qualities or spiritual advancement. If you leave this world at the same soul calibration you entered it, you have achieved nothing.

In Logion 28 of the Gospel of Thomas, Jesus says

"...They do not see. They came naked into the world, and naked they will leave it. At this time, they are intoxicated. [Only] When they have (shaken off) vomited their wine, they will return to themselves".

And at Logion 16 Jesus says "People may think that I have come to bring peace to the world. They do not know that I have come to sow division upon the earth: fire, sword, war".

Consistent with Darwin's depiction of evolution, just as species advance in an evolutionary way through times of famine, environmental dislocation and oppressive forces, so do human souls. This is why our material world is not a peaceful one, but riddled with suffering and frustration, not just at a macro level, but also at a micro very personal level; and so it challenges us constantly to "throw out our wine" and to rise to find our true perfected selves. This is the pathway to the true and ultimate Resurrection of the Dead.

Q - Who is Jesus? And, more importantly, do you need to believe in him to be saved? And its impact on Progressive Revelation and Universal Salvation.

I again address this key question here, albeit in a little further depth than previously, because it is the root of much of the religious unrest we have between faiths and cultures.

In fact, the Christian faith has for centuries been arguing about this (e.g. was Jesus God or not? if so is he fully human AND fully God? is he part of a Trinitarian God head? if so does each person in the trinity have a separate will? is he subservient to, or a lesser entity than, the Father? etc.). It has also been arguing, again for centuries and divisively, other technical religious issues (like Mary's Virgin status, her birth free of so-called Original Sin, the nature of con-substantiation during holy communion, the nature and meaning of certain sacraments etc.)

All such polemics have unfortunately distracted everyone from the main religious objectives; and have been the source of enormous and needless pain and destruction of life within Christian communities and at times beyond.

I believe Jesus (in the persona of The Christ, not merely the man born in Nazareth) is more than just a Messenger of God (which is a status that is amazingly awesome in itself). He is truly the Word or Logos (was temporarily made man for our benefit) and through him was created, and continues to be sustained, the material world (as opposed to the spiritual world of souls and spirit essences created, or at least moulded, by the Father).

Christ *sustains* the illusory material world; which as we have covered, is aimed at enabling us to recalibrate our soul essences via purification and love, so that we can truly ascend back into God's kingdom and have everlasting life in true happiness; without the need to any longer reincarnate or transmigrate to new worlds or dimensions (i.e. no longer the need to continue our School of Life lessons).

So for this reason, I totally believe Christ when he says, at John 11:25,

"I am the Resurrection and the Life".

But this does not mean you need to believe specifically in Jesus as being God in a Trinitarian sense, or that you need to love or worship him in a godly fashion, or even that you need know of his existence, in order to connect with God the Father.

A Muslim believer steeped in the Islamic faith can just as easily connect with God and eventually be saved, just as equally as a Christian. A Buddhist, born in remote Tibet and never knowing of Jesus, can still connect with God and find everlasting life provided he does what Jesus asked of us.

You must remember that even when Christ himself was asked: what does a man need to do to be saved? Jesus gave us only two key commandments. First, love God the Father with all your mind, heart, soul and strength. And second, to love your neighbour as yourself.

"Then one of them, which was a lawyer, asked him a question, tempting him, and saying, Master, which is the great commandment in the law? Jesus said unto him, Thou shalt love the Lord thy God with all thy heart, and with all thy soul, and with all thy mind. This is the first and great commandment. And the second is like unto it, Thou shalt love thy neighbour as thyself. On these two commandments hang all the law and the prophets."

— Matthew 22:35-40

And at Mark 12:30-31 (NIV)

"30 Love the Lord your God with all your heart and with all your soul and with all your mind and with all your strength.'[a] 31 The second is this: 'Love your neighbour as yourself.'[b] There is no commandment greater than these."

Jesus did NOT add to these that we must also recognise HIM as God, or godly in nature; or obey or worship HIM. **If to do so was key to our salvation, he clearly would have told us; and in no uncertain terms**.

In fact, Jesus clearly said that if you keep his commandments you will, by definition, love him anyway. And he will, in turn, love you - refer below.

◄John 14:21►

"Whoever has my commands and keeps them is the one who loves me. The one who loves me will be loved by my Father, and I too will love them and show myself to them."

And

◄John 15:10►

"If you keep my commands, you will remain in my love, just as I have kept my Father's commands and remain in his love."

Jesus therefore himself makes the point very clearly: if you do what I and my Father ask of you, you will by definition, love and believe in me. End of story. There is no better authority for us to receive on this than Jesus's own words.

It is therefore not for us, nor religious leaders, to interpret scripture in a way contrary to the plain and obvious reading of the text; let alone to invent a new commandment from words which are themselves contrary to what Jesus has said elsewhere, and in various Gospels.

I reject completely those who say that he meant differently simply because he said, at John 14:6,

"I am the way and the truth and the life. No one comes to the Father except through me."

What he meant by this is simply this. Jesus, as the Christ, is the Logos, or the Word, by which the illusory material world aimed to School and test us was made and is sustained. He is therefore truly, *the Way*; and in fact, in my hypothesis, he is the *only Way*, for us to find the Father.

God has entrusted the whole schema of the School of Life and our rehabilitation to Jesus, who emanates from the Father and is therefore godly in nature, a sort of mighty spirit. He is quasi God in nature, just as the sun's rays emanate from the sun, but he is, per se, not God. And he provides the mechanism for creation and maintenance of the material world (but not the creation of ourselves as spirit essences which God himself was responsible for although remembering, as per Genesis, God created us with the help of The Word - see later below).

This does actually accord with part of the Catholic belief system, in that, referring to Jesus, the Gospel of John notes,"*Through him*" ["my emphasis"] all things were made; without him nothing was made that has been made".(John 1:3)

Of course, Christianity regards him also as God, forming part of the Trinitarian notion of the Godhead.

Saint Paul also described Jesus, very telling in my view, in these terms :

"Yet for us there is but one God, the Father, *"from whom" ["my emphasis"]* are all things and we exist for Him; and one Lord, Jesus Christ, *"by whom" ["my emphasis"]* are all things, and we exist

"through Him" ["my emphasis"]." (1 Cor. 8:6).

Paul makes it so clear here. First, there is only one God and that is the Father. And from him all things are initiated. And we exist for Him (i.e. for him alone).

And second, there is Jesus, he is not referred to as God, but as "Lord'; and "by whom" (i.e. he is the mechanism by which) we exist. And "through Him" we exist, since we are subsisting in his projected illusory world that he operates for us so we can be schooled, tested and hopefully reformed and resurrected.

Of course, the Roman Catholic Church had for millennia proclaimed that everyone must come through Jesus to be saved (i.e. must be a Christian believer). If this were so, then the notions of Progressive Revelation and Universal Salvation, as I have described them in this work and as explained by the Baha'i Faith, could not be true.

The response to this, for the reasons outlined above, is that it is clearly not true to say that you only can connect with God and be saved if you are a Christian believing in Jesus as God.

Yes it might be true that Jesus, being the Logos and being God's son, was present with God at the outset; (in Genesis 1:16) when God said,

"Let US [my emphasis] make man in our image".

And although Christ may have been part of the "us" (i.e. Christ was God's instrument in creating the physical world intended to train and school us), God being all knowing, predicted the Fall of man by man's own freewill and therefore anticipated the need for the illusory material world needed to train the fallen souls; and which world and rehabilitative task, he entrusted to his "son" The Logos.

Christ is effectively the school principal and projector of our world; and so without getting through the school he set up, and which he continues to maintain, no one gets to truly reconnect with God (i.e. ascend to Heaven).

Jesus, when he says at John 14:6,

"I am **the way** and the **truth** and **the life**. No one comes to the Father except **through me**",

He is simply acknowledging this, (he even uses the words **"through me"**, and constantly distinguishes between himself and the "Father" who sent him).

He is therefore also acknowledging the need for all to rise through (i.e. **The Way**) being the School of Life (and discover our True selves i.e. **The Truth**) and thereby enter into God's kingdom (i.e. gain everlasting and non-recurring **Life**); rather than each soul having to believe in Jesus, or that Jesus is God, as a Christian might naively be told and therefore think that he or she needs to do in order to find God and be saved.

Again, as i covered earlier, after the second Vatican Council, the Catholic Church started to accept some notion of Universal salvation and now, despite the opposing and ignorance based views of many Christians, the Catholic Church finally seems to accept the legitimacy of certain other religions, in particular the Muslim faith, as a gateway to God and heaven for its believers. (Refer to Pope John Paul's II

Casablanca speech of 1985 mentioned earlier).

Interestingly, there's nothing in the Catholic Creed of Faith, the Nicaean Creed, which necessarily contradicts what I have said in this work; except for, as Origen also believed, the fact that I say that Christ is a lesser divine being than God the Father. But this is different to saying that Christ has no divinity whatsoever. The fact that he is "God from God" as mentioned in the creed below does not mean that when Jesus said we must love God, he meant we must also love and worship him as well.

Refer the words of the Nicaean Creed below [my emphasis in inverted commas],

"We believe in "one God,
the Father", ***the Almighty,***
maker of heaven and earth,
of all that is, seen and unseen.
"We believe in one Lord, Jesus Christ",
the only Son of God,
eternally begotten of the Father,
God from God, Light from Light,
true God from true God,
begotten, not made,
of one Being with the Father.
"Through him all things were made."
For us and for our salvation
he came down from heaven:
by the power of the Holy Spirit
he became incarnate from the Virgin Mary,
and was made man.
For our sake he was crucified under Pontius Pilate;

he suffered death and was buried.
On the third day he rose again
in accordance with the Scriptures;
he ascended into heaven
and is seated at the right hand of the Father.
He will come again in glory to judge the living and the dead,
and his kingdom will have no end.
We believe in the Holy Spirit, the Lord, the giver of life,
who proceeds from the Father and the Son.
With the Father and the Son he is worshiped and glorified.
He has spoken through the Prophets.
We believe in one holy catholic and apostolic Church.
We acknowledge one baptism for the forgiveness of sins.
We look for the resurrection of the dead,
and the life of the world to come. Amen.

—Episcopal Church Book of Common Prayer (1979), The Book of Common Prayer"

In my view, and by analogy, if God the Father was the sun, then Christ might well be the light that emanates from the sun, and the Holy Spirit (or the Divine Sophia as recognized in Eastern Orthodox Christianity) may well be the warmth that also emanates from the Father. Neither the light nor the warmth are, per se, the Sun or God in my analogy, but they have aspects of Divinity that trace back to the Father.In apparent conflict to what I say above, as it relates to the status of Christ as a lesser Spirit than

God the Father, is the first verse of John's Gospel; in that, if I believe as I do, that Christ is the Word through which the material world was made, then John 1:1 says,

"In the beginning was the Word, and the Word was with God, and the Word WAS [my emphasis] God".

As Saint Paul said, there is only one God and then there is our Lord, Jesus Christ. But Jesus is so intricately connected with God (in ways we find hard to understand admittedly), as to also be of a divine nature. And in this sense, you could therefore say he is of a Divine nature and so "God" to this extent.

Remember, as covered earlier, if the End Game is for all of those who "graduate" from the School of Life to achieve Theosis, or Enlightenment, or "become God like", i.e. Deification, or however each respective religion defines the ultimate consummation of our salvation, then surely we should not have an issue in Jesus himself having such a divine quality.

It is probably beyond our comprehension, certainly mine in any case, to understand how the Divine Nature will be ultimately shared between us, Christ and God, and possibly others. It is also best to avoid polemics of this nature, similar to the kind that has bedevilled Christian Theology in the past on many other issues.

However, what is readily comprehendible here is this key point. For the reasons explained earlier, regardless of the divine nature or otherwise of Jesus, neither God nor Jesus has ever suggested that we

must recognise and worship Jesus in order to be saved.

Consistent with what Origen of Alexandria (the greatest Christian scholar of his era, if not all time) maintained, Christ, although divine in nature, was nonetheless a different and lesser Being than God the Father (note, he is constantly referred to biblically as the "son" of God).

As a result, there's no inconsistency with the notion that Christ was both godly in nature, but not the one and only God the Father (or the God Consciousness) who is to be loved, praised and worshiped in the manner of many Faiths, as outlined earlier in this work.

Through Jesus, pre incarnate as The Word or The Christ, all things we see in this illusory material world were made; and he is the mechanism through which we can resurrect ourselves by being trained in the School of Life; that is, he is indeed the Light and the Life and the Resurrection; and yet he is NOT God the Father who is the only God, and who should be loved with all our heart, mind, soul and strength.

I reaffirm this point again and again here because it continues to be a sticking point for those who fail to both understand and accept the notions of Progressive Revelation and Universal Salvation.

Many of these accuse, for example, the Islamic religion of being a Satanic invention or false religion, simply because Islam does not recognize Jesus as God (although it does recognize him as a mighty prophet and messenger). These accusers say that Islam was ignited by the Dark forces, similar to what some

Jews said about the advent of Christianity. Such an accusation against Islam, as the Catholic Church now admits, is of course, utter nonsense based on the ignorance of the accusers and those who brainwash them, either intentionally or naively.

Consistent with the notion of Progressive Revelation and that all the key religions have at their heart a common starting origin, it is interesting to see that **in the Hindu faith, the God Vishnu seems to have similar qualities to Jesus the Logos, or the Word;** in that he is regarded as "projecting" the universe we live in and being pervasive throughout it.

In Hinduism, the cosmic functions of creation, maintenance, and destruction are personified by the forms of Brahma the Creator, **Vishnu the Maintainer or Preserver**, and Shiva the Destroyer or Transformer. Such deities compose "the Hindu triad" or "Great Trinity".

Although Wikipedia may not be the most authoritative source to reference, it is interesting to see what is said in it on Vishnu, and its similarities to what we have covered in sources such as Plato's Cave Allegory (freedom from bondage) and the Gospel of Thomas (present everywhere).

Wikipeadia

"Vishnu (Sanskrit pronunciation: [vɪʂɳu]; IAST: Viṣṇu) is one of the principal deities of Hinduism, and the Supreme Being in its Vaishnavism tradition.[1][2]

Along with Brahma and Shiva, Vishnu forms a Hindu trinity (Trimurti); *however, ancient Hindu texts do mention other trinities of gods or goddesses.[3][4]*

In Vaishnavism, Vishnu is identical to the formless

metaphysical concept called Brahman, the supreme, the Svayam Bhagavan, who takes various avatars as "the preserver, protector" whenever the world is threatened with evil, chaos, and destructive forces.[6] His avatars (incarnations) most notably include Krishna (often associated with Jesus) *in the Mahabharata and Rama in the Ramayana. He is also known as Narayana, Jagannath, Vasudeva, Vithoba, and Hari. He is one of the five equivalent deities worshipped in Panchayatana puja of the Smarta Tradition of Hinduism.[2]*

In Hindu iconography, a traditional depiction is Lord Vishnu reclining on the coils of Ananta (Ananta is an immortal, infinite snake), accompanied by his consort Devi Lakshmi, as he "dreams the universe into reality".

Yaska, the mid-1st-millennium BCE Vedanga scholar, in his Nirukta (etymological interpretation), defines Vishnu as viṣṇur viṣvater vā vyaśnoter vā, ***"one who enters everywhere".*** *He also writes, atha yad viṣito bhavati tad viṣnurbhavati,* ***"that which is free from fetters and bondages is Vishnu".[8]***

The medieval Indian scholar Medhātithi suggested that the word Vishnu has etymological roots in viś, meaning to pervade, thereby connoting that Vishnu is "one who is everything and inside everything".[9]

Vishnu means "all pervasive".[10][11]".

This also resonates with Spinoza's depiction of God as a pantheistic entity that was all pervasive; a notion of God with which Einstein coincidentally believed in.

It clearly has echoes of what was said in the

Gospel of Thomas at Logion 77,

(77) Jesus says:

(1) "I am the light that is over all. I am the All. The All came forth out of me. And to me the All has come."

(2) "Split a piece of wood — I am there.

(3) Lift the stone, and you will find me there."

Plato and Aristotle on the notion of "The Good" and "Nous".

The idea of Lord Vishnu, "dreaming the Universe into Reality" is an idea not foreign to the great Philosopher kings Plato and Aristotle.

I said earlier that God has entrusted the whole schema of the School of Life and our rehabilitation to Jesus the Christ, who emanates from the Father and is therefore godly in nature, a sort of mighty spirit; (he is quasi god in nature, just as the sun's light rays emanate from the sun, but he is "per se" not God) and he provides the mechanism for creation and maintenance of the material world.

Inherent in this is the notion that, God the Father, is the ultimate God and Jesus is, although difficult for us to understand, both his right hand man and yet an integral part of him. Jesus does what he does (namely, provides us with a path back to reunion with God and therefore is rightly called "Our Saviour") for God's sake.

The ancient Greeks had already determined that the Universe was created by some form of God, and the debate between Plato and Aristotle essentially turned on whether the God in question (i.e. the Form of the Good) acted alone in this creative feat (which appears to be Aristotle's view); or whether there was another God, or quasi God, involved who created the material world for the sake of the ultimate God (this was Plato's view, and he called this other God, "The Demiurge" or "Nous").

Whilst Aristotle believed the Form of the Good and Nous were one and the same, Plato believed them to be separate but that, nonetheless, Nous did things for the sake of the Form of the Good. This is, of course, reminiscent of the age old Christian debate as to whether Jesus, the Son of God, and the Father, are really one God, or separate persons within the Trinitarian notion of the Holy Trinity.

In his article entitled "Aristotle and Plato on God as Nous and as the Good", Stephen Menn makes the following observations:

"As Aristotle says in Nicomachean Ethics 1.6 and Eudemian Ethics 1.8, "good" is predicated in all of the categories. Nonetheless, it is easy to show that Aristotle takes both "the Good" and Nous to be names of the essence of God. Now Plato too takes "the Good" as the name of the highest divine principle; and Plato also uses Nous to name a (different) God, the source of order to the physical world. Plato says in the Philebus that "all the wise agree that Nous is king for us of heaven and earth" (28c6-8), and this Nous is identical with the "demiurge" of the Timaeus. I will try in this paper to show how Aristotle takes over, criticises, and modifies Plato's doctrines of the Good as the first divine

principle, and of Nous as an inferior principle, and how he presents as his alternative to Plato's theology his own doctrine of a divine principle which is both Nous and the Good."

"For Aristotle, as for Plato, "it is evident that that there is some eternal and unmoved substance from the sensibles "(Metaphysics 1073a3-5), and Aristotle is willing to describe this in deliberately Platonic terms as "something separate and itself-by-itself "(107a12-13)."

"Both the Good and Nous are posited as causes of other things. The Good should be the final cause (as in Eudemian Ethics 1.8), while Nous seems to be an efficient cause (as in Aristotle's account of Anaxagoras in Metaphysics 1), but these two causes are closely linked, ***"since Nous does what it does for the sake of the Good."["My emphasis"]"***

Finally, with specific reference to whether Nous can be even further associated with Jesus, who in my view as outlined earlier, "manifests and projects" the material world; along with the Hindu equivalent, Vishnu, who "thinks it into reality", Menn says the following in respect of the meaning of Nous.

"Translators have generally been at a loss with the word, and they are often forced to split it up into many different English words. Grammatically, Nous is derived from the verb noein, which can be as broad as "to think", but which often means, more precisely, to perceive or to intuit something intellectually. ... We may render Nous as "thought" or "intuition" when it denotes an action; but translation is more difficult in other cases."

There is therefore some synergy between Lord Vishnu's "dreaming the universe into reality"; Plato's Nous "thinking" the universe into reality (i.e. the demiurge of the Timaeus) and finally Christ as Logos, being the all-pervasive force that sustains the material world we live in as Principal of the School of Life.

Moreover, as we saw earlier in this work, modern science through the increasing understanding of quantum physics is now starting to depict our universe almost as a "living organism" with some form of all pervasive "consciousness", as opposed to the materialistic and mechanistic notion of the universe depicted by classical physics. Einstein's "Spooky Action at a Distance" observation we mentioned earlier may well have been not only anticipated, but also explained, by millennia-old Revelation.

So based on the above and earlier comments regarding the Greek Philosopher Giants of Pythagoras, Socrates, Plato and Aristotle, perhaps, when no doubt from time to time, that famous question is posed, which appears on its face to suggest that Philosophy and Theology must be studied separately; namely, the supposed Tertullian question being, "What has Athens to do with Jerusalem?" One should promptly and aptly respond, with great confidence, "Everything!"

Q - What role does Society have to provide access to Spiritual Salvation?

Given what has been said so far, as a society should

we not work hard to ensure that all our "down and outers" (i.e. people afflicted by Life's depressing vices) are given the opportunity to turn to God for assistance?

The purifying graces of God's spiritual presence can help these downtrodden souls. Importantly, if we truly want to help them, we should ensure that they are exposed to, and have the opportunity to practice, God's message of hope and salvation. Throwing such downtrodden people material and monetary welfare is not enough. We can help them beyond belief by exposing them to God's word.

For example, in the Australian context, I am convinced the only way for many of the unfortunate Aboriginal peoples to break the cycle of poverty, forlornness, welfare dependency and lack of self-esteem (created, of course, by many years of white man denials of freedoms and oppression) is to turn to God.

Since it is important for many of such peoples to retain their Australian Aboriginal heritage, then a religion similar to that of the Baha'i Faith may suit them best. Since the Baha'i Faith, incorporating notions of Progressive Revelation and Universal Salvation through many messengers and prophets (although perhaps not any ancient aboriginal ones), may allow them to continue to worship God by reference to their own aboriginal spirit messengers if they so choose (of which I know little or nothing about). Or alternatively, by reference to any of the more modern messengers of their choosing including, of course, Jesus and Bahaullah.

For those who wanted to follow Jesus in the fulsome context as "Lord of Creation and Saviour of All" then, of course, the pure Christian Faith would also offer that option.

The key point here is that God has enabled a variety of Faiths as pathways to his door, and he doesn't seem to mind which path we take provided we are prepared to undertake the pain and sacrifices needed to get there; and that in the end, we abide by the key commandments of loving both Him and our neighbours.

Accordingly, for people in a forlorn or downtrodden state, how one turns to God and spirituality generally, is varied and optional. God gives us many teaching options and the ability to choose the teacher that suits us best; although I suspect in reality, he also chooses that teacher for us rather than the other way around.

The important point here is that society should ensure that people are free to have exposure to spiritual teachings and not be left to fester and waddle in their forlorn states, without access to the most important reviving force available to them. And the more downtrodden, forlorn and lost they are, the greater the access that society should give them to the opportunity to be saved by God's message.

In our earlier example of the Sydney Central Railway violinist playing God's message, we should make sure that anyone who could not hear the busker due to infirmity, obstruction or other means was provided access to listen to God's message. Whether he becomes entranced by the busker's music is then up to him and God. It is not for society to thrust any specific religious beliefs down his throat, but I believe Society has a duty to enable access to God's word.

If it's true that all religions over time become decayed, dogmatic, lose their pure message to the point where what is taught to parishioners and students is not in fact derived directly from the original Holy Scripture, but rather from many man made onion layers of supposed "inspired "interpretation of the original scripture (read potentially "non-sense" if it's not directly found in the original scriptures), then what good are mainstream religions at leading individuals to the truth?; let alone to what is genuinely required of them to participate in a connection with God?

They are all poor substitutes for the original teachings. Indeed, that is exactly what Luther taught and what led to the cleansing Protestant revolution. Although Protestantism is itself not immune from such failings.

Does society have a role to ensure that its citizens are exposed to the original teachings; the original Holy scriptures? Surely if we conclude that our hypothesis is sound and that salvation and true happiness comes from connecting with God, then that is the highest good possible. ***If society does not help its citizens to reach the highest good, then really what's the point of it?***

Should not society, through the State and the judicial system, recognize the inherent fundamental human right of every citizen to have the opportunity to be exposed to some, if not all, of God's teachings contained in Holy Scripture?

The fundamental Human Right should not just be a right to Life, Liberty and the Pursuit of Happiness; but rather Life, Liberty and the Pursuit of Happiness including, and especially, Spiritual teachings.

If Life truly is God's School, then everyone should have the right to be able to listen to God's teachers - and to listen to their original teachings not just to the man-made muffled tones of the original recordings.

Schools should all teach as part of their core curriculum, the different religious and spiritual beliefs of the world, including a review of their similarities and differences. Understanding of the "other" is a key prerequisite of having compassion, and ultimately affinity, therewith.

Imagine if all children had access to understanding the key religious beliefs, including the Baha'i notion that the key religions flow from the same original source, how much less mistrust and misapprehension there would be among diverse Faiths? And the potential for a lot less racism and ignorance that leads to the persecution of others.

Q - Material versus Spiritual Superannuation

What is uncontroversial is that we are born, we live and we die. Why this happens is not uncontroversial, although I've tried to explain it in this work.

People generally believe that if we are lucky we might get to live a long life assuming it's a happy and healthy one. But even so, it passes by very quickly and, in the context of the immensity of time, is but a flutter of a butterfly's wings.

So why do we seemingly spend enormous time and energy trying to make money and build material wealth in priority to all else? Answer, of course, is that we don't see a better priority, and building material wealth helps us and our family's advancement in terms of access to healthcare, education, comfortable shelter, sustenance and worldly desires. But as we all know, neither we nor our families can take any of this with us when we die.

So we spend much of our lives toiling for something we cannot take with us after our brief sojourn on this earth. Wouldn't it be better to spend the incredibly short amount of time we have here to instead focus on something we *can* take with us, i.e. our spiritual superannuation rather than material superannuation?

As mentioned earlier, if we can grow the character of our souls by purifying them from worldly fancies and centre them on the love of God and Mankind in general, the evolutionary mutation that occurs to our souls from this can be taken with us because our souls survive physical death. Artful skills such as the love of music, literature, craftsmanship, the love of medicine or philosophy and theology, and much more, can also become embedded in our soul memories.

Moreover, given that our souls apparently learn best whilst we are clothed in a bodily form, we must maximize the limited life time opportunities we have to advance our soul purification and education process.

As mentioned earlier, not all souls will in my view be saved. At some point the school bell will ring, singling the end of school and the arrival of the so-called Judgement Day, when the Heavenly Bus will pull up at the school gate for those who have graduated. I don't know about you, but I certainly want to be on that bus. It's a ticket to eternal bliss. And as also mentioned earlier, the higher we calibrate our souls in this life, the more enjoyable the journey through many lifetime class years.

So is it not worth striving to accumulate this kind of spiritual wealth rather than simply striving for worldly things that we leave behind every reincarnated lifetime?

Finally, when the school bell will ultimately ring no one really knows. However, consider this - the master teacher, Jesus, has already been and gone! Also consider that if my hypothesis is correct and you are reading this work, you have had the benefit of receiving the great news of God's plan for us; you have clearly been exposed to the Sydney Central busker's music. What will you do with it in this life of yours? Will you have another lifetime to hear it again?

Q - What should we really be studying?

If the hypothesis put forward is correct then here are some suggestions as to what, as a society, we might wish to consider as worthy topics for scholarly study.

First, if there are three key things God would like us to do, namely, love him unconditionally (in effect reciprocating his unconditional love for us); love each other; and finally develop a resistance to any temptations that sway us from achieving the above two goals, then should we not be studying HOW best to achieve these three goals; and how to make such available to all Mankind? It logically follows that, of course, we should.

Second, (and all the following suggestions are not mutually exclusive from the first suggestion above) should we not understand much better than we do the whole notion of Karma and the use of multiple lifetimes to resolve it? I have never seen a school subject or university degree specializing in Karmic Studies, at least not in the western schools and universities I'm familiar with.

If mental anguish and depression can be caused by the fate and destiny that awaits us all from karmic forces, and if this can be better understood by rationalizing the lessons we need to learn to improve ourselves, might this not lead to an improvement in how people might handle anguish and depression?

For example, if someone who comes from a broken and abused family background better understood that the reason for it was possibly so he could learn something useful from his experience, and that in any event he may possibly have led previous lives of pomp and grandeur, and may indeed lead such lives in the future, he may be more resigned to making the most of the present life he has been given, rather than being depressed about the fact that his one and only shot at life is apparently a total disaster for no obvious reason or fault of his own.

Or an elderly couple (true story) who have recently buried two of their middle age children due to unexpected and unconnected illnesses, and cannot fathom why this should happen to them. Perhaps they may better be able to cope with the anguish if they realized that the two children are going to have many more lives in the future (potentially together with them), and that the two children's destiny was such to enable both the relevant deceased's own children and spouses to experience pain and anguish - for what reasons we, of course, do not fully know. But it could be, for example, to drive these remaining family members themselves to become closer to God; or to make them, or those around them, to understand that life is intrinsically an unhappy existence without a Godly connection; or in the case of this family, where the parents were already highly spiritual, to test the parent's spirituality by giving them a good reason to stop believing in God and seeing just how solid their belief system is.

I appreciate you might say that it must be a mean hearted God that would take away two of your children, just to test how strong your faith was. But that is potentially the nature of the God we are dealing with here. This is a tough school to be in, and especially to graduate from. And always remember that because the real "us" is our soul and spirit essences, God is of course, always compassionate in his treatment of all since the "real" children do not die in a spiritual sense.

How many suicides and cases of severe depression

might be avoided if people better understood God's plan? If people resigned themselves to making the most of what hand they were dealt with, knowing that in the next round they might get a much better hand, then perhaps they would gladly accept their lot and be more enthusiastic about playing the game as opposed to criticizing the dealer; or even worse, refusing to accept the existence of the dealer, on the basis that no good dealer can exist that would have dealt them such a bad hand.

Third, spiritual healing via prayer, laying of hands, etc. surely should be a key study topic for our ever cost bulging health industry. Imagine if people could be healed psychologically, or of physical ailments, by such means. If God is giving us a progressive education by sending us prophets, messengers and that special being called Christ (or as we would best try to comprehend him, His own Son), and if such persons healed the sick and cast out demons as they are reported to have done, then should we not be devoting serious scientific effort to understanding how this could be possible?

Fourth, understanding better why meditation works to uplift us is clearly a worthwhile topic of study. In a sense, meditation does for our mind what "fasting from the world" (to use a Jesus quote from the Gospel of Thomas) does for our body. It detaches from our mind distractive thoughts and allows us to sense our inner selves.

Fifth, as I mentioned earlier, how can we make spirituality available to the masses without all the baggage that old stodgy man made layered religious practices bring. Perhaps the work of people like Eckhart Tolle, Deepak Chopra and Joe Dispenza are examples of this.

Q - How should Philosophy and Theology be taught?
Together.

End.
2017

Appendix One

(Added January 2018)

Diversity of Faith in the Workplace

EY Approach to Interfaith Diversity : ARL = GP^2

Introductory Comments to an October 2017 Interfaith Event by Alf Capito, Hosting Partner, held at EY Sydney Office on the topic of Spirituality in the Workplace.

These introductory comments outlines EY's approach to Interfaith Diversity.

"This event is a high point to date in our Interfaith group's journey of achieving what the group set out to do two years ago - and that is to bring into the corporate world an ongoing, open and fearless dialogue about faith, spirituality and philosophy in a way that might encourage all EY workplace employees, and hopefully other workplaces as well, to be confident about bringing their spiritual belief system to work without fear or trepidation, and not having to leave it at that at the door on the way in every morning.

So what do we at EY believe when it comes to the Diversity of Faith?

Although I am not an avid Australian Rugby League fan, I think there's something admirable about the acronym ARL

To me it aptly summarises what we believe from a Diversity of Faith perspective; namely, to Accept, to Respect and to Learn from each other's faith systems.

We first must Accept the key faiths and philosophies that our people and clients espouse; and be willing to dialogue about such matters in the workplace without shame or trepidation. And here Acceptance means more than just Tolerance. One can readily consider one's own beliefs high above those of others and simply tolerate, in a subservient way, the views of others. That's not what we mean. We mean genuinely Accept by embracing the beliefs of others as Equal in nature to one's own views. Without that, the mindset needed to truly treat others as equals will be absent.

Second, and following on from true Acceptance, is Respect. To truly Respect the views of others one must be attuned to the rituals and other customs of divergent belief systems, including respecting and being sensitive to matters such as fasting, dress code, prayer, food and drink habits and other sensitive cultural issues. And naturally Respect includes the avoidance of pushing or proselytising your own views onto others.

And finally, to Learn from the belief systems of others; and learn not only insights from other faiths, but also to gain better insights into one's own faith or belief system by comparing, contrasting and ultimately validating one's own views, or even modifying them along the way.

And what are some of the things we might Learn from better understanding Faith systems?

We'll try these for starters:

Detachment from superficial worldly desires, including the control of the Ego and the Anger that often attaches to such Ego

Humility not Pride, or even worse, Arrogance

Honesty and Transparency

Courtesy and Manners to All Always

Patience

Forgiveness

The Power of Love and Compassion

Awareness, Appreciation and indeed Joy of our mere existence

And finally, the Power of Consultation and Inclusiveness, which no doubt has had a hand in bringing us all here together today; and, even though I'm not Baha'i, if I could respectfully borrow from the excellent Baha'i writings on the Power of Consultation and how it impacts on all Diversity & Inclusiveness topics – in particular, how Consultation leads to Understanding, how Understanding leads to Compassion, how Compassion leads to Friendship, and ultimately, how Friendship leads to Unity.

If we imbue ourselves with such virtuous learnings and the positive energy that comes from such learnings, we not only protect ourselves from the negative behaviours encountered in both workplace and life in general; but we can also be a lighted beacon of example to those around us.

To be truly in tune with such positive learnings

will leave no room for the negative corporate behaviours you read about in the business press on a daily basis. Behaviours such as:

Bullying or Harassment of staff

The Ego driven passions of CEOs, or Partners in Professional Firms, or Senior managers generally

Prejudices of all kinds, even unconscious ones

Dishonesty

Corruption

Self-interested behaviours couched in justifying "corporate speak"

And Unethical business practices of all types

So we believe Acceptance, Respect and Learning are important not just because they are basic Diversity & Inclusiveness Fundamentals, but because they also lead to both Personal and Professional Growth.

For those mathematically minded, or if you prefer a simple way to remember this discussion, you could sum it up as:

$ARL = GP^2$

Where GP^2 stands for Personal and Professional Growth, which in turn, elevates the Human Soul, which is primarily what Life is all about.

And here let me aptly refer to an often quoted old Aboriginal proverb, which is so steeped in immemorial antiquity, that its author is unknown:

"We are all visitors to this time, this place. We are just passing through. Our purpose here is to observe, to learn, to grow, to love... and then we return home".

Finally, I would like to make clear that our Interfaith Diversity framework caters equally for people who have no faith in a religion, god or spirituality as such, but nonetheless seek to achieve Personal and Professional Growth based on a philosophy of ethical and virtuous behaviour. I can find no better example of such a person than in an EY partner who I knew for over 25 years, and who recently retired from the firm. He held no religious or spiritual beliefs whatsoever and yet was one of the most virtuous and integrous people I've ever known.

So within that background and context, let me introduce the first of our speakers......."

Appendix Two

(Added November 2018)

November 21st 2018 Festival Of Light Celebration in the Workplace

Some opening comments.

"Hi everyone, my name is Alf Capito and I lead EY's Interfaith Group.

Today in our office we will hear specifically about the Hindu and Jewish Festivals of Light as we celebrate both Diwali and Hanukkah.

Before doing so, i would simply like to make a few preliminary observations and to also talk briefly about the importance of supporting and nurturing Interfaith Diversity and Inclusiveness in the workplace.

There's something special about Light.

Apart from those Faiths that we will talk about soon, all of the other great religions also mention the unique importance of Light.

In Islam, the Quran says that "God is the light of the heavens and the earth"

In the Baha'i faith, the Prophet Bahaullah notes that "So powerful is the Light of Unity that it can illuminate the whole earth"

Of course in Buddhism, the Buddha was said to be "Enlightened" as he sat under the Bodhi Tree; and is often depicted with the colours of the rainbow surrounding him.

And in Christianity, Jesus in the Biblical story of the Transfiguration becomes visible as a bright radiating light showing us a glimpse of his transcendent self.

Moreover, Holy persons, Saints, Prophets and many spiritually revered figures are often depicted with hallos of light surrounding them.

It is also instructive to note that Light features prominently in the history of some of the great iconic figures of science and philosophy.

Plato, in his famous Allegory of the Cave, pointed out that true reality is to be found outside of the cave; a cave in which mankind lives imprisoned by desire, fear and anger. And that this outside world is illumined by a brilliant Light that he called "The Form of the Good" or "The One".

Isaac Newton, the father of calculus, gave us our modern understanding of light and was the first to explain how refracted white light scientifically resolves itself into its component rainbow colours.

And of course Albert Einstein, revealed the famous mathematical equation $E=MC^2$, in which the only constant is the Speed of Light (represented by the letter C).

If I can be permitted to draw one more important parallel, between these iconic figures of Science and Philosophy, it is this. And this is a parallel which is often ignored by modern materialists who seem to be getting a lot of media these days.

These three great, arguably the three greatest, philosopher/scientists of all time, upon whose shoulders modern science and philosophy today now sits, were all spiritually or religious people. They all believed in some form of God or supernatural persona.

Plato, along with his famous student Aristotle, would debate amongst themselves whether God had an accomplice to help him, or alternatively, as Aristotle argued for, was alone in all respects.

Newton spent an inordinate amount of his study time trying to decipher what he thought were secret mathematical codes in the Bible; much to the bemoaning of his colleagues who thought he was wasting his genius.

And Einstein believed in Spinoza's non anthropomorphic God; a designer God. It is said he knew all too well the immense probabilities required for our world to have come about merely by chance.

And so Science and Philosophy should not be seen as being in obvious conflict with Faith and Spirituality.

The greatest scientific and philosophic minds that ever walked our planet did not see these disciplines as being mutually exclusive.

You don't need to sacrifice Faith and Spirituality in order to embrace Science and Reason.

And you certainly do not need to sacrifice Science and Reason in order to embrace Faith and Spirituality. These iconic figures are clear evidence that the two can coexist in us in tandem.

On the topic of Interfaith work practices, the EY Interfaith group has its own unique way of depicting the importance of Interfaith Diversity and Inclusiveness by an equation as follows:

$ARL = GP^2$

Where ARL stands for Accept, Respect and Learn and GP^2 stands for Personal and Professional Growth.

We first must Accept the key faiths and philosophies that our people and clients espouse; and be willing to dialogue about such matters in the workplace without shame or trepidation. And here Acceptance means more than just Tolerance. One can readily consider one's own beliefs high above those of others and simply tolerate, in a subservient way, the views of others. That's not what we mean. We mean genuinely Accept by embracing the beliefs of others as Equal in nature to one's own views. Without that, the mindset needed to truly treat others as equals will be absent.

Second, and following on from true Acceptance, is Respect. To truly Respect the views of others one must be attuned to the rituals and other customs of divergent belief systems, including respecting and being sensitive to matters such as fasting, dress code, prayer, food and drink habits, modes of greeting and other sensitive cultural issues. And naturally Respect includes the avoidance of pushing or proselytising your own views onto others.

And finally, to Learn from the belief systems of others; and learn not only insights from other faiths, but also to gain better insights into one's own faith or belief system by comparing, contrasting and ultimately validating one's own views, or even modifying them along the way.

To conclude I'd like to simply leave you with the thought that the GP^2 in this equation is effectively an approximation at calibrating just how well "enlightened" a person really is. People who are truly advanced both professionally and personally, have a certain "glow" about them that we all seemingly recognise when we see them.

At EY we believe that everyone should be free and uninhibited to search for and practice their own form of "enlightenment" – that is, how to grow themselves both personally and professionally.

And that an open workplace that supports both Diversity and Inclusiveness in the practice of Faith, Spirituality and Moral Philosophy should therefore be encouraged and nurtured."

End

About the Author

The author expresses no pre-existing skills or qualifications as an author, philosopher or religious expert. The impetus for this book comes from some personal experiences the author has had and which he explains in the Preface to the book.

The front and back cover of the book depicts a photo of a burning white cross the author saw coinciding with what he believes to be a clear mandate from higher sources to write the book. Apart from a clear sense that this book was 'guided' by a higher force, the author professes no Philosophic or Religious qualifications.

www.ingramcontent.com/pod-product-compliance
Lightning Source LLC
Chambersburg PA
CBHW030910090426
42737CB00007B/151
* 9 7 8 0 6 4 8 4 6 4 5 0 1 *